D1083229

LIBERTY
AND
NATURE

LIBERTY AND NATURE

AN ARISTOTELIAN DEFENSE OF LIBERAL ORDER

DOUGLAS B. RASMUSSEN

AND

DOUGLAS J. DEN UYL

Open Court

La Salle, Illinois

OPEN COURT and the above logo are registered in the U.S. Patent and Trade Office.

© 1991 by Open Court Publishing Company

First printing 1991

Printed and bound in the United States of America.

Library of Congress Cataloging-in-Publication Data

Rasmussen, Douglas B., 1948-
    Liberty and Nature: an Aristotelian defense of liberal order/by Douglas B. Rasmussen and Douglas J. Den Uyl.
       p. cm.
    Includes bibliographical references and index.
    ISBN 0-8126-9119-9 (cloth). — ISBN 0-8126-9120-2 (pbk.)
    1. Aristotle—Contributions in political science. 2. Liberalism.
3. Political science—Philosophy. I. Den Uyl, Douglas J., 1950-. II. Title

JC71.A7R37 199   090-20965
320.5' 1—dc20   CIP

You are advancing into the night, bearing torches toward which mankind would be glad to turn; but you leave them enveloped in the fog of a merely experiential approach and mere practical conceptualization, with no universal ideas to communicate. For lack of adequate ideology, your lights cannot be seen.

—Jacques Maritain, *Reflections on America*

CONTENTS

PREFACE

A work such as this certainly owes a great deal to friends and colleagues who have contributed in various ways to the shaping of its ideas and arguments. Among the most significant names in this category is Henry Veatch. Through letters, conversations, and criticisms of parts of this manuscript, he has done a great deal for us in the formulation of our ideas. As often as not, these ideas were not accepted by Professor Veatch and many still are not. But a significant contribution does not necessarily imply agreement.

Valuable suggestions were also provided by Paul Blair, Thomas Fay, Arthur Gianelli, David Gordon, Allan Gotthelf, Tibor R. Machan, Eric Mack, Fred D. Miller, Jr., David Ramsay Steele, and Theodore Vitali. We thank them and, of course, absolve them of all blame for any errors in this work.

We would also like to express our appreciation to the Center for Libertarian Studies and the Earhart Foundation for financial support, which helped to provide the time to research and write. We are grateful as well to St. John's University and Bellarmine College for reduced teaching loads and leaves which also provided additional time for research and writing.

Finally, we should thank the publishers of the *American Philosophical Quarterly*, *Public Affairs Quarterly*, *Reason Papers*, and *Vera Lex*, as well as the volumes *The Catholic Bishops and the Economy: A Debate* and *Man, Economy, and Liberty* for permission to use segments of our work previously published.

INTRODUCTION

It was only a few decades ago that political philosophy did not exist—at least within Anglo-American philosophy. There were, of course, Marxists and fellow travelers of the left among the faculty of philosophy departments. But for the most part political philosophy, if it existed at all, was relegated to a handful of people, many of whom were faculty members of political science departments. Today all that has changed. Why it has changed is perhaps complex. Yet certainly 'the sixties' had something to do with the emergence of political philosophy, not to mention the writings of certain individuals such as John Rawls or Leo Strauss.

There may, however, be a deeper reason for the emergence of political philosophy; a reason that lies beneath 'the sixties' and thinkers like Strauss and Rawls and that motivates the current flurry of activity in the field. This reason might be called the 'crisis of liberalism'. Liberalism—and the intellectual heritage that gave it birth (the Enlightenment) —are now openly and respectably attacked by such thinkers as Alasdair MacIntyre and Alan Bloom. Liberalism is also being vigorously defended by such thinkers as David Gauthier, Ronald Dworkin, James Buchanan, and F.A. Hayek—not to mention the seminal works of Rawls and Nozick. Although many of these thinkers differ significantly from each other, they all share a concern over the prospects of liberalism. This can be said without even defining what liberalism is, for the term often remains undefined, and part of the debate about liberalism is certainly connected with debate over what it means.

It is not implausible to argue that political philosophy, and probably philosophy in general, gains momentum at those points in history that are most unsettled or confronted by some crisis of conscience. The time of Plato and Aristotle was also a time when the Greek city-state was undergoing transformation, and modern philosophy was cultivated in an atmosphere of religious and scientific uncertainty and change. On a smaller basis, perhaps, the same process appears to be happening today with respect to our own moral/political understanding. The United States, for example, has little understanding of or consensus about what it stands for, where it is going, or what its founding principles mean. This represents a 'crisis of conscience' which undoubtedly motivates a number of intellectuals to fill the void with their own theories and prescriptions. If we are right about this crisis of conscience, it is little wonder that political philosophy has again re-emerged.

The re-emergence of political philosophy is primarily focused upon liberalism: its meaning, its principles, its nature, its logical structure. Whatever 'liberalism' may mean, it is unquestionably our political heritage. If there is a crisis of conscience today over political principles, reflection upon it will certainly center on liberalism. With the possible exception of Jürgen Habermas, who sees his 'discourse ethics' as an expression of the norms implicit in modernity, Marxists have stood outside the liberal tradition (at least from their perspective). They matter no more now to this debate than they ever have. The real debate will occur among liberals or former liberals themselves. That is to say, the impact this debate will have upon the future will come from among those who either consider themselves liberals or who once did, and not from traditional outsiders. It is our purpose in this book to enter the debate. Hence what follows is primarily a work of political philosophy.

The chapters which follow do offer discussions in ethics, metaphysics, epistemology, and related fields; but these fields are discussed to the extent that they have a bearing on political philosophy. One of our purposes in writing this work is to defend the liberal political heritage. The reader, however, will quickly discover that we do so from a rather nontraditional perspective, as such defenses go. We attempt to defend the liberal tradition from an Aristotelian foundation. Our first chapter is, therefore, meant to gain a foothold by claiming that Aristotelianism has not been philosophically defeated. In the chapter that follows, we try to outline and defend an Aristotelian approach to ethics. Using that framework, we offer a theory of rights in Chapter 3 and a discussion of the 'common good' of the political community in Chapter 4. Finally, Chapter 5 attempts to link certain features of a commercial republican order to Aristotelian themes. The concluding chapter, Chapter 6, is a brief summary of how we conceive our project.

Finally, some comments about terminology are necessary. In what
follows the terms *Aristotelian* or *Aristotelianism* are used in a certain
sense. To understand the sense in which these terms are used, it is helpful to use a set of distinctions James Collins claimed applied to most
modern thought. We believe, however, these distinctions apply to philosophical thought of any period and provide us with three senses in which
Aristotelian or *Aristotelianism* might be employed. Using Collins's explanation of his distinctions, we can, *mutatis mutandis*, note the following senses of *Aristotelian* or *Aristotelianism.*

1. *Originative:* the personally developed thought of Aristotle as expressed in his writings;

2. *Continuative or School-Tradition:* the work of those thinkers who
   analyze, clarify, defend, and develop teachings of Aristotle within
   the framework of his own principles and methods;

3. *Recurrent-Thematic-Classificatory-Polemical:* work which involves the novel use of positions of Aristotle, but without necessarily being historically linked with Aristotle or working within
   Aristotle's framework and method. Such work thematizes
   Aristotle's ideas within a new intellectual context in a manner
   which is apart from the systematic interconnections they held in
   Aristotle's philosophy. Such work uses the term *Aristotelian* both
   to classify fundamental positions regarding philosophical problems and as a convenient starting point for criticisms. Such work
   is more schematic than historical, more argumentatively dictated
   than based on any independent examination of Aristotle's texts.
   (James Collins, *Interpreting Modern Philosophy* [Princeton, New
   Jersey: Princeton University Press, 1972], 54–55.)

When we use the terms *Aristotelian* or *Aristotelanism* to describe our
position or approach to certain issues, it will be primarily in the
recurrent-thematic-classificatory-polemical sense. What this Aristotelian
position or approach is and how we use it should become clear in the
first two chapters.

It will also become clear to the reader that the type of liberalism
we defend is closest to what has traditionally been called classical

liberalism. Yet since our defense of the political and social principles most often associated with classical liberalism differs from the usual defenses, we are certainly contributing to the crisis of liberalism previously mentioned, if not to its solution.

1

GAINING A FOOTHOLD

Isn't it high time, then, that we returned once again to something like an Aristotelian telos or a naturally obligatory end? For what else can give meaning to our lives as we actually live them and in terms of the actual purposes and projects to be pursued and striven for?
—Henry B. Veatch, 'Telos and Teleology in Aristotelian Ethics'

INTRODUCTION

How can an essentially Aristotelian natural-end ethics overcome the problem of moving from an 'is' to an 'ought'? How can it provide an account of human nature that is at once plausible and capable of showing where one's ethical obligations lie? How can an Aristotelian ethics provide a basis for Lockean rights? Can the Aristotelian claim that man is a social and political animal be reconciled with Lockean rights? Can Lockean rights be reconciled with the Aristotelian claim that government should promote the common good? And, finally, can an Aristotelian account of human nature and ethics provide any support for the commercial society? These questions we must answer, but we must first deal with some outstanding criticisms that have been made against Aristotelian ethics. By rebutting these criticisms we hope to set the stage for later chapters, which offer positive theories that may contribute to answering the foregoing questions.

In this chapter we will look at some contemporary thinkers who accord primary importance to human freedom or autonomy and yet who also see no value in defending freedom from an Aristotelian framework. These thinkers hold competing theories of ethics and human nature to the one we seek to defend (and to each other). Our purpose in this chapter will be, then, twofold: (1) to respond to criticism[1] of Aristotelian ethics, and (2) if the plausibility of the rebuttal requires it, to show the weaknesses of the competing theory.[2] Once these recent critiques of Aristotelianism have been deflected, the legitimacy of the following chapters should be clear.

Before considering the alleged defects of an Aristotelian ethics, some preliminary observations must be made. The first observation concerns our use of the term *Aristotelian*. We intend to use this term to designate a tradition rather than an individual. A number of individuals, besides Aristotle himself, fall within this tradition. These individuals would include such diverse thinkers as Thomas Aquinas and various contemporary Thomists, Henry Veatch, Ayn Rand, Alasdair MacIntyre, Jacques Maritain, John Finnis, and David Norton. By using 'Aristotelian' to designate a broad tradition, we allow ourselves the flexibility to offer our own variations on the basic themes of this tradition. Moreover, we do not feel obligated to locate every position we take within the texts of Aristotle himself, thus avoiding the impression of interpreting those texts.

All Aristotelians share some basic beliefs. These include the commitment to teleology, eudaimonism, the grounding of ethics in human nature, the natural sociability of man, the primacy of reason over passion, the rejection of reductive materialism, and realism. We shall not directly defend these theses, but allow their meaning to develop as the chapters evolve. In this chapter, for example, we presuppose some familiarity on the part of the reader with these basic tenets of Aristotelianism. Given this presupposition, we then proceed to rebut various criticisms of some of these basic tenets. The result will be that later chapters can assume the plausibility of the Aristotelian paradigm without our having to devote additional space to establishing the validity of that paradigm beforehand—a project that we believe would require another book.

The preceding paragraph has explained one of the senses in which this and the next chapter are concerned with foundations. Another sense in which we are looking at foundations has to do with substantive content. It could be argued that the foundations of Aristotelian ethics begin with metaphysics. In this chapter, however, we are concerned with exploring some basic theories about human nature. Some may regard our examination of human nature as itself metaphysical. If so, then we have a metaphysical starting point. However, many within the Aristotelian tradition would think of *metaphysics* as referring to an examination of being in general (rather than human being). These same individuals may also hold that metaphysics in this latter sense must be done to provide the basis for an Aristotelian ethics. We do not wish to dispute those who see the necessity for metaphysics, but we must provide some limits to our inquiry. Thus, although metaphysical issues are not completely ignored in what follows, we do believe that focusing upon human nature is sufficiently foundational for purposes of this book.

Finally, we will more than likely not include an argument or position the reader believes should have been considered. This problem seems to us unavoidable, since so much has been written on these topics. We do hope, however, to be cognizant of at least some important contemporary themes in the discussion that follows. On the other hand, the reader will note that we have made an effort to discuss a diverse group of individuals.[3] Thus the different individuals and diverse general themes (indicated by section titles) should go some distance in providing the foundational legitimacy for the chapters that follow. By discussing some rather recent and specific criticisms, we hope that our responses will be of contemporary relevance.[4]

RELATIVIST ATTACKS ON ARISTOTELIANISM

Charles King's works represent one of the best defenses of a non-Kantian and non-Aristotelian commitment to freedom. Although King may not be well known in some circles, his influence upon those who value freedom has been extensive. Moreover, he has directly challenged an Aristotelian approach to ethics (our own) with clear and interesting arguments. We therefore believe the reader will be instructed by a discussion of some of King's points and that the purposes of this chapter will be furthered by such a discussion.

King argues that there are two basic approaches to moral theory: approaches which base morality on authority and approaches which base morality on individual interest.[5] King considers 'prescientific' and medieval approaches to morality to be wedded to a cosmology which has God as the ruler of the universe. Under this conception, morality consists of obedience to God's laws. King believes this cosmology to be undermined by modern science. He therefore regards individual interest theories as the alternative to "the simple picture of morality as grounded in God's commands".[6] Since the medieval world view is no longer applicable, men must make their own values. They must base their morality on what actual men actually desire.

Before considering King's 'morality of interest', it should be noted that the two alternatives presented are not jointly exhaustive of the moral theories that can be advanced. The Aristotelian approach to morality stands between King's alternatives. Aristotelians (even Aquinas) do not ground morality in authority. Rather, the good for man is to be found in the actualization of his nature. This teleological conception is based neither on authority nor mere interest. Thus we need not accept King's dichotomous picture of moral theories.

King believes that moral theory must be concerned with general principles. But general principles must be understood in light of the two concepts of moral scepticism King advances. Cognitive moral scepticism concerns whether truth conditions can be found for moral judgments, and motivational moral scepticism concerns whether reasons can be given for why one should act in accordance with certain moral judgments. While King believes there is no reason to accept cognitive moral scepticism, he does believe that the motivational sceptic's question—namely, 'Why should I act that way?'—is the essential test that any would-be moral theory must pass. For this reason King holds that the eudaimonic, utilitarian, and Kantian theories of ethics fail. Each of these theories fails because their foundational principles do not answer the question of the motivational sceptic.

Given the importance King attaches to the motivational sceptic's question, we need to examine the kind of answer that would satisfy this sceptic. According to King, only a moral theory which advances principles that connect with the actual desires of actual people can satisfy the motivational sceptic. If a moral principle cannot appeal to a person's desires, and thus make a claim on his conduct, then that moral principle fails to be the "final court of appeal".

Though it is certainly true that moral theories must be capable of making a claim on human conduct, it is also true, King admits, that moral principles must be sufficiently general so as to guide a variety of persons in a variety of circumstances. It is at this point that a problem appears. Actual human desires are directed towards specific ends. Yet moral principles, if they are to aid us when confronted with numerous alternatives, must not be defined in terms of actual desires or circumstances. For among the alternatives we consistently face is whether a given desire is worthy of pursuit. Thus there seems to be no way, on King's account, to develop from a foundation of actual desires the kind of general guidelines required by moral principles. The moral issue is not simply one of choosing the means necessary to satisfy a desire, but rather whether the desire is worth pursuing in the first place.

In response to the foregoing argument King would want to contend that moral principles do not determine which desires are worthy of pursuing but are rather only maxims guiding the satisfaction of our desires. King states that "neither philosophy nor any other study can show persons what their most deeply felt desires should be".[7] But is this true? It seems to us that ethical theories can (and have) motivated people on the deepest level. For as Spinoza noted long ago, *anything* can serve as a source of motivation,[8] which must also apply to ethical theories. Thus King's objection to an Aristotelian ethics could not be that it necessarily fails to motivate (or satisfy our "most deeply felt desires"), but rather that such a theory is false.

We wonder, however, why truth or falsity of an ethical theory matters to King. For false theories can motivate a person to act as well as true theories and thus pass the motivational sceptic's test. King cannot respond that false theories *really* do not motivate or satisfy desires given the willingness people seem to have to believe in programs advocated by such figures as Hitler and Mao Tse-Tung. Perhaps King would want to claim that moral principles must consistently appeal to everyone's desires. Hitler may have appealed to some but not others. But if this line of response is taken, then King is no longer talking about actual desires, since what is evident is that actual desires are not consistent. Moreover, why should one desire consistency on King's account if one does not now have that actual desire?

Though King talks as if the truth of an ethical theory matters,[9] the foundations he lays for ethics seem to require only effective persuasion. As long as one can present a persuasive account of how one should behave and can effectively appeal to people's actual desires, the motivational sceptic is satisfied. Thus advertisers would have more interesting insights into moral theory than would moral theorists. It seems to us that moral truths are only necessary if moral principles do more than guide us to the satisfaction of our actual desires. King could respond by claiming that following a false moral theory will destroy or make impossible the attainment of other desires we hold. Suppose, for example, we desire to follow the false teachings of a prophet who claims that playing golf is the highest of sins; yet we still desire to play golf. King might claim that we should abandon this false theory so that we could continue to play golf. But why, on King's view, is the desire to play golf any more worthy than the desire to follow this prophet? Only if there is a distinction between right desire and desire can this complaint be justified. An Aristotelian theory provides this distinction; King's theory does not.

The reason King has no conception of right desire is because desire is conceived separately from the requirements of life. In this connection King has an explicit attack on one version of Aristotelianism—namely, that values exist because of the needs and requirements of living beings.[10] King denies that there is any necessary connection between values and life. Since it is possible to imagine a being that is indestructible and has the capacity to desire, there is only a contingent connection between life and values. This argument is offered in rebuttal to our own conclusion that it is life that makes values possible.

Though it is highly dubious that imaginary claims are ever sufficient to show a lack of necessary connection,[11] we shall nevertheless consider King's account of the indestructible desirer. As King puts it, "the mere removal of the possibility of destruction would not remove a whole range of interests or desires of ordinary human life". [12] Notice that King asks us to imagine a being characterized by both life and indestructibility. We, however, find such a notion incoherent and agree with Aristotle that life means "self-nutrition, growth *and* decay". In any case, let us consider this indestructible desirer while ignoring the question of life for the moment.

Is it the case that the indestructible desirer is in every sense 'indestructible'? First of all, desires cannot exist without there being something that is desired. Thus, since we can imagine that all possible objects of desire for this being have been removed, as King puts it, "by whatever means" (including the being's ability to conjure up those objects), this being, *qua desiring* being, can cease to exist. What this shows is that desiring and attaining the objects of one's desires must make a difference to the existence of this being as a desiring being. So when faced with the prospect of continuing to exist as a desiring being versus ceasing to exist as a desiring being, it is the possibility of being destroyed as a desiring being that generates the possibility of values for this being. That is to say, if satisfying its desires were not an end which was crucial to its identity and thus existence as a desiring being, those desires would have no value for it, and it would cease to take actions to maintain itself as a desiring being. Therefore, desiring and conditionality of existence as a certain *type* of being are necessarily connected even if, as in this *per impossibile* example of King's, the being could not entirely pass out of existence. This last point is significant because it reminds us that value and conditionality of existence as a certain *type* of being are always and necessarily connected, that one's 'existence'—at least a certain form of it—is the object of one's actions, or, to put it differently, that values are the sort of thing one holds because they make a difference to oneself. Our broader point is that life is an inherently conditional state and thereby an inherently value-laden state. King's example, in asking us to forget life for the moment, inadvertently forces us to recognize that feature of the nature of life (its conditional status) that is so central to the origin of value.

King further claims that the capacity to desire is all that is necessary for the existence of value. "[V]alue finds its beginning in desire, not merely in the process of life".[13] This claim is, however, false. For if values are that which an entity acts to gain and/or keep (a claim King accepts), then plants have values or ends, though they cannot be said to have desires. This point raises a question about the relationship between life, teleology, and values. We shall discuss this relationship more fully in Chapter 2. At this stage, however, we feel justified in concluding that King has not given us sufficient reasons for rejecting an Aristotelian meta-ethics.

One other feature of King's critique of an Aristotelian ethics is worth noting here—his view of reason. He claims that "the faculty of desire or inclination remains separate from reason".[14] Furthermore, the only function of reason is to serve desire or discover facts. Therefore, King sets up a false dichotomy between reason either being the 'slave of the passions' or the passions being the slave of reason. The Aristotelian tradition once again offers a middle ground between these extremes—

namely, the possibility of rational desire.[15] Aristotle is willing to admit that desire is necessary for action. He is unwilling, however, to consider desires as brute facts unconnected with and uninfluenced by reason. Rational desire is made possible in an Aristotelian ethics because of the distinction between right desire and desire (actual desire). King's unwillingness to make this distinction leaves him with no choice but to create this false dichotomy.

Gilbert Harman is another thinker who is both an advocate of freedom and a critic of Aristotelian ethics. Recently, he has directly challenged[16] Aristotelian ethics by claiming (1) that no account of human nature is sufficient to validate one conception of human flourishing rather than another and (2) that Aristotelian ethics implies consequentialism and is thus incapable of providing a normative foundation for rights. Harman's first charge will not be handled here, for it is quite similar to Alan Gewirth's criticism of the "naturalistic determination thesis" and so our reply to Gewirth in the last section of this chapter can be applied to Harman's first charge. His second charge will be specifically dealt with when our conception of man's natural end is developed in the second chapter. It should, however, suffice for now to say that the natural end for man need not be conceived as an end which requires that all other ends are only valuable as a means to it. Harman's charge of consequentialism, as we shall see in the next chapter, is too quickly made. What we will consider here is his own account of morality. His adherence to relativism and conventionalism is *in itself* an attack upon an Aristotelian approach to ethics (as well as some other approaches). Thus a response to that approach will fulfill our purpose of opening the way to the legitimacy of the Aristotelian paradigm.

Like King, Harman does not believe that there is any a priori source for morality, nor does he believe that morality could arise from God or human nature. Instead, morality is a matter of convention. It arises from shared moral attitudes which result from "continuing implicit negotiation bargaining and compromise".[17] Harman believes that moral judgments,[18] which state what some person ought or ought not do or what is right or wrong for that person, make sense only if the person who makes the judgment and the moral agent agree regarding the moral principle(s) by which the agent's actions are judged. He states that "it makes no sense to ask whether an action is wrong, period, apart from any relation to an agreement".[19] Harman maintains, then, two theses: (1) there is a type of moral judgment which implies that the person judging and the moral agent share similar moral principles; and (2) these moral principles arise from an implicit agreement or a tacit understanding regarding what moral principles will be followed.

Harman's view of morality is, of course, a version of ethical relativism. "All morality", according to Harman, "consists in conventions that are the result of continual tacit bargaining and adjustment".[20] His purpose as an ethical theorist is thus to explain how it is that certain moral principles come to be held. He does not attempt to evaluate a moral principle by a standard 'outside' the context of those who share it, or if he does, he does not regard such an evaluation in a normative sense.

Harman's argument for thesis (1) amounts to an appeal to a form of the ought-implies-can principle. Just as there would be something logically odd about telling someone that he ought to attempt to escape from a prison which is absolutely escape-proof, so too there is something logically odd about telling someone he ought or ought not do X when the person has no reason to follow the advice. To illustrate his thesis, Harman asks us to consider a contented employee of Murder Inc. who has been raised to respect the members of the 'family' but to have no regard for the rest of society and who has been assigned the task of killing a certain bank manager. Harman claims that our judgment that this employee of Murder Inc. ought not to kill the bank manager "would be a misuse of language. . ., since that would imply that our own moral considerations carry some weight with him, which they do not".[21] We may judge him as a criminal, or even say that murder is something morally wrong, but we cannot judge that *this person* ought not to kill the bank manager. In making such a judgment we suppose him susceptible to the moral considerations upon which *we* base our judgment. The employee is, however, beyond the pale, beyond motivational reach; we are not entitled to judge him.

Harman's argument for thesis (2) amounts to an appeal to the argument from best explanation. Harman claims that only a view of morality as something which arises from an implicit or tacit process of negotiation, bargaining, and compromise can account for why we ordinarily place greater importance on the negative as opposed to the positive aspects of morality—that is, why we believe that it is worse to harm someone than to refuse to help them. If morality consisted of an agreement about facts, there would be no reason to suppose that negative duties would be regarded as more important than positive duties. Yet, if we hold that moral principles are adopted by people with different powers and resources who adopt principles which are in their interest, given that others do also, then it seems plausible to view the adoption of moral principles as a process of implicit or tacit negotiation, bargaining, or compromise. People who were well-off would not accept a principle whereby everyone would do as much as possible to help those in need, for this would mean that the poor would get all the benefit from social life.

> A compromise would be likely and a weak principle would probably be accepted . . . . [A]lthough everyone could agree to a strong principle concerning the avoidance of harm, it would not be true that everyone would favor an equally strong principle of mutual aid.[22]

So Harman claims that moral principles result from an implicit agreement or tacit understanding. Morality must be conventional if it is to provide people with reasons to take action.

Harman's arguments for theses (1) and (2) do not work. We will consider his argument for thesis (1) first. There seem to be three problems with this argument.

a. While it is true that to tell the employee of Murder Inc. that he ought not to kill the bank manager it must be possible for him to follow this judgment, this does not mean that the person judging the employee's actions and the employee must share the same moral principles. Rather, all that is necessary is that the employee, or any human being for that matter, possess the ability to reason and choose and thus be capable of discovering why he ought not kill the bank manager. Simply because the employee does not share our moral principles and thus would not at this time be motivated by a judgment made in accordance with them does not mean that he could not discover the truth of these principles and thus be capable of acting in accordance with them. 'Ought implies can' need not be interpreted so narrowly.

b. Though it is certainly true that the employee of Murder Inc. does not know of any reason to follow the moral judgment that he ought not to kill the bank manager, it does not follow that the employee has no reason. If morality is indeed something with foundations in human nature, it would not be impossible to show the employee that he has reasons not to kill the bank manager. And unless we assume that objective moral knowledge is impossible, it does not follow that this employee cannot be given sufficient reasons. Harman cannot logically assume the absence of objective moral standards in an argument designed to show that certain moral judgments are relative. Moreover, he cannot logically assume that lack of moral agreement proves that moral knowledge is impossible.

Yet, Harman's example of a professional criminal is of someone who is described as fully rational and cognizant of all the relevant facts, who neither overlooks nor misunderstands any feature of the reasoning as to why he should not kill the bank manager and does not suffer from 'weakness of will' and still, nonetheless, sees no reason he should not go ahead with the murder. This example represents an alleged possibility with which Harman threatens any would-be nonrelativist conception of morality. He believes that the burden of proof is on the nonrelativist to show that his account of morality can handle this purported possibility. This threat is, however, not as great as Harman supposes. For to shift the burden of proof to the nonrelativist Harman must present an actual case. *Stating* that something is possible is not the same as *demonstrating* it. We suspect there is more to these requirements than Harman realizes, leaving the burden of proof with him to demonstrate the possibility. Furthermore, there is a question that needs to be asked—namely, what does Harman take a sufficient reason to be? In many places Harman notes that a person's reasons depend on that person's interests, desires, plans, intentions, and values; but if these are the ultimate source of human motivation, and nothing else is involved, then a familiar and fundamental objection appears.

c. As we noted when considering King's ethical views, the Aristotelian tradition recognizes the possibility of reason motivating someone to act—that is to say, rational desires are possible—and so it is not necessary to understand a motivation only in terms of the desires or interests one already has. Human motivation is not so narrowly circumscribed. People can be motivated by what is good or right as well as what they desire. Harman's view of what motivates a person seems to share King's failure to consider the possibility that reason could discover the values that human life needs and motivate a person to act in accordance with them. Harman should at least tell us why he does not consider this possibility.

There is only one problem with Harman's argument for thesis (2). It is, however, a major one. Since morality is supposed to be the result of an implicit process of negotiation, bargaining, and compromise, there is the problem of why anyone *ought* to keep the agreement. This question looms large given Harman's view of morality, for there is no standard to which one can appeal to say that one ought to keep his agreements and understandings. Harman is, however, unimpressed by this question. He notes that this question (objection) rests on treating an agreement as a kind of ritual, and such treatment of agreements is a mistake.[23] To agree to follow a moral principle is, for Harman, more than just saying one will. Rather, it is to intend to do something—in this case, to follow a moral principle—and if one intends to do what a moral principle states, then there is no problem of motivation. In other words, we would already have a reason to keep our agreement. Yet does this reply actually succeed? Granted that once we intend to do something, we have reason to do it, why ought we develop the intention to follow certain moral principles in the first place?

Harman states that persons accept certain values and principles "mainly because it is in their interest to do so, given that others also do".[24] Further, he states that "what a person has reason to do depends on that person's various desires, plans, intentions, and values".[25] Yet how is one to determine where his interests lie? Are no courses of action better for someone than others? And if there are better courses of action, what is the basis for determining where one's real interests lie? If, on the other hand, interest is understood as merely the satisfaction of our actual desires, then why would one ever agree to some *general* principle of action? Harman is, of course, an ethical relativist and does not have to claim that morality arises outside of convention. Thus these questions need not bother him when it comes to *evaluating* persons who do not develop the intention to follow certain moral principles. Yet Harman is attempting to *explain* how certain ethical principles arise, and if he cannot provide the best account of why these moral principles exist, then his claim that morality rests on implicit agreements and tacit understandings fails. Therefore, the questions of why someone should ever agree to some general principle of action or why someone should ever *intend* to follow a moral principle are extremely important.

Harman's account of ethical principles fails to answer these questions. He claims that people agree to follow moral principles because it suits their interests, desires, and plans, but since he offers no standard by which to differentiate one's true interests from merely apparent ones, it seems quite likely that one would (implicitly) agree to follow a moral principle only until there was a conflicting interest. Harman's account of why ethical principles are adopted fails to explain why anyone would ever be *obligated* to follow a moral principle in a situation in which one has a conflicting interest. There is, of course, no basis for obligation in Harman's theory, because acting from obligation has something to do with acting from principle, and principled behavior is precisely what Harman's theory removes. Moreover, the logic of Harman's approach creates the incentive to participate in bargaining only if it increases one's power over others. If one can maneuver oneself into a position of power, then the breaking of a moral principle will be costless, since others can do nothing about it. Of course, most attempts to grab power fail, and one would have to be very careful and circumspect in one's power lusting. Nevertheless, there would be no moral reason, no obligation on one's part, to treat others as anything more than a means to increasing one's own power.

Since Harman has not provided a reason for why one would follow a general moral principle, and indeed, since his theory dictates against that possibility anyway, he has not provided the best explanation of morality. We would suggest that the best explanation of morality cannot ignore principled actions and the standards for justifying such actions.

Such standards can be found in that province Harman has dismissed from consideration, namely, human nature. It is here we may find why we should follow moral principles.

Perhaps Harman would consider this final objection unfair, for he may not regard his purpose to be one of explaining why someone is obligated to follow a moral principle when his interests conflict. Harman may wish to deny that moral principles should be interpreted in such a manner. Denying that moral principles obligate where one's interests are in conflict is, of course, nothing new and would be a possible move for Harman to make. [26] There is, however, a problem with this move. How would Harman then justify his claim[27] that his version of moral relativism implies tolerance of other moralities?

Harman argues that if we suppose that everyone agrees that morality is a matter of convention, then no one will claim to have some privileged insight into what *the* true moral principles must be. Thus, one will recognize that as a practical matter some understanding with others will need to be reached and "that is where the pressure for tolerance comes from".[28] It may be true that there are some practical pressures towards tolerance, but that does not show why one *ought* to be tolerant and thus, once again, why one should develop the intention to follow a moral principle of toleration. Since human history has taught us that the practical pressures for intolerance are as great or greater than those for tolerance, Harman's theory may actually result in the opposite of what he intends. To wit:

> If relativism signifies contempt for fixed categories and men who claim to be the bearers of an objective, immortal truth . . . then there is nothing more relativistic than Fascist attitudes and activity. . . . From the fact that all ideologies are of equal value, that all ideologies are mere fictions, the modern relativist infers that everybody has the right to create for himself his own ideology and to attempt to enforce it with all the energy of which he is capable.[29]

Both King and Harman approach ethics in a similar fashion. The Humean thesis on the primacy of the passions is taken as given and so is the Humean position on the nature of facts and their relation to values. In both cases, present actual desires, nonteleologically understood, are the ground upon which ethical theory is to be built. These foundations lead to a general problem with which we would like to conclude this part of the chapter—namely, the problem of generating an ought from an is. Since both King and Harman embed their doctrine in an 'is', it seems to us difficult or impossible to generate any 'oughts' (as Hume himself might have predicted). For if actual desires or actual agreements are the decisive criteria, it seems unlikely that a case for acting in ways other than one desires to act can be made. The best one can hope for is to discover some less than fully articulated present desire to appeal to, or to show how more of one's present desires can be fulfilled by one course of action rather than another.

Kant seems to have understood the point we are making quite well. Having accepted the Humean vision of the 'phenomenal' self, Kant knew he needed to generate norms from some other source. Should Hume's conception of man turn out to be correct, Kant is likely to have concluded that ethics would reduce to a branch of anthropology. The ethicist would wither away, leaving the serious work of explaining why people desire what they desire or agree to what they agree to to the social scientist. In other words, the task at hand would be explaining behavior—not recommending alternative courses of action. The 'is' is especially troublesome for a thinker like King, because King seems to hold a vision of a liberal social order. Although we are sympathetic to King's vision, we believe that given his theory of human motivation and given current desires and institutions, a liberal society would surely be a mere fantasy. Harman, on the other hand, is more circumspect. He does not actually argue for a new order; he merely describes why certain norms have an appeal. Such a procedure is to be expected when actual agreements are the ground for ethical theorizing, for within such a program the 'ethicist' can do no more than explain why the norms that exist have arisen. The 'ethicist' cannot justify why those norms ought to be pursued independently of the reasons given for why they arose in the first place. Thus, although we admire King's commitment to freedom, we believe Harman's noncommittal descriptivism to be more consistent.

A FORMALISTIC ATTACK ON ARISTOTELIAN ETHICS

Robert Nozick does not share in the main problems that beset Harman. He escapes these problems by rejecting one of the main Humean theses from which Harman operates, and he tries to take the middle ground that an Aristotelian would also wish to hold:

> We should not be surprised that objective value can be specified apart from what a person actually desires. . . . However, value is not completely divorced from motivation simply because it need not be tied to actual motivation under any and all conditions.[30]

Nozick does, however, share with Harman a rejection of the Aristotelian paradigm, although he does make more of an effort to incorporate some of that paradigm's insights on flourishing.[31] Moreover, Nozick shares with Harman and ourselves an interest in liberty. It should therefore be advantageous to our purpose here to examine some of Nozick's views as they directly affect our topic.

Some years ago Nozick published an explicit attack on one version of Aristotelianism.[32] A few years later we published our own response to that attack.[33] It seems pointless to resurrect that debate here. In any case, we cannot be certain that the views Nozick held then are still held by him today. We therefore wish to focus on what he has to say in *Philosophical Explanations* about Aristotelian ethics. We will concentrate upon Nozick's objections to the Aristotelian concept of flourishing.

We shall begin by examining Nozick's most direct attack upon Aristotle which is contained in a section entitled 'Flourishing'. Nozick claims that "Aristotle held that what is special to a thing marks its function, and so fixes its peculiarly appropriate form of behavior, its mode of flourishing".[34] The problem with such a view, asserts Nozick, is that there is no necessary connection between uniqueness and flourishing. An entity E might possess property P, which no other entity possesses, but P might nevertheless contribute nothing to the flourishing of E. Moreover, if Aristotle were right and we discovered some other entity E_1 who possessed P, then that would seem to imply that P's importance to flourishing (assuming now that P contributes to flourishing) would cease to exist. Thus possessing unique property P cannot adequately serve as the foundation for a concept of flourishing.

Nozick's basic mistake in the foregoing analysis comes from believing that Aristotle holds that possessing properties is analogous to possessing objects—what has sometimes been termed the pin-cushion theory of substance. This mistake is reflected in Nozick's opening sentence quoted above. Aristotle did not hold that a thing's function was determined by its distinguishing characteristic.[35] Rather Aristotle held (1) that uniqueness alone was not decisive, but that distinctiveness mattered only insofar as it expressed a thing's essence, (2) that the distinguishing characteristic would necessarily serve as the faculty through which other faculties would be developed if flourishing were to occur, and (3) that development of the distinguishing characteristic would be valuable for its own sake. Suppose, for example, that reason is the distinguishing characteristic. Knowing the differentia would not be enough for Aristotle to develop a concept of flourishing. One must also know the genus, say animality. Flourishing, then, could not be constituted by disembodied reasoning, nor is that our function.[36] Fulfilling our function would also include the development of faculties shared by other animals (such as pleasure and health). What the distinguishing characteristic does do for us that is unique is to characterize the modality through which the development of these other faculties will be successful.

The distinguishing characteristic is not valued for its uniqueness, for Aristotle was aware of other unique features we possess (such as risibility). Rather, the distinguishing characteristic serves to *identify* the kind of being for whom flourishing is possible and thus the kind of flourishing appropriate to that being. Even Nozick cannot escape this sense of 'distinguishing characteristic', for he devotes numerous pages to what courses of action are appropriate for human flourishing. In this sense, too, Nozick gives human beings a distinct identity from which he judges success or failure. This is certainly not the place to engage in discussions of Aristotelian real definitions or the role of the doctrine of the predicables. It is enough to note that what Aristotle does with his differentia in a real definition is not unlike what Nozick does with his notion of a "value-seeking I". Both thinkers attempt to identify what it is about the thing in question (human beings) that can serve to synthesize and explain the diverse factors of human existence.

The foregoing explains why P is not merely contingently related to the concept of flourishing for Aristotle. It is only if one views P as some separable property of a substance (a pin in the cushion) that one can carry through Nozick's first criticism. Thus we have no objection to the proposition that a unique property may not contribute to flourishing, but we do object to the idea that an essentially differentiating property could be conceived to be only contingently related to what will count as flourishing for that kind of thing—whether the thing be plant, animal, or man. Yet there is still the second criticism concerning the discovery of some other creature with this same distinguishing characteristic. Would we now have to give up P as a measure of flourishing once this creature is discovered?

Given our description of what Aristotle was after with his concept of a differentia, it is obvious that discovery of another creature with P would not mean that P no longer defines the mode of flourishing for us simply because P is no longer unique to us. Nozick's question, however, seems to involve more than this: suppose we discover another creature, who also possesses P, that is differentiated from ourselves only by our having Q, and Q is not a property of us that is particularly significant for our flourishing. Would Q now take on added significance for us simply because it is now the only differentiating factor? The answer here must be no, since Q was already defined as not contributing to flourishing in the first place. The case would be analogous to discovering for the first time that there are dark-skinned (or light-skinned) people. Thus, to make Nozick's criticism go through, we must suppose that Q *is* significant for our flourishing but is somehow not P.

To accept the idea that Q is significant for our flourishing but does not necessarily involve P is a move we refuse to make, since it requires us to philosophize in an un-Aristotelian way.[37] Since P and Q are not properties tacked on to a being that can be understood separately from it, we would be required to imagine P-ing in ways exclusive of Q-ing. But since Aristotelian real definitions intend to capture an *integrated* conception of the entity, QP-ing must be part of what we mean by possessing P.

The only remaining alternative, therefore, is to use analogical reasoning. Let us call this new entity, following Nozick,[38] an angel. This angel bears some similarity to us in the sense that it can engage in syllogistic reasoning P,[39] but failing to possess any animality Q, its flourishing does not include such things as pleasure, health, and human love. Here we would argue that the angel only analogically possesses P, since

P is not exercised in the way P is exercised for us. P still serves to identify what is essential for our type of flourishing. The only difference now is that certain operations we thought peculiar to our form of P are now recognized to be possessed by others. To some, even admitting this much looks like a major departure from Aristotelianism. But there is nothing in the nature of real definitions as Aristotle conceived them that does not permit revision or that precludes the existence of borderline cases, even if there is some dispute about whether Aristotle himself recognized these possibilities. What *is* clear is that Nozick fails to understand the Aristotelian conceptions of substance and real definitions, and thus, flourishing.[40]

In general this misunderstanding comes from an attempt to use dichotomous categories that Aristotle would reject. These categories are roughly similar to the rationalist/empiricist dichotomy of modern philosophy. Notice that Nozick treats the issue *formally*, as if the question at hand could be adequately treated in terms of Ps and Qs. If that were true, then the discovery of dark- (or light-) skinned people would be a significant problem for Aristotelians. Since that is not a problem, one comes to realize that the type of empiricism Aristotelianism (at least as we interpret it) represents, requires more than the merely formal presentation given to it by Nozick. On the other hand, the preceding section demonstrates that Aristotelianism is not reducible to the kind of Humean empiricism to which Harman's theory is subject. Although Nozick's criticism of Aristotelian flourishing was rationalistic, Nozick's philosophy does not strike us as *exclusively* rationalistic. Certainly that philosophy is not merely formal. Gewirth, on the other hand, is expressly rationalistic in ethics. Strangely enough, however, his criticism of Aristotelianism is not nearly as formalistic as Nozick's criticism.

A SUBSTANTIVE RATIONALIST CRITIQUE OF ARISTOTELIANISM

In the preceding sections of this chapter we have examined some contemporary advocates of freedom representing different schools of ethical thought. In this section we would like to conclude with one more advocate of freedom—Alan Gewirth. By now it is common knowledge that Gewirth considers freedom to be a necessary and generic feature of

action. The same claim is made for 'welfare', but it is Gewirth's advocacy of freedom that justifies his inclusion in this chapter. Equally important for our purposes is the fact that Gewirth is perhaps the finest rep-
resentative of Kantianism that analytic philosophy currently has to offer.
However, our claim that Gewirth is a Kantian should not be misunderstood. He does not base his ethics on the formal characteristic of reason
alone, as Kant seems to, but adds substance by considering the generic
features of human action. Nevertheless, Gewirth's formal application of
the generic features of action, his emphasis on the centrality of contradiction, his view that ethics is primarily concerned with the other, and
his rejection of teleology as the basis for ethical standards makes him a
Kantian in a similar way in which we are Aristotelians; variations on the
tradition are not enough to place him (or us) outside of it.

Gewirth's major work, *Reason and Morality*,[41] does not contain any
sustained critique of the Aristotelian tradition, although there are numerous references to the inegalitarian (and thus defective) nature of that tradition. Fortunately, Gewirth's breadth of scholarship allows us to look
elsewhere for such a critique. At a symposium in honor of the retirement
of the Aristotelian scholar Henry B. Veatch, Gewirth presented a long
and sustained attack on the Aristotelian ethical tradition. This paper,
'Natural Law, Human Action, and Morality', has been published, along
with the others given at the symposium, in a collection of essays on
Veatch's thought.[42] Our focus, therefore, will be upon this paper. The
response we give to Gewirth below should be taken as an attempt to reject the claim that the Aristotelian tradition cannot serve as the basis for
a sound ethical theory. Our remarks should not be construed as necessarily a refutation of Gewirth's own ethical theory.

The bulk of Gewirth's criticisms of the Aristotelian natural-end tradition are expressed by two theses: the "naturalistic determination thesis"
and the "rationalistic thesis."[43] The first thesis holds that "the good of
human beings is based on or is determined by their nature." The second
thesis holds that "this basis is ascertained by reason."[44] It is with the
naturalistic determination thesis (henceforth NDT) that Gewirth begins
his main critique.

Since the NDT holds that man's good is determined by his nature,
the question arises whether this nature is a necessary or a sufficient condition for determining the good for man. Gewirth is willing to admit that

some conception of human nature is a necessary condition for determining the good. Indeed, "human nature sets the outer limits on what can count as the good of man, but it does not exhaustively define or constitute the good".[45] Thus Gewirth's criticism is that despite the claims of the Aristotelian, human nature is not a sufficient condition for defining the good for man. In this connection, Gewirth's tactic is to raise problems about what constitutes the good and thus show that since the answers are ambiguous or not forthcoming, the Aristotelian cannot claim that human nature provides a sufficient condition. One of the issues raised by Gewirth concerns Aristotle's claim that it is our *distinctive* mode of being (that is, rationality) that should guide us in defining the good. Gewirth's criticism is similar to the one leveled by Nozick, and since we have dealt with that above, we shall not repeat ourselves here.

Gewirth does not leave the reader without a standard for determining when sufficiency has been reached. He says:

> By a basic principle being "determinate", I mean that it has or entails definite contents, such that the *opposite* contents are ruled out or prohibited. So the question of determinacy may also be put in this way: Do we get a single, consistent set of characteristics for the content of man's good if we try to derive it from man's nature in the sense just indicated? Can we read man's good off from man's nature in this sense? [46]

Gewirth's answer to these questions is no, and our own conception of what is implied by human nature must await the next chapter. But it is worth noting at this stage that Aristotelians may object to the standard Gewirth has just laid down. For it is not at all clear that the thinkers of this tradition have claimed that man's good can be 'read off' from his nature as one 'reads off' sales figures from a sales chart. Since a traditional realist theory of knowledge does not claim that knowledge can be 'read off' from reality, and since man's good is an object of knowledge, there is little reason to suppose that the Aristotelian must adhere to the standard Gewirth proposes. Man's good may require the same process of effort and discovery needed to realize any object of knowledge.

Nevertheless, Gewirth does seem justified in demanding that some standards be implied by human nature, and thus he may be correct in claiming that "the concept of human nature. . . is too diffuse and varied to provide a determinate set of contents for natural law".[47] The evidence

Gewirth offers for this last claim is that distinctive features of human nature can imply morally objectionable or contradictory results. For example, self-aggrandizement is distinctively human, but is morally objectionable.[48] Reason may be distinctive, but it can be used for good *or* evil.[49] Thus even what is distinctive about man is too "diffuse and varied" to function well as a standard for ethics.

However, such criticisms either indicate a fundamental lack of understanding of the theory Gewirth is attacking (which is difficult to believe), or they indicate that Gewirth assumes the validity of a meta-ethical principle contrary to the one used by the theory he is attacking. No Aristotelian holds that a distinctive human faculty (such as reason) can be understood in separation from the rest of human nature or from man's *telos*. Because of the act/potency distinction, how one actually reasons does not, by itself, speak to the value of such reasoning with respect to achieving our natural end. Moreover, as we indicated in our discussion of Nozick, 'reason' is most likely understood by the tradition to involve more than the linear kind of deductive reasoning prevalent in modern conceptions (and exemplified by such thinkers as Descartes, Hume, and Kant). Thus, although reason is a distinctive faculty of human nature, a complete understanding of this faculty cannot be obtained by examining it in separation from the other features of human nature. What Gewirth offers us is more along the lines of *reasoning* than it is of reason itself, since all he has shown is that it is possible for people to employ a process of reasoning and arrive at false conclusions.

Gewirth, of course, is free to reject the notion of final causality as well as the non-Humean idea that what is distinct is not necessarily separable. He is not, however, free to assume the falsity of these positions while making his criticism. Had he not assumed the validity of these non-Aristotelian theses in his critique, he would have realized that the fact that reason can be used for good as well as evil says nothing at all about whether a feature of the faculty in question (reasoning) may be capable of ignoring its own conclusions about the good, or whether it is possible to proceed from ill-considered or false premises, or whether it is possible to fail to make the effort to discover the good in the first place. The ethical imperative of classical Aristotelianism is that one live a rational life, not that one live simply a reasoning life. Reason, as Gewirth understands it, is clearly not our *telos*, for all men can reason but not all have achieved their final end. Hence it should have been obvious that the attenuated understanding of reason Gewirth presents *could not* be the one held by Aristotelians when considering questions of the human good.

Gewirth's arguments go astray because his basic conviction is that any particular behavior of a person with a rational nature is just as natural as any other behavior. Thus the mindless existence of a drug addict would be no less natural than the examined life of Socrates. Of course, on some level both types of lives are natural in the sense that they are not miraculous or illusory. But to argue this way would be like saying that the stunted and sickly condition of an organism is as natural as a healthy one. Again, they are both natural in the senses just mentioned and in the sense that the sickly condition of organism P is necessarily dependent upon P possessing the nature of a P. But surely the point is that P's nature enables us to say something about the difference between health and disease for P. And the ability to make this distinction reflects a certain (teleological) conception of nature—one that Gewirth does not recognize or fails to endorse. In short, Gewirth's arguments, in virtue of their dependence upon a particular interpretation of *natural*, beg the question about whether deviant forms of behavior qualify as natural.

In a similar light, a major part of Gewirth's attack comes in the fifth section of his paper, where he argues that Aristotle himself held that human nature was not sufficient to ground the good for man. Gewirth puts the substance of his point as follows:

> But—and this is the crucial point—these potentialities can be turned in many different directions so far as concerns the various virtues, vices, and other ethical conditions that may be developed on the basis of them. This is the *diffuseness* to which I referred before. . . . Thus Aristotle emphasizes that the development of the various states of character cannot be accounted for by *nature* (*physis*), where nature is the efficient and formal cause that drives entities along the path from potentiality to actualization. . . . Hence, moral virtues must have a different source than nature, including human nature, and this source consists in the way in which our passions or emotions are *conditioned* in one direction rather than others.[50]

Gewirth's point here is simply that since some other element is needed to establish the good—in this case habituation—human nature cannot be the sufficient condition for establishing the good. Thus although we must locate our good within our function (necessary condition), our good is not the same *as* our function and thus not a sufficient condition for determining the good. Gewirth caps off his discussion by noting that

> [Aristotle] defines the human good not simply in terms of certain facts of human operations or activities, but rather in terms of the good performance of those activities. He goes on to say that such good performance means that the activities are carried on "in accordance with *virtue*" i.e. with excellence.[51]

The foregoing passage, however, fails to note that what counts as excellence or virtue may itself be determined in terms of human nature. And Gewirth's refusal to interpret 'function,' 'nature' or 'activity' teleologically accounts for why he believes that the *good* performance of a function must be determined by some standard unrelated to the function itself".[52] Indeed, in the passage just prior to the preceding, notice that Gewirth understands 'nature' in Aristotle *without* final causality! Furthermore, Gewirth seems to believe that Aristotle is culture bound in the sense that he (Aristotle) interprets good functioning in terms of "his own class, time, and place".[53]

We suspect that the problem here is again tied to Gewirth's conception of nature. He simply cannot understand how a human being's development toward excellence can possibly be natural, if such development requires the cultivation of intellectual and moral virtues. Deliberate planning and effort seem to fall under the category of art rather than nature for Gewirth. But this too begs the whole question. For Aristotelians the fulfillment of our nature requires deliberation and planning. Thus, for Aristotelians, civilized man is *natural* man, whereas for many modern thinkers (such as Hobbes and Rousseau) natural man is best characterized by savage or primitive man.[54] Gewirth seems to fall into this latter category, and his arguments put the issue in clear focus. For when the question is asked, 'When is man most natural?' one paradigm posits a creature whose capacities and excellences have been developed; the other paradigm calls forth a creature ruled by unreflective instinct and desire.

Section 6 begins Gewirth's discussion of the "rationalistic thesis". The rationalistic thesis (hereafter RT) holds that it is reason that determines the good for man. Although Gewirth offers some relatively minor objections to this thesis,[55] his main approach is to examine reason in Aristotle and Aquinas separately and show the defects of each thinker's conception.[56] The basic conclusion of these remarks is the same as Gewirth's conclusion about the NDT: the conceptions of reason offered by Aristotle and Aquinas are too indeterminate to serve as a clear standard for the good of man. There are, however, some different arguments offered in these sections, and we shall look at a few of the major ones.

In the section on Aristotle, Gewirth's main objection to the RT seems to be the following:

> In the case of the body, there are trans-culturally recognized norms of physical health that specify the ends toward which the physician must work. It is these norms that constitute man's bodily good; and reason can operate to ascertain the means to this end. But there are not similar trans-culturally recognized norms or ends in the case of the moral virtues. What constituted a good man in Nazi Germany, for example, was different in important respects from the criteria upheld in the Soviet Union, and both of these were different from the criteria upheld in the western democracies, in various parts of Asia and Africa, and so forth.[57]

After this passage Gewirth asserts that Aristotle inserted the values of his own culture when trying to give a determinate account of man's good, indicating that the RT fails or is indeterminate. But this kind of argument contains two elementary errors: (1) even if Aristotle does insert his own culture's values into his theory, it does not follow from that that the theory itself is defective; and (2) the fact that different conceptions of the good exist does not show that they are all equally justified on the basis of Aristotle's theory, *nor* does it show that they are all justifiable. On the basis of this kind of argument one could argue that since not all communities advocate the kind of egalitarianism and welfare statism that Gewirth does towards the end of *Reason and Morality*, Gewirth cannot claim that egalitarianism and welfare statism are rationally justified.

One can, however, challenge Gewirth's argument more directly. Is it in fact true that "norms of physical health" are transculturally agreed upon?[58] Certainly, there is no transculturally accepted form of medicine, thus showing that there is no transculturally accepted way (no rationally justified way?) of correcting ill health. Moreover, there do not seem to be transculturally recognized forms of diet and exercise. Indeed, even within our own culture there is much debate (for instance) about the value of natural foods and about which diets and exercise programs will ensure health. Thus Gewirth must be claiming that a healthy person can be *recognized* as such transculturally, even if there is dispute about the means to that end. We suspect that even on this count, the matter is not so clear cut as Gewirth makes it seem; but Gewirth's claim here is not implausible, so we shall accept it now at face value.

Aristotle, as Gewirth himself notes,[59] would have predicted that there would be more of a chance for agreement on physical health than on moral health, since the object in question (the body) is itself, more limited and determinate than the soul. But after all, is it really the case that an analogous argument for the soul cannot be made as Gewirth has made it for the body? We think not. Like a healthy individual, persons of vision, principle, achievement, and integrity seem to shine through the limits of their own culture such that other cultures—(indeed, other ages)—can admire their moral qualities. The following words by Henry Veatch illustrate this point:

> . . . in the context of our present argument, what is significant is not merely the fact that both Socrates and [the Earl of] Ormonde, each in their respective ways, might be said to have lived examined lives, but also that we today as we read the accounts of such lives are able to appreciate the excellence of their examples. For in the circumstances and conditions of our lives we are as different from both Socrates and Ormonde as they were from each other. Yet the requirements of human excellence are discernible in human life wherever it may be found, with the result that we all, with but few exceptions, have at least some inkling of the kinds of claims which our very human nature makes upon us.[60]

It would seem, therefore, that although there may be disagreements over specifics, and perhaps more to learn or discover about moral behavior, some basic moral truths do manage to be recognized transculturally.

In the end, however, Gewirth's criticism comes down to a single point—the lack of determinacy, which characterizes Aristotelian ethics. It is this indeterminacy that supposedly keeps this tradition from ruling out evil actions as being natural, that keeps the tradition from generating a theory of obligation with deontological force, that fails to rule out as logically inconsistent actions that are not good, and that fails to provide any helpful guidance for our actions. It is thus time to meet the indeterminacy argument head on.

The central defect of Gewirth's critique is that what he regards as the weakness of Aristotelianism is in fact its very strength and plausibility. Gewirth is correct to claim that the human good cannot be 'read off' from human nature, thus leaving some degree of indeterminacy. But Gewirth's conclusion about the tradition is only a problem if one assumes beforehand that it is the purpose of and appropriate to ethical theorizing to remove all elements of indeterminacy from ethical reasoning and judgment. This assumption can and should be rejected. The value of the Aristotelian tradition may be analogous to the value of the U.S. Constitution—both have staying power precisely because they do not attempt to speak to every issue in every circumstance. In practice, flexibility or indeterminacy translate into a recognition of the value of diversity, pluralism, and a basic commitment to individual judgment and responsibility. Such values are lost in an approach to ethics that relies almost exclusively on a priori and deductive resolutions of ethical issues [61]

Gewirth shares the modern preoccupation with rules and formal deductive processes. The tendency of this approach is to confuse ethics with law in the sense that the goal of ethical reasoning becomes the creation of a deontological rule for every situation. When Kant removed prudence from the list of classically accepted virtues, he did more than indicate a scepticism about there being any relationship between morality and self-interest. In effect, Kant defined ethics in terms of the Cartesian conception of rationality—a move Descartes himself was reluctant to make.[62] What was once thought essential to an understanding of prudence (and the other virtues as well) was now thought accidental and even distracting to ethical theory. The contingencies of practical action—differing circumstances, risk, uncertainty about the future, culture, self-interest, personal judgment, and differing talents and abilities—were either ignored completely or relegated to what the deductive process could not cover at the time. [63]

It is questionable whether the Kantian (Gewirthian) approach to ethics is an improvement over what it sought to replace. The price of 'determinacy' has been a bifurcated human nature, especially with respect to the appetites. Where Aristotle could meaningfully speak of

appetitive rationality or rational appetites, modern philosophy dichoto-
mized reason and appetite to such an extent that they become irreconcil-
able, leaving the ethical theorist to choose between the two (for example,
relativism or Kantian formalism). The evidence for this is Gewirth's own
arguments. As we saw above, Gewirth's discussion of reason and rationality indicates the extent to which he separates reason from the rest of
human nature. The result of this approach has been modern man's vacil-
lation between sentimentality and/or hedonism on the one hand and
deontological rigidity in ethics on the other. A further price paid by the
adoption of the Cartesian framework has been the loss of personal responsibility and judgment. Since contingency *is* a feature of practical
action, the effort to remove it necessitates conformity of will and action.
Today there is virtually no human problem that someone has not claimed
requires a national policy or set of standards. And what is allowed to
qualify as 'good' is also admitted only if it applies in precisely the same
manner to everyone equally. Since neither actions nor persons are reducible to precise formalization, the very egalitarianism advocated by
Gewirth and others is, as one thinker so aptly put it,[64] a "revolt against
nature". It is, therefore, by no means obvious that contingency and indeterminacy are the vices that Gewirth supposes them to be.

It is important that our remarks here not be misunderstood. Our
claim is not that the Aristotelian tradition holds that the human good is
at root indeterminate. Rather, our claim is that this tradition formulates
principles whose degree of determinancy is appropriate to the variety of
circumstances to which those principles are to apply. Gewirth, on the
other hand, 'proves' too much and ends up contradicting himself. He
grants in the opening pages of his paper that human nature can set some
necessary boundaries for what will count as the good. If this is so, however, then it follows that some acts can cross those boundaries and thus
violate the principles of the system. But Gewirth's arguments amount to
saying that human nature provides no boundaries at all. Obviously one
cannot have it both ways.

If human nature—considered in abstraction from particular circumstances, cultures, times, and places—can serve as the basis for any moral
values, however minimal in specific content they may be, then perhaps
that is all that this aspect of the theory was ever designed to do. In other
words, perhaps it is the case that human nature is both necessary and

sufficient for establishing the minimal (but necessary) boundary conditions that can be applicable cross-culturally and irrespective of circumstances. Veatch's principle of living the examined life may be a case in
point. Man's *telos* and rational nature generate an obligation to lead an
examined life; but what exactly that life will look like cannot be deduced
from the concept of human nature alone. In our own case, we believe a
theory of rights (such as the one outlined in Chapter 3) can be grounded
in human nature. Rights, by their very nature, establish boundary conditions, not specific rules for behavior in concrete situations. Thus human
nature may be both necessary and sufficient with respect to answering
some moral questions, even if it is not both necessary and sufficient with
respect to all moral questions.

Human existence can be given more content if we consider human
nature in conjunction with other factors that are part of human living.
These factors would include circumstances, personal aptitudes, prudential judgment, habituation, cultural surroundings and values, and risk and
uncertainty. If some of these factors are used to further enhance our concept of human nature, we can start to develop additional boundaries
within the general boundaries mentioned above. Aristotle's doctrine of
the virtues would be an example here. Recognizing the importance of
habituation for moral behavior, as well as differing personal aptitudes
and cultural surroundings, the ethical theorist can begin to elaborate a set
of guidelines for virtuous behavior. As Aristotle himself recognized,
these standards will still contain a large measure of indeterminacy. We
may be able to set reasonable limits (extremes) for, say, courageous and
cowardly behavior, but where any individual will fit can vary. Again,
this indeterminacy marks the virtue of the system, not its failing. The
ethical theorist, given his remoteness from actual specific situations, can
only offer guidance—not definitive solutions. The more experience and
knowledge the ethical thinker gains (Aristotle's "man of practical wisdom"), the more trustworthy the advice. But even the wise man's advice
cannot be a substitute for responsible personal judgment on the part of
the individual to whom such advice may be offered.

Gewirth, operating within a rationalistic framework where moral
truth can be *deduced* categorically from basic premisses, is uncomfortable with systems that place a heavy burden on personal judgement.
After all, a system like Aristotle's could allow for varying judgments

under the same set of circumstances depending on the individuals involved. Thus Kant and Gewirth push the Cartesian method in ethics to
the point where individual judgment is (and must be) replaced by a definitive rule covering that situation. Diversity is tolerated only if it is
quantitative and not qualitative diversity; that is, as long as the rule does
not specify the number of individuals it covers, diverse individuals are
allowed to act under that rule. It is not, however, permitted that there be
diverse interpretations or applications of the rule by qualitatively diverse
individuals. It is no accident, therefore, that in Gewirth's own ethical
theorizing what constitutes a moral principle is that which cannot be rejected on "pain of contradiction". And it is worth speculating on what
the world would be like if businessmen, athletes, engineers, and the like
could only follow moral recommendations that were incapable of being
overturned except on "pain of contradiction".

The Gewirthian criticisms of the Aristotelian tradition in ethics fail
not because those criticisms are inherently weak, but rather because they
fail to comprehend an approach not grounded on the same set of assumptions and methodology as his own system. If this summary statement is correct, the student of ethical theory is left with some fundamental choices between an approach like Gewirth's and one like Aristotle's.
In this connection, Gewirth has done a service to ethical theorists; for
Gewirth's basic point about indeterminacy is, in some sense, on target.
The final significance of that point must therefore be that personal freedom, judgment, and responsibility are given primacy of place in the
Aristotelian project. An approach like Gewirth's, on the other hand, must
struggle hard to find a place for such values.

2

IN DEFENSE OF
A NATURAL-END ETHICS

Yet many men, being slaves to appetite and sleep, have passed through life untaught and untrained, like many wayfarers; in these men we see, contrary to Nature's intent, the body a source of pleasure, the soul a burden. For my own part, I consider the lives and deaths of such men as about alike, since no record is made of either. In very truth, that man alone lives and makes the most of life, as it seems to me, who devotes himself to some occupation, courting the fame of a glorious deed or noble career. But amid the wealth of opportunities, Nature points out one path to one and another to another.

—Sallust, *Bellum Catilinae*

In Chapter 1 we showed that it was not necessary to adopt ethical relativism and that neither a Kantian nor a formalist critique of an Aristotelian ethics succeeds. Yet it remains to be seen just what an Aristotelian ethics amounts to and how it would address the basic meta-ethical issues that have plagued much of modern and contemporary philosophy. Further, the exact character of an Aristotelian ethics as a normative theory needs to be examined; for we are concerned to show that an Aristotelian ethics provides the moral foundation for the natural right to liberty. This chapter will describe, develop, and defend an Aristotelian ethics; Chapter 3 will use the moral foundation established in this chapter as the basis for its account of the natural right to liberty.

In the first main section of this chapter we intend to outline some of the main features of an Aristotelian ethics. Our purpose here is to briefly familiarize (or refamiliarize) the reader with these features, many of which are discussed in more detail in the sections that follow. We also intend to correct some common misunderstandings that have been associated with these concepts. In the second main section of the chapter we discuss some of the central issues surrounding an Aristotelian meta-ethics, and in the final main section we indicate how some of the principles discussed in earlier sections have an effect on Aristotelian normative theory.

BASIC FEATURES OF AN ARISTOTELIAN ETHICS

Aristotelian Essentialism and Cognitive Realism

An Aristotelian ethics derives its characterization of a good human life from a knowledge of human nature. Accordingly, it assumes that human beings have a nature and that this nature can be known. Overall, this assumption reflects the metaphysical view of essentialism and the epistemological view of cognitive realism. Most generally stated, essentialism is simply the claim that to exist is to be something. Every being *in rerum natura* is necessarily what it is. (We will see a more precise formulation of essentialism shortly.) Cognitive realism is the claim that things can be known as they really are and not merely as relative to some conceptual or linguistic scheme. Essentialism and cognitive realism are respectively the basic metaphysical and epistemological features of an Aristotelian ethics.

It is important to understand that an *Aristotelian* essentialism (as contrasted with a Porphyrian essentialism) does not regard the essence or nature of a being as some metaphysical constituent—something which exists 'in' the individual as its most important 'part'. Rather, a being's essence or nature constitutes its mode of existence and characterizes it in its entirety. Thus, the natural-kind term *man* signifies (though it does not specify) the whole identity of an individual human being, not just 'manness'. Aristotelian essentialism does not assume that the meaning of a natural-kind term is confined to some criterion-in-mind and allows for the possibility of growth and development in our account of the nature of a being. The real definition of a human being, therefore, is not the result of an *inspectio mentis* procedure[1] but is discovered through a scientific, empirical process.[2] An Aristotelian ethics, then, appeals to all that the various sciences can tell us regarding the nature of a human being in developing its account of the good human life and does not confine itself to some a priori definition.

It is also important to understand that cognitive realism does not require that we know *sub specie aeternitatis*. Human knowledge is relative
in the sense that it is achieved in pieces, step by step, and thus should
not be considered a static, timeless snapshot or picture. Yet it does not
follow from the fact that human knowledge must 'start somewhere' and
does not grasp everything in all its detail all at once that we are barred
from knowing the real. Our account of what a human being is, to continue the example, can tell us what individual human beings really are,
even though we may need to revise this account at some later time,[3] and
even though our relevant interests and needs may determine what features of a human being we initially investigate.[4] Only by requiring that
human knowledge be God-like, or by assuming that our manner of
knowing creates the very character of what we know, would cognitive
realism be impossible.[5] An Aristotelian ethics thus claims to really know
the nature of man and accordingly to develop its account of human well-
being on the basis of this knowledge.

An Aristotelian ethics acknowledges that if our knowledge of the
nature of man changed radically, then the account of human well-being
would also change. Yet to say that human knowledge can change is not
to imply that any given proposition might change. There is a difference
between saying that human knowledge can change and saying that there
is some evidence that this instance of human knowledge might change.
Most generally put, there is a difference between saying X is possible
and saying X is *always* and necessarily possible. Thus, whether any
change in what human well-being consists in is possible would depend
on whether evidence for such a change were forthcoming.[6]

Human Nature, Potentiality, and Teleology
The nature or essence of a being, call it X, is not only that without
which X would not exist, it is also that which sorts X from other beings
and in terms of which X can be grouped with other beings into a class.[7]
The nature of a human being for an Aristotelian ethics is that of an animal whose consciousness can, when self-directed, apprehend the world
in conceptual terms. Man is an animal that has no automatic knowledge
and can only live by the use of his mind. Man is an animal who needs to
bring his intelligence and understanding to bear on the problems and issues his life presents. Whether he uses his conceptual capacity

is, however, up to him. As Aristotle notes toward the end of *De Anima*
II, 5:

> Actual sensation corresponds to the stage of the exercise of knowledge. But
> between the two cases compared there is a difference; the objects that ex-
> cite the sensory powers to activity, the seen, the heard, & c., are outside. The
> ground of this difference is that what actual sensation apprehends is indi-
> viduals, while what knowledge apprehends is universals, and these are in a
> sense within the soul. That is why *a man can exercise his knowledge when
> he wishes,* but his sensation does not depend upon himself—a sensible
> object must be there.[8]

Conceptual awareness depends on the individual human being exercising
the effort necessary to initiate and maintain it, and the ability to engage
in this form of awareness is the fundamental distinguishing feature of a
human being.[9] Though there may be other distinguishing features of a
human being—such as the ability to laugh, to love, to hate, to use words,
to make complex tools—these distinguishing features do not make possible or explain the greatest number of other features of a human being.
Neither do they make possible or explain each other. Man's ability to
engage the world in conceptual terms does, however, make possible and
explain the greatest number of his other features, and it makes possible
and explains these other distinguishing features of the species as well.
Thus, for an Aristotelian ethics, the real definition of a human being is
rational animal. As noted earlier, this definition is the result of a scientific, empirical process and is not merely some criterion-in-mind. Rather,
this definition is a condensation of a vast number of facts pertaining to
man and captures in formula-like fashion that which most fully characterizes this being.

   The nature of a human being in an Aristotelian ethics is also a potentiality that can be actualized. An individual human being can only
grow or develop into a certain sort of thing; a person cannot choose to
become a different kind of being. A person can, of course, fail to take
the actions necessary to actualize his nature, but a human being cannot,
contrary to the implications of existentialism, choose what kind of being
he will be. Yet, human nature is not a Platonic form; it is always indi-
viduated and thus is not like a master die in accord with which individual human beings are struck off. Though particular advocates of Aristo-

telian ethics may not have always paid sufficient attention to the great pluralism and diversity that humans exhibit, there is plenty of room for pluralism and diversity within Aristotelian ethics. Indeed, a person's generic [10] potentialities are never separate from a person's individuative potentialities. There is no such thing as a person actualizing himself as a human that is not a case of actualizing his unique potentialities as an individual; and by the same token, a person cannot actualize what is unique to himself and at the same time fail to actualize those potentialities that he has in virtue of his humanity. A human being is both a *who* and a *what,* and though we can conceptually distinguish individuative and generic potentialities, they are never separate in the individual human being.

Yet understanding human nature as involving a determinate set of potentialities that can be actualized would have no relevance for ethics if there were no need for the actualization of these potentialities. In other words, there must be some reason these potentialities are to be actualized. Simply because something is a potentiality does not in and of itself tell us why it is to be actualized.[11] In Aristotelian ethics this question is answered by the notion of natural functions or ends—in a word, teleology. The actualization of a being's potentialities is needed because a being cannot remain in existence, cannot be the sort of thing it is, if it does not actualize its potentialities, and remaining in existence as the sort of thing it is is the natural end or function of a being. Thus, an entity's potentialities are to be actualized because it could not fulfill its natural end without doing so. We shall see in the second section of this chapter what basis there is for claiming that remaining in existence is the inherent function or end of an entity and to what class of entities this claim applies. Yet we can see that in an Aristotelian ethics being an animal that lives by the use of his mind is not just a potentiality which can be actualized, it is the natural function or end of a human being. In other words, living rationally or intelligently[12] is that-for-the-sake-of-which all human actions are done and that which constitutes the standard by which actions are to be evaluated. The precise manner by which specific actions are to be evaluated will be discussed in the third section of this chapter, but for now it should be noted that the crucial element in an Aristotelian ethics is the idea that living rationally or intelligently is the natural end, function, or *ergon* of a human being.

Human Flourishing

In Aristotelian ethics living rationally or intelligently is described as *eudaimonia*, a state of well-being which is achieved by self-actualization and characterized by maturation. Though usually translated as 'happiness', this can be misleading if not qualified.[13] Happiness should not be understood as simply the gratification of desire; rather, it is the satisfaction of *right* desire—the satisfaction of those desires and wants which will lead to successful human living.

> The happiness of a human being is not a state of sensory pleasure, although such pleasures are also necessary for a successful human life, since man is not *only* a rational being but an animal with the biological capacity and need for sensory experiences as well. Instead the happiness or successful life of a person must involve considerations that *depend* upon his conceptual capacities. Man must be a success *as* a rational animal. He must live in such a way that he achieves goals that are rational for him individually but also as a human being. The former will vary depending on *who* he is. The latter are uniform and pertain to *what* he is. . . [H]is goal as a human being must be to do what is his unique capacity: live rationally.[14]

Living rationally or intelligently is, therefore, not merely a matter of employing intelligence or reason to achieve whatever ends one happens to desire. Living rationally or intelligently prescribes or determines the ends themselves—the ends one needs to desire—and these ends in turn constitute the overall end of human life or, as some philosophers have aptly called it, human flourishing.

The central difficulty in interpreting the concept of human flourishing in Aristotle has to do with the nature and arrangement of 'final ends'. Some years ago W. F. Hardie posed the question of whether eudaimonia was a single dominant end to which all others were subordinate, or whether eudaimonia could be characterized as an integrated or inclusive set of final ends.[15] Moreover, how to interpret the relationship between means to ends and final ends to each other has also posed some perplexing problems of interpretation. If, for example, there is a single final end to which all others are means, then the value of those other ends is completely dependent on the final end to which they are a means. Furthermore, such a picture of eudaimonia would seem to reduce Aristotelian ethics to a simple consequentialism.

We wish to avoid the pitfalls of a dominant-end or strictly conse-
quentialist interpretation of eudaimonia, and some of the discussion
found in later sections of this chapter is designed to do just that. Nevertheless, the most common misunderstanding of eudaimonia is the one
with which we opened this section—the equation of happiness with the
satisfaction of desire. The happiness-equals-pleasure principle as an interpretation of Aristotelian ethics is destructive of the very possibility of
ethics. This point was noted by Kant in his critique of eudaimonistic ethics, and we believe that interpretation has been instrumental in turning
the understanding of Aristotelian ethics in the wrong direction. Thus a
moment spent on Kant's arguments should clear the way for more plausible interpretations, such as the one we offer below.

In his effort to separate happiness from morality, Kant offers three
main arguments.[16]

1. If happiness were in fact our natural end, then nature blundered by giving
   men reason; for since most people are not happy, instinct rather than
   reason would have been a more efficient means to happiness. But nature
   doesn't make such blunders; therefore happiness is not our natural end.

2. The more reason applies itself to the enjoyment of life, the less enjoyment
   one finds. Indeed those who live most by reason are the most dissatisfied
   and come to envy those who seem to get along by their passions alone.
   This is because the more one lives by reason, the more one understands
   the amount of misery in the world. Thus there is no necessary connection
   between reason and happiness.

3. Happiness, as Aristotle says, depends on circumstances such as a good
   childhood, intelligence, a pleasant disposition, good looks, and so forth,
   which are beyond our control. Thus a person may be happy and not deserve it, or a person may deserve happiness and not get it. Kant says that
   the only thing more repellent to contemplate than a person who is happy
   who does not deserve it is one who does deserve it and is not happy. In
   an ideal world happiness and virtue would correspond, but this is not the
   world we live in.

The upshot of these arguments is to claim that happiness and morality are at best only contingently related. Acting on moral principle is
what matters, and that can be done without a resulting feeling of happiness. Indeed, more often than not, doing what is right is contrary to what
would make one happy. But Kant's arguments only succeed if one

accepts two of Kant's starting assumptions. The first is that Kant takes happiness to be the satisfaction of all of our inclinations. [17] Kant does not deviate from the Humean conception of man as a being of two distinct and separate powers—reason and desire or inclination. Since it is obviously true that merely satisfying inclinations necessarily produces neither happiness nor moral behavior, Kant can claim that a moral theory could never establish more than a contingent relationship between happiness and moral life. As we noted above, however, Aristotle clearly never saw happiness in terms of the mere satisfaction of inclination or desire. Thus, if Kant's arguments are to have a target, Bentham might be better suited than Aristotle.

The other assumption Kant makes is that moral virtue or perfection consists in the rejection of desire in moral action. This conception is developed at length into a full-fledged moral theory with all the attendant distinctions, such as acting from duty versus acting according to duty, self-interest as prudence and not morality, and the obedience to rules for their own sake. Thus, for Kant, a person who overcomes contrary inclinations and acts from duty is morally superior to one who does his duty and likes it. For Aristotle, on the other hand, a person who knew what was right, did what was right, but found no pleasure in it would be a person who has yet to achieve moral perfection—that is, he would be a person who has yet to achieve a state of flourishing. [18] These contrasting paradigms of moral perfection stand on their own merits, and the reader can judge for himself which of the two is actually an example of perfection. But as far as Kant's arguments go with respect to defeating the Aristotelian connection between 'happiness' and morality, the existence of unhappiness or the possibility of right action without happiness does nothing to show the defects in the Aristotelian position. [19]

From what we have said it should be clear that the concept of human flourishing cannot be correctly understood in terms of much of the conceptual baggage modern man brings to such a topic. But neither is the Aristotelian conception of eudaimonia opaque to our understanding. Thus perhaps our message about flourishing in this section amounts simply to this: Aristotle's doctrine is not easily assimilable into categories most of us are used to employing when talking of happiness, virtue, and moral perfection.

The Primary Importance of the Person

An Aristotelian ethics not only requires that we know the good, we must also do the good. Yet even this is not sufficient for an Aristotelian ethics, for the whole point of such an ethics is not merely that we have ethical knowledge or even that our actions are in conformity with the principles that human flourishing calls for. Rather, we must *be* good. As Aristotle states, "Actions, to be sure, are called just and temperate when they are such as a just and temperate man would do. But the doer is just or temperate not because he does such things but when he does them in the way of just and temperate persons". [20] It is thus the person himself who ultimately counts, not the knowledge or even the actions the person may possess or exhibit. An Aristotelian ethics regards the natural end of man to be the "practical life of man possessing reason" and does not regard this end to be something which exists in the abstract. Rather, it is an end that each and every individual human being has and can only be achieved through the knowledge, action, and choices of each individual person. Knowing and doing the good cannot be separate from the person's own choosing.

The foregoing point is best illustrated in contrast with a distinction common in contemporary ethics—the distinction between agent and action morality.[21] The former is thought to deal with the person's intentions or character, while the latter concerns the person's actions. Utilitarianism is thus thought of as primarily an action morality, while Kantianism is thought to be oriented largely towards an agent morality. For purposes of analysis this distinction serves well enough; but for an Aristotelian what is distinct is not necessarily separable. Thus an Aristotelian ethics would regard the separation of agent morality from action morality as ultimately mistaken. It is neither the actions nor the intentions alone that qualify as the desiderata for moral life. The unity of the person reflects a need to unify these analytically distinct elements of moral theory. Consequently, when we claim that Aristotelian ethics gives primacy of place to the person, we mean to indicate that such an ethics seeks to integrate the various elements of human behavior into a coherent pattern of personal existence.

We can see the integrated conception of moral personhood that Aristotle seeks from these three conditions that must be met if our knowledge and actions are to enable us to *be* good: "(1) The agent must act in full consciousness of what he is doing. (2) He must 'will' the action, and will it for its own sake. (3) The act must proceed from a fixed and unchangeable disposition."[22] Only by each of us gaining the knowledge, performing the actions, cultivating the proper habits of character, and exercising the correct choices can we realize the type of person who can be said to have achieved moral excellence. It must be remembered, therefore, that eudaimonia is a state of well-being that is attained by a process of *self*-actualization, and both can exist only through the choices and actions of the person. In an ontological sense, the person is a unity seeking further actualization of the self. But since further actualization depends upon choice reflected through action, the degree to which action and choice are consistent affects the degree of success the individual will have. One can choose as if intentions and actions were separable components of personhood. The result of such choices is dysdaimonia. Eudaimonia, on the other hand, maintains the original ontological unity of the self over time. The Aristotelian eudaimonic person is not characterized by an aggregation of intentions, desires, or actions. It is rather that one's intentions, desires, and actions come to be manifestations of a single core self developing towards its own further realization.

Ethics and Politics

Before considering the meta-ethical foundations of an Aristotelian ethics, it should be made clear what we take to be the relationship between ethics and politics. Given that there is ethical knowledge and given that governmental action is characterized by the legal use of physical compulsion, interference, or coercion, there is a question about the relationship between ethics and politics that needs answering—namely, what matters of morality, if any, are to be matters for governmental action? We understand the natural right to liberty to be the standard which determines what matters of morality are to be made matters of governmental action, but this must wait for the development of the next chapter. Aristotle himself saw a necessary connection between morality and politics because the state exists for the sake of the good. We would concur with this general assessment, but there are a number of ambiguities surrounding the use of the term *state* as a translation of Aristotle's *polis*.[23] For the most part, our task in the following chapters will be to outline the conditions under which the state is justified in using its coercive powers.

If *state* is understood in a general communitarian fashion, such as that offered by Alasdair MacIntyre, the necessity for community in achieving the good is uncontroversial. But MacIntyre more specifically understands his communitarianism to require opposition to natural rights as those rights were defined by such Enlightenment thinkers as Locke and Jefferson. We, on the other hand, see the concept of community as essentially bound up with the protection of natural rights. To some our claim that an Aristotelian ethics provides the moral foundation for natural rights, particularly Lockean rights, might seem equivalent to an attempt to square a circle; for Lockean rights are generally viewed as standing on the extreme individualist end of the political spectrum. An Aristotelian ethics is ordinarily thought to be a middle position in which a notion of the political 'common good' prevents the development of a political philosophy that goes to either extreme. Indeed, as the argument usually goes, government's nature is not characterized by coercion, but rather by authority, and is thus an agency by which the commonweal is achieved. The role of government is, then, to be determined by the demands of man's social and political nature and not by the natural right to liberty or any other extreme individualist doctrine. These arguments, as well as some of the more particular views of the advocates of this conventional wisdom, will be considered in Chapters 3 and 4.

THE IS-OUGHT PROBLEM

Facts and Values

Given that human beings have a nature and that this nature is a potential that can be actualized, why ought a person to actualize his nature? Why should a human being live in accord with the requirements of human flourishing? Or even, why should a person satisfy his desires? In other words, how do we move from an 'is' to an 'ought', how do we ever find values in a world of facts? In one sense, there can be no answer to this question; for if the world of facts is totally and completely separate from values, then there is no way one can move from an 'is' to an 'ought'. So, the problem faced is not so much one of how one derives an 'ought' from an 'is' as it is the problem of whether there is any conception of the 'is' that would allow for the existence of values.

Traditionally, the answer to the is-ought question has been supplied by a teleological conception of reality in which beings had a purpose given them by their nature or God, and thus there was an ontological source of values. Yet it cannot be denied that much of the progress that science has achieved over the last few centuries has been the result of rejecting teleological explanations. In fact, to many people the very words *teleological explanation*, when applied to natural processes, seem to connote the fallacy of anthropomorphism. Further, the notion of teleology is associated with a theistic conception of the universe and arguments for the existence of God, which are generally regarded as not succeeding. Thus, the very idea that a teleological conception of reality might provide a way out of the is-ought problem must seem as an instance of dubious metaphysics from the classical and medieval past. For many contemporary thinkers, the only ends in the universe are those that a human being sets for himself. There are no natural ends.

Some would further claim that the situation is even worse for the teleological view of reality than has been stated. It is not simply the case that there are no ends in nature except those set by man, or even that there is no reason he should choose this end instead of that end. Rather, there is the question of whether human action is to be regarded as teleological in the first place. Do human beings really act for ends? Some thinkers, such as B.F. Skinner, [24] would deny that teleological explanations have any authentic role to play in understanding human behavior. Thus, the problem of trying to determine what ends man should choose in a universe which provides no standard for such choices is to some already a problem of a bygone era. When the reductionist thinkers have finished with the human being, he is no longer an entity that acts for ends or makes choices at all.

Instead of being pushed into a debate regarding Skinner's view of human nature, let us take a step back and ask if the case against there being natural ends or functions is something that has been decided once and for all. It depends. It depends on what teleology involves. Teleology need not be regarded as universal in order to be defended. Neither is it the case that one needs to adopt a theistic conception of the universe or have a specific view regarding the origin of the species.[25] All that is necessary is that there be some facts which cannot be adequately understood without appealing to a natural end or function. Is there something which requires teleological explanation? In *De generatione animalium* 2.1 734b19–735a4, Aristotle states:

> . . . we may allow that hardness and softness, stickiness and brittleness, and whatever qualities are found in the parts that have life and soul, may be caused by mere heat and cold, yet, when we come to the principle in virtue of which flesh is flesh and bone is bone, that is no longer so; what makes them is the movement that is set up by the male parent, who is in actuality what that out of which the offspring is made is in potentiality.

When it comes to understanding what living things are and how they grow and develop, teleological explanations seem to be required. Thus, the question of whether teleology exists comes down to the question of whether the laws in terms of which organic phenomena are explained can be reduced to laws which make no mention of the end or goal of the living process but only of how the material constituents interact. Allan Gotthelf has put this issue as follows:

> In the case of organic development, can one give an account of the process of development solely in terms of the laws of chemical interaction, laws which make no mention of the end to be realized, so that in principle one could give a chronological list of sets of chemical transformations of initial and added material such that the end result is a correct chemical description of a mature living organism, without any laws of transformation making any reference to the end result?[26]

If such a reduction *cannot* be made, then there is a case to be made for teleology when it comes to understanding what living things are and how they function.

Whether the reducibility thesis has any real possibility cannot be answered from the philosopher's armchair. Yet it was Aristotle's belief that the evidence did not warrant it, and though Aristotle's account of the physical mechanism through which final causes take effect was certainly mistaken, the idea that teleology is an "irreducible potential for form" is supported by developments in contemporary biology. As Michael Bradie and Fred D. Miller, Jr. note:

. . . the core of Aristotle's teleology has been vindicated by modern biology. For the point is that life processes are self-regulating in virtue of inherent forms or structures. The type of movement required on Aristotle's account for a potential for form is the type of movement exemplified by the DNA molecule. The genetic "program" contained in the molecule's structure directs and limits the organism's growth in the manner set forth in Aristotle's biological writings.[27]

Further, Gotthelf has argued that for Aristotle the primary use of *for the sake of* concerns the development of living things.

Aristotle's teleology is neither vitalist and mystical nor "as if" and mechanical. The notion of an irreducible potential for form supplies the proper content to the awareness that for Aristotle organic development is actually *directive*, without implying (as the "immaterial conscious agency" interpretation does) that it is direc*ted*; and it identifies the ontological basis of the awareness that the existence and stages of development can be understood only in terms of its end—by establishing that the *identity* of the development is its being *irreducibly* a development to that end, irreducibly the actualization of a potential for form.[28]

What living things are and how they develop cannot be understood except insofar as they are understood as functioning for the sake of the mature state of the organism.

It is precisely the capacities for successful living which are not explainable in terms of element-potentials, it is these for which there must be potentials over and above the element-potentials. And why are these potentials potentials for the mature state, and not for youth, old age, or death? Surely because all others are explainable from the existence of a capacity for the mature state, but the latter are not explainable from them. If the potential were for death, we would have no explanation of growth and development (and death can in any case be explained from element-potentials). If it were for some state of lesser efficacy relative to survival than the mature state, we would have no explanation of the development from that state to the state we now call maturity (if the state in question came before the mature state) nor of the development to maturity which occurred before the state was reached, (if that state came after maturity). But movement *to maturity* does occur, and needs explanation. Only a potential for development to maturity would explain that. [29]

The process of pursuing and maintaining ends is the result of the very nature of living things. Teleology, then, has a place in nature, not because the universe has a cosmic purpose, or even because God has created and endowed each being with a purpose. Rather, teleology exists because the very nature of living things involves the potential that is irreducibly for development to maturity.

The point is not merely that a being must be alive to pursue ends; it is, rather, that end-oriented behavior is necessitated (not merely made possible) by the fact that a being is a *living* thing. The process of pursuing and maintaining ends is required by the fact that a living thing could not exist as a living thing if this process did not occur. Pursuing and maintaining ends is an essential feature of life which results from its conditional nature. That is to say, since a living thing faces alternatives, since its actions can attain ends or fail to, and since the consequences of a living thing attaining or failing to attain ends make a difference to its existence as a living thing, it is a being which must act for ends. It is the conditional character of a being's life that creates the requirement or need that its pursuit and maintenance of ends be successful—actualize its potentialities. This process, when successful, is the requirement that accounts for the existence of a living thing. The existence of a living thing is necessary for the satisfaction of this requirement. Thus, since the function of a thing "is its use or enactment in regard to the satisfaction of the requirement which explains the existence of that thing",[30] pursuing and maintaining ends that satisfy a living thing's needs is the natural function or end of a living thing. This function is defined in virtue of the objective features of a living thing and is not determined by the uses to which a living thing can be put and cannot be altered by one's intentions or desires.[31] A living thing simply has this function in virtue of what it is. Satisfying its needs—which requires actualizing its potentialities—is that-for-the-sake-of-which a living thing's end-oriented actions occur.

If we understand valuation as the process of pursuing and maintaining ends or goals, then the successful performance of this process (namely, satisfying a living thing's needs—actualizing its potentialities) explains the existence of values. "The fact that living things exist and function necessitates the existence of values."[32] The natural function or end of a living thing is its ultimate value. This idea can be expressed as follows:

> Without an ultimate goal or end, there can be no lesser goals or means: a series of means going off into an infinite progression toward a non-existent end is a metaphysical and epistemological impossibility. It is only an ultimate goal, an *end in itself*, that makes the existence of values possible. Metaphysically, *life* is the only phenomenon that is an end in itself: a value gained and kept by a constant process of action. Epistemologically, the concept of "value" is genetically dependent upon and derived from the antecedent concept of "life". . . . It is only the concept of "life" that makes the concept of "value" possible.[33]

Yet, to fully appreciate what is meant here, it should be realized that life does not exist in the abstract and thus there is no single end or goal that constitutes the value 'life'. Living is not the same thing in different beings. Living as an amoeba is not living as a plant; living as a plant is not living as an animal; and living as an animal is not living as a human being. The mature state of a living being—the full and complete actualization of a living thing's nature—is how the life of a living thing is achieved. The life of a being cannot be attained by action that does not conform to a particular living thing's nature. It is 'life' understood in this sense that is an end in itself—the natural end or function of a living thing.

If the foregoing account of teleology is correct, then the world of facts is not totally devoid of values. There is a biocentric basis for values. Values exist in the sense that there is an end or function that a living thing has in virtue of its nature, and this end or function is the source of all other ends or functions (values) the living thing might have. Now, a living thing's acts of valuation are said to be good if they satisfy the needs of a living being, namely, if they allow it to actualize its potentialities, but when these acts are chosen, when there is an agent who chooses these acts, then they are morally good. Moral goods will, however, be discussed later. For now, we see that if there are natural ends, and if their attainment is understood as a process of actualizing potentialities, goodness can be defined in terms of this process of a living thing actualizing its potentialities. We will discuss this 'definition' of goodness shortly, but we must first consider another version of the is-ought problem. This problem concerns what it is, if anything, that makes the natural end of a human being obligatory.

The Source of Obligation

There is another version of the is-ought problem. This version does not claim that there is some unbridgeable gulf between facts and values. Rather, the is-ought problem results from a difficulty intrinsic to ethics itself. The difficulty is simply this: How do we justify a prescriptive premiss? Either there is an infinite regression of prescriptions, or there is a most basic prescriptive premiss (or set of prescriptions).[34] If we adopt the first disjunct, then the justification of ethical claims is impossible, and if we adopt the second disjunct, then we face the problem of explaining why this most basic prescriptive premiss (or set thereof) is obligatory. Either a human being cannot disobey this most basic prescriptive premiss, or he can disobey. If a human being cannot disobey this most basic prescriptive premiss, then this premiss is not a matter for moral concern, because there is no point in saying that we should not disobey a moral principle if we cannot disobey it in the first place. If a human being can disobey this most basic prescriptive premiss, and thus he can choose either to follow this basic moral principle or not follow it, then we must ask what would justify this decision. Is there a still more basic moral maxim (with its attendant question of what would justify it) or is this most basic moral principle truly the most basic and thus not in need of additional justification? If we cannot appeal to anything else to justify our decision and are indeed trying to decide whether we will obey or disobey this truly most basic prescriptive premiss, then there seems to be no way we can be obligated to follow it. As long as we can either obey or disobey it, we can ask why we should follow it, and at this level, there is no further normative foundation to appeal to.

If we try to respond to this difficulty by appealing to the natural end or function of a human being and argue that we ought to follow this most basic prescriptive premiss because it will tend to bring about well-being and fulfillment for us, we can still ask 'Why?'. If we want to have well-being and fulfillment, then we ought to follow this most basic prescriptive premiss, but why should we want well-being and fulfillment? It seems, then, that an Aristotelian natural-end ethics cannot justify its ultimate prescriptive premiss. How can it justify the claim that we ought to seek fulfillment and well-being? The problem has again only been moved back one step. Yet, the difficulty faced by an Aristotelian natural-end ethics is even more extreme; for if it is claimed that we have no choice with regard to our natural end or function—namely, we must act for our well-being and fulfillment—then what sense could there be in claiming that we *ought* to behave this way? The existence of natural ends or functions does not seem sufficient to move us from an 'is' to an 'ought.'

An ineluctable natural end certainly does seem to be morally value-less, for it is pointless to say that we should live in accord with our nature if it is impossible to do otherwise. Yet this objection is made too quickly. It fails to distinguish between what is potential and what is actual. Our natural end can be ineluctable as a potentiality and yet not be ineluctable as an actuality. As an inherent potentiality for a certain end and nothing else, our natural end is ineluctable—a human being cannot be something other than what his potentialities allow—but it does not follow from this that our potentialities will necessarily be actualized. The attainment of our natural end is a highly contingent matter dependent on circumstances and human decision. Yet this contingency does not conflict with the applicability of the natural end as a standard for evaluating our choices. The natural end of a human being is always applicable as a standard for evaluating choices, if we are dealing with a creature with an irreducible potential for that end. Since we are teleological beings, the mode by which an end is achieved is distinct from the end itself, so that misdirection in the former does not invalidate the latter as either a standard or value. Thus, the fact that all human actions must, in terms of potentiality, be for the sake of well-being and fulfillment does not mean that all human actions must actually be directed toward well-being and fulfillment. The natural end or function of a human being remains the standard by which human actions are to be judged and is thus not morally valueless.

It is important to note here that human freedom for an Aristotelian natural-end ethics is not, as it is for Sartre, a freedom with respect to what is the natural function or end of a human being. Human volition has a teleological character. Though the exercise and direction of specific volitional acts is entirely dependent on the individual human being, volition as an inherent power of a human being is for the sake of human well-being and fulfillment. Thus, the ability to willingly act in a manner contrary to the requirements of human flourishing is not sufficient to show the nonobligatory character of the natural end. Moreover, and as already shown when considering Gewirth's objections to Aristotelian ethics, the ability to disobey an ultimate prescriptive premiss is not a theoretical problem for an Aristotelian natural-end ethics.

There is still, however, a problem to be handled. How does one show the obligatory character of an ultimate prescriptive premiss? How would an Aristotelian natural-end ethics establish the obligatory character of its ultimate prescriptive premiss? How would the obligatory character of 'One ought to live in accord with the requirements of one's nature' be established? It must be remembered that an Aristotelian natural-end ethics does not take the existence of values for granted. It does not suppose that one can talk of obligation or morality without there first being such a thing as values, and it does not suppose that one can determine which values are good or bad separate from that which gives rise to the requirement that one pursue values which satisfy a living thing's needs. The conditional character of life creates the requirement that the values pursued satisfy a living thing's needs. Actualizing the potentialities of a living thing satisfies this requirement and constitutes the function of valuation, the natural end of a living thing. The natural end of a living thing makes possible and necessitates all acts of valuation and is the basis for determining what satisfies a living thing's needs. Actualizing our potentialities, finding fulfillment and well-being, is just what it is for us to be good. It is in terms of our attaining this good that our obligations arise.

Actualizing our potentialities is not made good by the fact that we choose or desire it. Rather, what we choose or desire is made good when and if our choices or desires in fact actualize our potentialities. Thus the obligatory character of 'One ought to live in accordance with the requirements of one's nature' results from the fact that this is the good for a human being. The demand that we justify the obligatory character of this statement supposes that something else is required for there to be values that are good. It supposes that this ultimate prescriptive premiss is in fact not ultimate. This demand ignores the facts which give rise to obligation. Furthers it fails to realize that in ethics, as well as elsewhere, an infinite regress in justifications is not possible, and there must be something ultimate; something which is simply the case.

From the fact that the obligatory character of 'One ought to live in accordance with the requirements of one's nature' does not require justification (nor could any be given), it does not follow that nothing can be said in defense of this ultimate prescriptive premiss. There is a close and instructive parallel between Aristotle's argument that the denier of the principle of noncontradiction must accept this principle to deny it and our defense of this ultimate prescriptive premiss.[35] Our argument does not attempt to demonstrate or prove the obligatory character of this ultimate prescriptive premiss, but it does attempt to show by 'negative demonstration' that the person who challenges this ultimate prescriptive premiss actually accepts it.

The person who asks why he should live in accordance with the requirements of his nature has a value he is trying to attain. He wants an answer to his question; he is seeking this value. Yet wants or values are not metaphysically primary. Having an answer to a question is a value only to a being for whom knowledge is a value and for whom possessing knowledge as opposed to not possessing knowledge could make a difference in its existence or functioning. Otherwise, there would be no ultimate difference between possessing knowledge or not possessing knowledge and thus no basis for knowledge being an object of pursuit for this being.

It is, as argued in the previous section, the natural end of a living thing which necessitates and makes possible the existence of values— including the existence of the value of having an answer to the question, 'Why should one live in accord with the requirements of one's nature?' Someone could not, therefore, value the answer to this question—the answer *qua* value and *qua* object of choice would not exist—if it were not true that one should live in accord with the requirements of one's nature. The very fact that the person values an answer to his question requires the truth of the principle he is questioning. In asking his question, in seeking an answer, the person accepts the principle he is questioning. In this way, then, the obligatory character of 'One ought to live in accordance with the requirements of one's nature' can be defended. It should be stressed, however, that this 'negative demonstration' does not prove this ethical first-principle. Only an understanding of how values arise and what the human good is will allow one to grasp the obligatory character of this ultimate prescriptive premiss.

Since the obligatory character of 'One ought to live in accordance with the requirements of one's nature' is based on what a human being is and needs, it might seem that an Aristotelian natural-end ethics is still, despite everything that has been said, only a 'hypothetical' imperative and not a 'categorical' one. There is a sense in which this is true. An Aristotelian ethics does make morality dependent on what a human being *is* and does define moral goodness in terms of what is fulfilling; and if these facts were not the case, then the obligatory character of 'One ought to live in accordance with the requirements of one's nature' would indeed dissolve into nothing. Yet Aristotelian ethics is not 'hypothetical' in the sense that the obligatory character of its ethical first-principle depends on whether one desires or chooses fulfillment. Desires and choices are for the sake of fulfillment. The human good is objective. Unless one is bewitched by the Kantian claim that an ethical first-principle must be independent of the facts of nature, that it cannot be based on facts of nature without destroying its 'categorical' status, there is no reason to regard the first-principle of an Aristotelian ethics as hypothetical in the sense of being somehow less than fully obligatory.

More importantly, the natural-end character of an Aristotelian ethics has the advantage of being able to explain the obligatory character of its ethical first-principle. It can appeal to the facts that give rise to moral concerns. It does not try to establish or prove the obligatory character of its ethical first-principle by showing how one who fails to accept it contradicts himself. An Aristotelian natural-end ethics realizes that the fact that one is guilty of a contradiction only shows that logically one is in an untenable position; it does not show that one ought to do anything about it. Without an ethical justification of the claim 'Do not hold contradictory positions', there is no moral reason why one should change their actions. The is-ought problem is not solved by Kantian 'transcendental arguments'; instead, we must know what the human good is.

Defining the Good—Part I

One of the central obstacles to an Aristotelian natural-end ethics has been the claim that goodness is not something definable and that one commits the 'definist fallacy' in any attempt to define goodness. The definist fallacy "is the process of confusing or identifying two properties, of defining one property by another". [36] Accordingly, any attempt to

define goodness in terms of a natural end or any natural feature is subject to G. E. Moore's open-question argument—namely, if it is meaningful to ask of a putative definition of goodness 'But is it good?' then the
definition fails as a definition. The basis for this is as follows: if it is
meaningful to question a definition, then the definition's denial is not
self-contradictory, and if the definition's denial is not self-contradictory,
there is a possibility the definiendum could exist without the definiens.
Yet, if this were so, we would not have a definition. A definition must
state what something necessarily is; it cannot have a denial that is not
self-contradictory and is hence possible. For example, if it is meaningful
to ask whether a living thing that actualizes its potentialities is good,
then it is not self-contradictory to deny this definition; and hence the
possibility exists of there being a living thing whose potentialities are
actualized without achievement of the good. Indeed, just what sort of
definition of goodness can this example be, if the contradictory of what
the definition claims goodness to be is not precluded? For much of the
twentieth century Moore's open-question argument has been the device
by which all naturalistic and natural-end accounts of goodness have been
destroyed.

For Moore, the inability to define goodness coincides with his belief
that goodness is *sui generis*, an indefinable, non-natural property. For
thinkers after Moore, the inability to define goodness was taken as evidence for the belief that ethics was noncognitive, that is, not anything
about which we could have knowledge. It is, however, not our concern
to take up the many twists and turns that have occurred in meta-ethics
since Moore,[37] nor is it even our concern to try and discover all the
things Moore could have meant by "naturalistic fallacy". [38] What we will
do is see if an Aristotelian natural-end theory can both avoid the definist
fallacy and overcome Moore's open-question argument. Further, we will
note where the definition of goodness that is presented in our account of
an Aristotelian natural-end ethics differs from some other interpretations
of that tradition.

The first thing that needs to be said is that the definist fallacy presents a difficulty for the naturalistic account of goodness only if it is true
that goodness is an indefinable, non-natural property.[39] It is most certainly a fallacy to attempt to define something in terms of what it is not
or to confuse one thing with another. Yet this in and of itself does not

show that goodness is something indefinable or that a naturalistic account of goodness could not succeed. In other words, the definist fallacy is not the basis for the claim that goodness is indefinable. Rather, it is a *conclusion* of the claim that goodness is indefinable. To use it as a premiss for the argument[40] that goodness is indefinable is to beg the question.

The only way that the definist fallacy could be used as a way to establish the indefinability of goodness would be if it were assumed that all genuine definitions are tautologies, that the definiens merely repeats the single meaning that was expressed in the definiendum. If this were so, then it would be true that any definition of goodness that did more than repeat 'goodness is goodness' would be guilty of defining something in terms of what it is not. Yet this criterion demands too much, for to require that definitions be tautologies is to make them useless. If all genuine definitions must be tautologies, then no definition can tell us anything new. All attempts to define what something really is must be abandoned if this criterion is followed: for example, 'Water is H_2O' does not meet this criterion. Of course, if goodness is *sui generis*,[41] then it certainly seems wrong to suppose that it can be defined in a nontautologous manner. Yet whether goodness is *sui generis*—at least in the sense that it is something which cannot be characterized in a nontautologous way—is the point at issue. This point cannot be assumed by the definist fallacy without, to note once more, begging the question.

Though requiring that definitions be tautologies will not suffice as a criterion for a definition, it remains nonetheless true that all definitions must have denials which are self-contradictory. One might object to this criterion by claiming that a definition is a synthetic a priori truth which states what something necessarily is and yet does not have a self-contradictory denial. Yet unless a Kantian turn is made (not an attractive option for an Aristotelian natural-end ethics), it is most difficult to understand how a definition could state what something necessarily is and still have its denial consistent. Further, it is not strategically necessary to argue that real definitions are synthetic a priori truths, because having a denial which is self-contradictory does not prove that the definition is a mere substitution-instance of a logical truth; and even if that *were* the case, this would not be sufficient to show that its truth is the result of purely formal or linguistic considerations.[42] Rather, the crucial issue is how we determine whether a definition's denial is self-contradictory.[43] According to Moore's open-question argument, if it is *meaningful* to ask of the naturalistic definition of goodness 'But is it good?', then this supposedly shows that the naturalistic definition cannot preclude the possibility of the definiendum existing without the definiens. If so, then no naturalistic account of goodness can succeed.

Yet there are at least two things wrong with this open-question argument:

1. If by 'But is it good?' we mean 'Have you got things right?' or 'Are you sure you are not mistaken?' then we are noting that we are not dealing with a tautology and want to make sure that we have got the facts straight. Being open to this sort of question is the price we pay for not dealing in trivialities and for not being omniscient. Yet even being open to this question does not establish the possibility that *we* might be wrong or even that *this* definition might need changing. Rather, all we know is that people can be mistaken or that definitions can be revised, but we do not know that this might be the case in some specific instance. As noted before, there is a difference between something being possible and something being *always* and necessarily possible, and until and unless evidence for such alleged possibilities is forthcoming, there is no reason to regard the naturalistic definition as flawed.

2. The meaningfulness[44] of the question 'But is it good?' cannot always be determined from the philosopher's armchair. It may indeed be self-contradictory to ask of a naturalistic definition of goodness 'But is it good?' and yet not be evidently so. Consider once again the definition that water is H_2O. A person who is ignorant of the chemical composition of water could use an argument analogous to the open-question argument to show that H_2O is not necessarily what water is. This person would agree that water is necessarily water, but would claim to meaningfully question whether water is necessarily H_2O. If what is meant by *water* is confined to what he knows, explicitly considers, or can deduce

from some criterion-in-mind, or if what is possible for water is determined by what he can imagine (picture)—for example, he imagines a clear fluid that looks, smells, tastes, and acts like water in every way but does not have the chemical composition of H_2O—then his claim to have shown that water is not necessarily H_2O has merit. Yet if what water is and is capable of doing and becoming is not determined by what someone has in mind or imagines, but rather by water itself, and if we break free from the unnecessary assumption that the *meaning* of water is determined by an *inspectio mentis* procedure, then this claim does not succeed. Rather, what water is, as well as the relevant sciences can determine it, would be the basis for determining whether water is necessarily H_2O. There is no reason to assume that what something necessarily *is* is to be determined a priori,[45] and the philosopher's armchair is certainly not the place from which to determine natural necessities.

For the very same reasons, then, when it comes to trying to determine what goodness necessarily is, there is no reason for us to assume that the ability to apparently ask 'But is it good?' without self-contradiction shows that it is possible for the definiendum to exist without the definiens. Instead, we must consider what we have learned about values, why they exist and what gives rise to their pursuit. We must consider the question 'But is it good?' in light of everything that we know about goodness and from that basis determine whether it is self-contradictory to separate the definiens from the definiendum. In other words, we must consider all that a naturalistic theory has established (in our case, what an Aristotelian natural-end theory has been able to show regarding all the issues in meta-ethics and normative ethics) in relation to whatever problems, inadequacies, or objections that are outstanding to determine if it can offer an adequate definition of goodness. When judged in this fashion, the naturalistic account of goodness is not guaranteed success, but neither is it denied the possibility of success. Thus, the open-question argument does not constitute an insuperable barrier to a naturalistic account of goodness.[46] It is then to an Aristotelian natural-end ethic's account of goodness that we should now return.

Defining the Good—Part II

In its most general sense, goodness is the actualization by a *living thing* of the potentialities which make up its nature. Yet there is no single identical property in every living thing that constitutes goodness. Rather, goodness is always a good *for*. It is the *relation* between what is actualized and what is potential in a living thing that provides the basis for calling it good. In other words, it is the actual as opposed to the potential that is what it is for a living thing to be good. However, in an Aristotelian ethics goodness does not exist in the abstract. As noted earlier, what is good is determined by the nature of a living thing, and so what is good for one sort of living thing may not be good for another. Yet this is still too abstract; for there is no such thing as the actualization of the potentialities of a being's nature that does not involve the actualization of its individuative potentialities (or vice versa). Thus, an Aristotelian ethics not only understands the actualization of potentialities to be the actualization of the potentialities of an individual living thing, it also understands the actualization of potentialities to be consequent (supervenient) upon the satisfaction of the individual living thing's needs. Goodness is always what is good *for* the individual living thing and is not some abstract property or relation.[47]

An important difference between our account of goodness and that of some interpretations[48] of an Aristotelian natural-end ethics should be noted at this time. We do not hold that goodness is *any* actualization of potential, that is, we do not claim that goodness exists wherever potentiality is actualized. Rather, goodness exists only if the actualization of a potentiality is an end, that is, a value. If the actualization of a potentiality were not an end, then there would not be any basis for why the actualization of a potentiality needs to occur. The *fact* that something has a potentiality does not in and of itself provide any reason its actualization is an end, a value. Neither does the *fact* that a potentiality has been actualized in and of itself provide any reason for this occurrence being something which is good. Thus, we do not speak of goodness as the actualization of a potentiality apart from that process being end-oriented. As Gotthelf states, "The good must be understood not merely to be actuality: it is actuality *which is aimed at*."[49] And since it is the needs and requirements of living things that make the actualization of a potentiality an end, we do not speak of goodness as the actualization of a potentiality apart from a living thing. Teleology is absolutely crucial to an Aristotelian ethics. Yet since we do not see any reason to regard all of reality as end-oriented,[50] but do think there are excellent reasons for believing that ends or values exist as a result of the needs and requirements of living things, we define goodness as the actualization by a living thing of its nonelemental potentialities and endorse the following observation:

> There are no intrinsically beautiful or good or right things, only things that are good, right, or beautiful in relation to living entities *for* which things can be good, right, or beautiful in terms of purposes or goals.[51]

Goodness is neither an intrinsic feature of things or actions, nor is it simply a subjective phenomenon of consciousness. Rather, goodness is an aspect of reality in relation to the needs or ends of a living thing.

Of course, the question 'What is the nature of goodness?' is, as far as we can tell, a question only a human being asks. We have no knowledge of other living things having debates over the nature of goodness, nor do we know of species from other planets who ponder this question. Goodness is an issue for human beings precisely because we can exercise the effort to understand this issue and act on the basis of our knowledge or fail to. It is for this reason that we speak of moral goodness. Moral goodness is differentiated from the foregoing account of goodness by the fact that the actualization of a potentiality results from decision or choice. It is for this reason that we can morally blame or praise human beings for the actions they take. We need, therefore, to examine what kind of normative theory an Aristotelian ethics is. We need to see how moral judgments are made, and what they are made about.

Yet, before doing so, we want to note that if the foregoing account of values and goodness is correct, then something is morally good or right, not because it possesses some intrinsic feature, nor because it is merely a matter of opinion; rather, it is morally good or right because it is good *for* a human being—it satisfies human needs.[52] Morality is neither a set of commandments written across the starry sky, nor merely the expression of emotion and preferences—be they of one person or of the masses.

ARISTOTELIAN NORMATIVE THEORY

A Different Kind of Normative Theory

There are two common approaches to contemporary normative theory: a teleological one and a deontological one. A teleological theory, according to the contemporary understanding, defines the good independently of the right and judges the rightness of actions by whether they are productive of good consequences. What is good thus determines what actions are right. A deontological theory judges the rightness of (at least some) actions independently of whether they are productive of good consequences. What is right is (at least in some cases) not determined by the good.[53] Generally speaking, an Aristotelian ethics is described as a teleological theory. W.D. Ross states:

> Aristotle's ethics is definitely teleological; morality consists in doing certain actions not because we see them to be right in themselves but because we see them to be such as will bring us nearer to the "good for man".[54]

Certainly this description is true in the sense that there is a natural end for a human being which constitutes the standard for moral evaluations. Yet it does not follow from this that the good in an Aristotelian ethics is defined independently of the right. Neither does it follow that the moral worth of actions is judged merely by the consequences they produce, namely, action X is to be preferred over action Y simply because it leads to more human well-being and fulfillment than Y. An Aristotelian ethics is more complicated than this and, in fact, constitutes a way of transcending contemporary approaches to normative theory. As John M. Cooper notes:

> For although [Aristotle] agrees with Kant in rejecting maximization schemes of all kinds in favor of a definitely structured life, he does not think of moral constraints themselves as imposed on persons without regard for (and even despite) their own good, as Kant (together with most of his modern opponents) tends to do. In Aristotle's theory human good *consists* (partly) in virtuous action, so his theory, while decidedly not teleological in the modern sense, is also not deontological either.[55]

Yet in order to see how an Aristotelian ethics could ever transcend these two approaches to normative theory, we need to consider certain presuppositions of an Aristotelian approach to ethics.

It is sometimes asked[56] why we need to use principles in ethics. The answer to this question is, for an Aristotelian ethics, found in both our knowledge of human beings and the nature of human flourishing. We do not have any automatic course of action by which to live, and our particular way of dealing with reality requires that we use our minds in a certain manner—namely, we must engage in conceptualization. Both of these facts require that we deal with the world by means of principles. In the former case, we need to develop something that does, in effect, the work of an automatic course of action: principles which would serve as guides for action. In the latter case, we need to *understand* how the various and numerous specific actions we take can be related to our natural end through the action guiding principles which are themselves understood as components constitutive of our natural end. What nature provides to animals more or less automatically must be understood and chosen by man. Principles, therefore, provide the twofold function of not only indicating how certain courses of action will impact upon our lives, but also of providing us with the very standards of successful living itself. Here we are thinking of principles as ends in themselves. There may be other principles we need to learn to tell us how to achieve certain ends and which have no value except insofar as they help us achieve those ends. But ethics is properly concerned with principles which are ends in themselves and not merely means. In this case, Kant was correct to argue that it is only to rational beings that such principles have value.[57] And although we have rejected the formalistic understanding of rationality so characteristic of Kant, we would agree that only rational beings can conceptualize a principle and then use that principle as a standard for evaluating action.

Since we need to conceptualize principles for successful living (flourishing), it is important to understand the general nature of these principles, or at least the ones most properly associated with ethics. The principles we have designated as ends in themselves are also known as 'virtues'. These principles or virtues share a characteristic which transcends the usual consequentialist/deontological way of considering rules: actions which instantiate the principles not only contribute to the achievement of our natural end (consequentialism), but the very performance of the action is itself what constitutes our natural end (deontologism). Aristotle was clear that eudaimonia was an *activity*.[58]

The principles which guide us towards flourishing are both productive of that condition and expressive of it.[59]

Accordingly, it is a mistake to try to develop a normative theory which tries to assess the morality of a particular action by calculating its consequences. Consequences, like desires, need principles of evaluation to judge their appropriateness and define their legitimacy. The contemporary pull towards deontologism is reflective of this truth.[60] It is, by the same token, also a mistake to try to discover normative principles without reference to the final ends of human flourishing. Human flourishing not only demands that principles for human action be developed, it demands that these principles be made to reflect the final ends that constitute human flourishing. If the life of a human being were not something to which the consequences of its actions could ultimately make a difference, then there would be no need for ethical principles. It is, metaphysically speaking, correct to say that considerations of consequences are fundamental while, epistemologically speaking, considerations of principles are fundamental. In an Aristotelian normative theory neither sort of consideration is ignored. The morality of our actions is judged by normative principles, not consequences, and yet these principles are based on the final ends of human flourishing which, when achieved, constitute that-for-the-sake-of-which morality (normative principles) exists.

We noted earlier in this chapter that W.F. Hardie drew a distinction between a dominant- and an inclusive-end theory of eudaimonia. What we have been saying above (and what follows below) depends upon the adoption of an inclusive-end approach to teleological eudaimonism. The possibility of an action being both productive and expressive of eudaimonia depends upon eudaimonia not being a single end which competes with all other ends and thus allows no other ends to have value except as a means to it. We can reject the dominant-end approach and arrive at the conclusions we are arguing for because it is possible within an Aristotelian normative theory for something to be done for its own sake and also for the sake of something else *without just being a necessary preliminary to something else*. For example, maintaining one's integrity or having a friendship is something which is good, not merely because it is a necessary means to human flourishing, but because it is an end in itself. Maintaining your integrity or having a friendship is good because each is an essential aspect or feature of human flourishing; each is one of the things meant when we speak of human flourishing. In order to know that maintaining one's integrity or having a friendship is a right thing to do, it is not necessary to examine whether the consequences of maintaining one's integrity (if it is truly a case of maintaining one's integrity) or having a friendship (if it is truly a friendship) will promote human flourishing. Rather, we just need to know that maintaining integrity or having a friendship is one of the final ends which constitute human flourishing. The natural end provides us with final ends from which principles to guide our actions may be based.

Because the natural end for man includes final ends which constitute human flourishing, an Aristotelian ethics can judge the morality of specific actions by principles that are based on these final ends. These principles guide our actions and determine what is right conduct. If a specific action is an instance of one of these principles, then it is right and ought to be done. If a specific action is in conflict with one of these principles, then it is wrong and ought not to be done. There is no need to argue over whether this or that action ought to be done because of its consequences. Rather, the argument will be over whether an action is truly an instance of one of the principles of right conduct or whether a principle properly expresses one of the final ends of human well-being. In an Aristotelian ethics normative principles determine whether an action is right, not the calculation of the specific consequences of an action.

An Aristotelian ethics, then, is a normative theory that is teleological in the sense that human flourishing constitutes *the* standard upon which all moral evaluations are ultimately based, and yet not teleological in the sense that the morality of specific actions is not judged by whether the specific consequences of those actions promote human flourishing. Further, an Aristotelian ethics is a normative theory that is deontological in the sense that it is normative principles, not consequences, that determine an action's moral worth, and yet not deontological in the sense that the normative principles are based on the final ends that constitute human flourishing. An Aristotelian ethics is a normative theory with a view of goodness that is capable of generating principles of right—principles that cannot be trumped by considerations of consequences. We shall see how a theory of rights can be based on an Aristotelian natural-end ethics in Chapter 3. It is, however, sufficient for now to simply note that an Aristotelian ethics is a normative theory that transcends characterization as either a teleological or deontological normative theory. It is a different kind of normative theory.

One final word is necessary on the different sort of normative theory an Aristotelian ethics is. An Aristotelian ethics gives primacy of place to the self and not to others. And it is for this reason that an Aristotelian teleology stands in contrast to the modern presupposition that what is in one's interest or will benefit one is uncontroversial[61] and that therefore the focus of ethics should be on our relations with others. We believe the following words best summarize this difference and consequently explain our emphasis upon self-perfection, human flourishing, or eudaimonia.

> In teleologies of the modern type there has been a radical displacement or shift of incidence of duties and obligations and, hence, of morals and ethics as a whole. The moral life is no longer thought of as consisting principally in the individual's pursuing his rightful end or goal or telos just as a human being and trying not to be deflected therefrom by the myriads of chance impulses and drives and inclinations and likings and preferences that never cease to manifest themselves in the life of any one of us. No, morality will instead be largely an affair . . . of the individual's having to try to bring himself to be other-regarding rather than exclusively self-regarding. His duties . . . are not towards himself at all, but only towards others. . . . [62]

Human Flourishing and Rationality

As noted in the first chapter, Gilbert Harman has charged that Aristotelian ethics treats human flourishing or eudaimonia as the only thing that counts without regard to how it is attained.[63] This charge is, however, mistaken, because it treats human flourishing as a dominant end. It is not. To further understand just how mistaken this charge is, we should consider a significant, but usually overlooked, comment by Aristotle regarding eudaimonia.[64] He says in *Politics* VII, 1323b24–29, that his own view of eudaimonia is supported by the facts about god,

> who is eudaimon and blessed, but not on account of any external goods but on account of himself and because he is by nature of a certain sort—which shows that being fortunate must be different from flourishing. For the goods external to the soul come of themselves by chance, but no one is just or temperate by or through chance.

Human flourishing or eudaimonia must be attained through a person's own efforts and cannot be something that is the result of factors that are beyond one's control. As Cooper states: "For Aristotle, *eudaimonia* is necessarily the result of a person's own efforts; success, of whatever kind, could only count as *eudaimonia* if due to one's own efforts".[65] Thus, when it comes to identifying the exact nature of human flourishing, a distinction needs to be made between what is actually a constituent part of flourishing and what is merely a necessary condition for flourishing.[66] One must be careful not to confuse "those things which one must have in order to flourish with the condition of flourishing itself".[67] Human flourishing does not consist in the mere possession and use of the goods required for successful human living.[68] Rather, human flourishing or eudaimonia consists in a person taking charge of his own life so as to develop and maintain those ends (those virtues) for which he is alone responsible and which in most cases[69] will allow him to attain the goods his life requires.

Regarding the goods life requires, such as health and wealth, it should be noted that they do not exist independently and apart from human actions to attain them;[70] they only exist as goods insofar as they are objects of human effort. If a person is to flourish, he must *direct himself* to their attainment as best the circumstances will permit. Human flourishing should not be interpreted to involve or require 'goods' which are not the object of human effort or which are in principle beyond the range of human action.

The foregoing point is best understood within the context of an inclusive-end interpretation of eudaimonia. Health and wealth may always be 'goods' in an abstract sense, but the degree to which they are 'goods' will vary significantly in the concrete. In the first place, such goods must be the object of human action; but this means that they must be the object of actions taken by individuals. Since the interests, circumstances, and aptitudes of individuals vary, the particular 'mix' of such goods will vary as well. For the businessman, for example, more emphasis would be placed upon the achievement of wealth than upon health. For the athlete, however, the opposite might be the case. And with respect to individuals within these broad categories even further refinements and variations of the mix would be expected. Therefore, we must not only understand such goods in terms of their being objects of action (rather than in terms of possession or use), but we must also realize that the value of such goods is in practice relative to the individual. Although it is quite incorrect to describe an Aristotelian ethics as a form of relativism, it nevertheless shares relativism's most appealing feature: pluralism.

The appropriate mix of goods in one's life is not something one necessarily knows intuitively. Similarly, the appropriate courses of action to take with respect to such goods are not given either. All the elements of the mix, as well as the associated actions, must be conceptualized into a compossible set appropriate to the individual's own condition of flourishing. As a human being, the individual must conform to certain general requirements of human flourishing dictated by human nature itself. But as an individual, unique circumstances, aptitudes, and interests will particularize the mix. What is interesting about an Aristotelian ethics is that the central general virtue is also the central particular virtue. In other words, that which is required for successful personal flourishing is the same for any and all persons: rationality.[71]

The cardinal virtue, and that which is the the source of all other virtues, is rationality.[72] This involves first and foremost a commitment to the policy of identifying and dealing with the world by means of concepts. Conceptually attending to the world is how we acquire knowledge. It is no part-time affair and involves more than forming a few simple abstractions or using a few words. Conceptually dealing with reality requires that our convictions, values, desires, goals, and actions be based on knowledge and understanding and that we do not act blindly from impulse and habit. Exercising the effort to conceptually attend to the world comes in many forms: in seeking clarity as opposed to vagueness, in persevering in the attempt to understand instead of giving up, in willingly seeing and correcting errors as opposed to maintaining them, in being open to new knowledge rather than being close-minded, and in general being concerned with coherence and evidence instead of being unconcerned.[73] Conceptually attending to the world is the *method* of using our mind and constitutes the distinctively human way of living.

To say that human beings need to employ their conceptual faculty to know and deal with the world is not to say that human beings have to deny their desires and attempt to live without them. As Henry B. Veatch, commenting on Aristotle, states:

As Aristotle sees it, for a man to live intelligently is not merely an affair of what he calls in his technical language, "intellectual virtue"— the virtues of skill and know-how when it comes to determining what needs to be done or ought to be done. No less is it an affair of so-called "moral virtue"—such being the virtues of choice, through the acquisition and possession of which man comes to consistently to want and prefer just those courses of action which reason dictates as requisite and needing to be done.[74]

In order to know and deal with the world in a rational or intelligent way, then, we need to learn how to use and control our desires. Our desires move us toward objects of apparent benefit and away from objects of apparent harm. Yet our desires can be mistaken. They can direct us toward something that is not in fact beneficial or away from something that actually *is* beneficial. The solution to this problem is, however, not to deny our desires and to attempt to live without them. Neither is it a solution to abdicate on any attempt to direct our desires toward those things we know to be actually beneficial and away from those things that are indeed harmful. Rather, we must discover what the true goods of human life are and strive to harmonize our desires with our knowledge of these goods. How we feel and react to a particular situation "should not be a mere uncritical and undisciplined response, but rather the sensible and intelligent reaction which the particular situation calls for".[75]

If we fail to learn how to use and control our desires, then we will be persons caught in self-contradiction—we will be moved toward two different actions at once, or else, when the desires are not of equal strength, we will only be capable of acting half-heartedly. We will be dysdaimonic. We will be perpetually distracted, never fully committed to or involved in any course of action. We will be at variance with ourselves, as Aristotle notes, and "have appetites for some things and rational desires for others. [In this state] our soul is rent by faction, and one element in it grieves when it abstains from certain acts, while the other is pleased, and one draws [us] this way and the other that, as if they were pulling [us] in pieces".[76] If we, however, do learn how to use and control our desires, then our life can take on a 'wholeheartedness' in which we are fully present in our actions and experience the whole of our life in every act. David Norton has noted that it can be said interchangeably of the eudaimonic individual that "'He is where he wants to be, doing what he wants to do' or 'He is where he must be, doing what he must do'".[77] The 'must' here, Norton observes, is a moral 'must' and stems from a person's own choice. Thus, we have within our power the ability to make our own soul; and what we make of it is reflected through the mix of goods we have either intelligently or unintelligently pursued.

Living rationally or intelligently is, then, not a single dominant end. It is not a specific end which competes with other ends and is thus judged as having more importance than all other ends. Rather, living rationally or intelligently is achieved through the attainment of specific ends which constitute this way of living. Living rationally or intelligently characterizes an integrated set of activities (virtues); each of which is valuable because each is an essential feature of this way of living and not merely a necessary means. Thus, living rationally or intelligently is an ultimate end in the sense that it is "the *most* final end and is never sought for the sake of anything else because it includes all final ends". [78] But the ultimate end does not include the other final ends as a box might include its contents. Rather, such ends are 'included' in the ultimate end as expressions of it. They become so, however, when they express intelligence or rationality. Even such a moral virtue as justice or a good such as friendship would not qualify as ends in themselves if intelligence were absent.[79]

We believe that what we have said could easily lead into a discussion of many other necessary virtues for flourishing: honesty, integrity, productivity, courage, and justice would all have to be mentioned. But an analysis of these virtues would carry us too far afield. Our main emphasis has been on the central role of rationality. These other virtues, we believe, stem from that and would tend to flow naturally from one committed to rationality or intelligent living. We do, however, believe a very brief word about friendship would be in order here. This is because our discussion so far has shown that Aristotelian ethics does not consist essentially in conformity to rules or calculations of the general welfare. Rather, it consists in self-improvement. What bearing, therefore, does all this have in our relations towards others? The answer to this question is the concept of friendship. We discuss various aspects of this concept again in Chapter 5, but how friendship relates to flourishing itself needs to be mentioned here.

Friendship is an essential ingredient of human flourishing. Whether the friendship be merely a friendship based on attainment of mutual pleasure or advantage, or whether the friendship is a character-friendship[80] based on the recognition of good qualities of character, friendship is an essential constituent of human well-being. Friendships, and here we will be primarily speaking of character-friendships, are needed for one to (1) know the goodness of one's life and (2) continuously engage in the moral and intellectual virtues that go to make up a flourishing life.[81]

1. As was noted in the first section of this chapter, human flourishing does not consist merely in conformity to the principles one's natural end requires; rather one needs to know the facts about oneself—how one's life is going, specifically the nature of one's own character—and to self-consciously make choices regarding how to live in light of this knowledge. Yet, how can one know that the qualities in himself he thinks are virtuous are indeed so? Or how can one know what are really one's faults? And, maybe most importantly, what are one's real motivations? Self- knowledge is most difficult to achieve, but not impossible. One has the best chance for self-knowledge through a relationship in which there is a close affinity of values. One cannot study one's own actions and self as easily as that of another's, and in a character-friendship the affinity is strong enough so as to allow a greater mirroring of one's own character. As Cooper notes: "Here the presumption is that even an intimate friend remains distinct enough to be studied objectively; yet, because one intuitively knows oneself to be fundamentally the same in character as he is, one obtains through him an objective view of oneself".[82] Such a friendship will serve as the needed bridge by which objectivity about the other can be converted into objectivity about oneself.

2. An entirely private life is not the best possible life for a human being. Shared activities with others are essential to the well-being of human beings, for shared activities enable a person to discover that others also find the same things interesting and worthwhile. By allowing the person to expand the scope of his activities by acting with others, shared activities also enhance a person's interest and pleasure in his own activities and thus deepen and secure

his commitment to them. A shared activity is an activity in which everyone shares and mutually knows the goal to be achieved, everyone knows the role to be played by each person in the activity, and everyone agrees to do his share in this common effort.[83] All the forms of friendship are shared activities and are thus essential for human flourishing. Character-friendships are, however, particularly vital forms of shared activities. In a character-friendship one knows that the other party is committed to the same moral values, and this knowledge allows a person to deepen and secure the moral and intellectual activities (virtues) that his well-being involves. For this reason, one cannot have a character-friendship with a superficial acquaintance, but only with someone one knows very well.

> A human being cannot have a flourishing life except by having intimate friends to whom he is attached precisely on account of their good qualities of character, and who are similarly attached to him: it is only with such persons that he can share the moral activities that are most central to his life.[84]

It might seem that the view of friendship endorsed by an Aristotelian natural-end ethics is one which treats persons in such relationships as merely instruments to be used for attaining human flourishing. Yet this is not true: for as we have seen, it is possible for something to be an end in itself and still contribute to another end. It is possible for a friend to be someone one values for their own sake (as indeed Aristotle states), and it still be the case that this friendship is a vital constituent of one's personal well-being. What is true about friendship (and all other eudaimonic ends as well) is that it is constitutive of the process of self-perfection. In this sense, although the link to and concern for others is not lost, the emphasis is still upon the self.

Practical Rationality and Versions of Human Flourishing

Though by no means exhaustive, the account of human flourishing sketched earlier gives us some idea of what must be considered if one's life is to have any chance of being all that it can and should be. Yet knowing in what human flourishing consists is no a priori matter. The final ends which constitute man's natural end are not determined in a deductive fashion from some abstract conception of human flourishing. Rather, the constituents of human flourishing are discovered by everything we can learn from experience regarding the needs of human life— be they physical, psychological, sexual, environmental, educational, economic, political, or whatever.

Though the most crucial and central principles of human flourishing can be known, an Aristotelian ethics does not provide the moral agent with an a priori rule or rehearsed procedure for what should be done in a concrete situation. Determining the exact course of action to take in a concrete situation is something that requires deliberation on the part of the individual moral agent. It is, however, not the case that moral deliberation is finished before the time of action so that all the moral agent needs do is to note the particular instances of the type of action decided upon beforehand. Rather, as Fred D. Miller, Jr. has recently shown in his article 'Aristotle On Rationality In Action', [85] moral deliberation is for Aristotle completed only at the time of action, and insight on the part of the moral agent is required in the concrete situation in order to know what action to take. In *Nicomachean Ethics* VI, 11 Aristotle states:

> And insight is of ultimate things in both directions; for insight and not reasoning is of the primary bounding principles and of ultimate things, and insight, *in demonstrations*, is of immutable bounding principles, whereas insight, *in matters of action*, is of the ultimate and of the contingent and of the minor premise. . . .[86]

The moral agent's insight is the recognition that that which could have been otherwise is of the sort that will allow for the attainment of the agent's goal. For example, if one has the goal of having friends, the process of deliberating about whom to be friends with will be properly completed only when one sees that a particular person among one's acquaintances is indeed someone with whom a friendship can be achieved and decides to pursue a friendship with this person. One's insight is necessary to identify that this person is the sort of person with whom one could be friends. Knowing the right thing to do is for an Aristotelian ethics impossible without the moral agent exercising practical rationality, and practical rationality ultimately calls upon the individual human being to exercise his own insight and judgment in regard to what actions to take. The process of deliberating is something that the person must do for himself; it cannot be done for him by others. An Aristotelian ethics, as Miller has shown, places extreme importance on the person not only knowing the constituents of human flourishing but also knowing how to attain these final ends. What ultimately counts is that it is the person himself acting in the concrete situation to attain the ends which constitute human flourishing.

Not only are there no a priori recipes by which a person can live his life, it is simply false to assume that human flourishing could ever be anything other than what each individual person can work out for himself. As we have noted, one's generic potentialities are never separate from one's individuative potentialities, and every person needs to develop his own version of human flourishing. For example, one person may spend a comparatively larger amount of time and effort developing his personal relationships than someone else, while another person may spend more time and effort developing his physical health. To ignore either would obviously be a mistake, but the emphasis put on each is a matter of degree; and the proper balance or 'mean' is only something that the individual can determine for himself in light of his own unique potentialities, needs, and circumstances.

Moreover, the development of moral character, whereby one comes to desire what is actually good and to not desire what is in fact bad, is something that must result from the individual's own insight and judgment [87] regarding himself and the situations faced. Developing the habits that constitute good moral character cannot be achieved by following a course of action others have determined to be right for a person if one does not himself understand and value this course of action. This is true even if others are correct in their judgments and the person incorrect. Moral character also depends upon understanding and judgment. Yet if this last point is to be adequately understood and appreciated, the relationship between the final ends which constitute human flourishing must be explained.

The Importance of Autonomy

Even though human flourishing is not a single end which is more valuable than all others but is instead an end which is achieved through the attainment of those final ends that constitute it, there can still be an end that is more fundamental than all the others that make up human well-being. In other words, there can be a 'lexical ordering' of the final ends of human flourishing.

As we have seen, the final end that is always to be preferred over all others is that which makes possible and explains the existence of other final ends; it is that final end without which all the other ends could not exist. For a human being, this final end is rationality. Living rationally or intelligently is the overarching end or virtue which integrates and unifies all the other ends of human flourishing. Living rationally or intelligently is a human being's unique excellence—*arete*. There is not a single human action that is right or end that is good that does not involve the exercise of one's intelligence. The 'rightness' of an action or the 'goodness' of an end could not for a human being exist if the action for the sake of the end were not an exercise of human reason or intelligence.

Yet human reason or intelligence is not automatic; effort is required. To deal with the world rationally or intelligently a human being must exercise the effort to initiate and maintain a conceptual grasp on what he is doing, and since there is no collective human mind or being, it is the individual human being directing and using his own mind to take actions to achieve ends that is absolutely necessary for human fulfillment. He needs to act from his own knowledge and understanding and thereby exercise control and direction over his actions. Thus, autonomy or self-directedness is an inherent feature of any activity being constitutive of human well-being. No feature of human rationality or intelligence is so central or basic.

It might be objected that self-directedness or autonomy, though necessary for human well-being, is no more necessary than such goods as health, wealth, pleasure, and friendship. One could not live well without these goods. In fact, in extreme situations, one could not even begin to use reason or intelligence without some or all of these goods. Thus, there really is no basis for saying that self-directedness or autonomy is a more important feature of rational or intelligent living than any other of the goods that constitute or make possible human flourishing. This objection, however, misses its mark. Though it is certainly true that health, wealth, pleasure, and friendship are necessary for human well-being and that in cases of extreme deprivation of some or all of these goods human intelligence or reason cannot even function, it does not follow from this that all the goods of human well-being are of equal importance. It should be remembered that human needs cannot be satisfied and potentialities actualized in *any* manner. If a human being were attached to a machine which satisfied his every need and thus made it possible for him not to have to do anything, this would not constitute a worthwhile human life. Rather, human needs and potentialities have to be dealt with by actions that are generated and maintained by the the human being himself.

If something is to be a human good, it must be an object of human valuation. It must be something which in some way a human being has acted to gain and/or keep. Even receiving a gift from a friend is only expressive of friendship if one has taken actions in creating and maintaining the friendship. If one had not acted in any way to create the friendship and thus the item, in effect, appeared out of the blue, then it would not be a way of experiencing friendship and would not fulfill this human need. Thus, human flourishing does not merely require that a human being possess health, wealth, pleasure, and friendship; he must rather attain these goods through the exercise of his own reason and intelligence. Thus, self-directedness or autonomy remains the central or primary feature of rational or intelligent living.

It is often claimed that a human being is an end-in-himself, but what does this claim mean and how can it be justified? In an Aristotelian ethics man's natural end, human flourishing, is the ultimate, final end—that final end which includes all other final ends—and since human flourishing does not exist in the abstract, there is no such thing as human flourishing separate from the activities which constitute the flourishing of individual human beings. Thus, the ultimate end of human action, the basis for all moral judgments, is the fulfillment of the individual human being. There is no higher moral purpose, no other end to be served than the well-being, the flourishing, of the individual human being. Nothing else is needed to morally justify the existence and actions of the individual human being. A human being's moral worth and value are not to be determined by any other would-be moral standard. Thus, actions taken by a human being that self-actualize (perfect his nature) are actions that are ends-in-themselves, and when these actions constitute the individual human being—specifically, when these actions result from principles of actions (virtues) which constitute his character—then the individual human being is an end-in-himself.

Each and every human being is potentially an end-in-himself, but to actually *be* an end-in-himself, the individual human being must take the appropriate actions—namely, actions that self-actualize. In effect, a person must earn this status. Being an end-in-himself, like every other aspect of morality, is something that must be accomplished by the individual human being and is something for which he alone is responsible.[88] Autonomy or self-directedness is central to the process.[89]

Kant claimed that one should "act in such a way that you always treat humanity, whether in your person or in the person of any other, never simply as a means, but always at the same time as an end".[90] This claim has, of course, been subject to skepticism and confusion; for not only has it never been clear just how it might be justified, it has also never been clear what has exactly been meant by it.[91] The centrality of self-directedness or autonomy in rational or intelligent living allows an Aristotelian ethics to provide a clearer meaning and justification of this claim. Yet to understand how an Aristotelian ethics would begin to interpret and justify this claim, some additional observations about self-directedness or autonomy are necessary.

First, it must be understood that self-directedness or autonomy does not in and of itself guarantee that a human being will take the right actions or pursue the proper goals. To describe a person as autonomous does not necessarily mean that he is living rationally or intelligently. All that autonomy or self-directedness guarantees is that a human being will be using his own reason and intelligence in determining what ends to pursue or principles to follow.

Second, even though autonomy does not guarantee that a person is living as he should, it is nonetheless important for morality. Self-directedness guarantees the fundamentally essential humanity of the person—the exercise by the person of his own judgment and choice. If a human being were not autonomous, then he could be neither praised nor blamed. His actions would not be subject to moral appraisal.

Third, autonomy also preserves the possibility that others can deal with a person in a manner that respects his humanity. Since a self-directed person is living by the exercise of his own thought and judgment, he is open to reason. He can be dealt with as a being to whom reasons can be given for why he ought or ought not do something. A self-directed person may, of course, not find the reasons offered for why something ought or ought not to be done adequate, and he may or may not be correct in his evaluation of the reasons given. Yet he is living as a human being—as a creature to whom reasons can make a difference, not merely as a creature who is caused to act by this or that desire.

Fourth, self-directedness or autonomy are inherent powers in the individual human being. One does not choose to be self-directed or autonomous; rather, choice *is* self-directedness or autonomy.[92] One can, of course, exercise self-directedness or fail to do so, but it is not something others can provide.

Fifth, even though autonomy or self-directedness does not guarantee that a person is flourishing, it is not external to the essence of human flourishing. It pertains to the very essence. Fundamentally speaking, human flourishing is an activity, not a static state, and an individual human being directing and using his own mind to take actions to achieve ends—living according to his own choices—is the very form, the only form, in which life in accordance with virtue (human flourishing) can be lived.

From what we have learned about human flourishing, together with the foregoing comments about autonomy, we may conclude that if a person fails to develop integrity or refuses to seek friendships, or if he abdicates the responsibility of controlling and using his desires or engaging in productive work, or if he cares nothing about reason at all, then he is misusing himself, acting contrary to his natural end, and treating himself simply as a means.[93] If other persons use a person for purposes he has not chosen, regardless of the purposes to be attained, then the person is being misused, his natural end is not achieved, and he is being treated simply as a means.

To achieve a better understanding of Kant's claim, it should be noted here that only *certain* specific actions by a person constitute a misuse of himself and a failure to treat himself as an end-in-himself; however, *any* use of a person by another person which prevents him from using himself (namely, which does not allow self-directedness or autonomy) is a misuse of him.[94] Neither can the natural end of a human being, human flourishing, be achieved, nor can a human being be treated as a being with a potential to be an end-in-himself, if his autonomy is not respected. We shall see in Chapter 3 how a theory of natural rights can be developed from an Aristotelian understanding of the claim that human beings are potential ends-in-themselves. The existence of a natural end for human beings and the primary importance of self-directedness for rational or intelligent living will be crucial components of such a theory.

Aristotelian Ethics

At least as we have developed it, an Aristotelian natural-end ethics is a profoundly humanistic and individualistic ethics.[95] It is humanistic because human flourishing is the ultimate moral standard; it is individualistic because human flourishing is always understood as the flourishing of the individual human being. An Aristotelian ethics is in no way subjectivistic; for the individual human being has a nature and cannot find fulfillment by choosing any course of action he might desire. There is moral knowledge, and the individual human being needs to learn in what his fulfillment and well-being truly consist. An Aristotelian ethics is neither narrowly egoistic nor atomistic. Human beings are social and political animals and live best in a human community that has the rule of law. In Chapter 4 the social and political nature of a human being will be examined and the relationship between what we call Lockean rights and the common good of the political community will be explored.

In this chapter we have examined how an Aristotelian ethics provides a foundation for moral values. We have described the basic features of an Aristotelian ethics, dealt with the central meta-ethical issues, and explained the unique character of an Aristotelian normative theory. We have not attempted to explore in detail every feature of an Aristotelian ethics but have instead concentrated on those features that will best assist us in revealing how such an ethics offers the foundation for a Lockean conception of natural rights. An Aristotelian ethics offers fertile ground for the construction of a political philosophy which judges liberty as the primary social and political value. We shall, however, not attempt to construct a Lockean political philosophy in all its forms. Rather, we shall confine ourselves to showing how an Aristotelian natural-end ethics can justify Lockean rights and avoid many of the difficulties associated with rights theory.

3

NATURAL RIGHTS

The idea of natural right must be unknown as long as the idea of nature is unknown. The discovery of nature is the work of philosophy. Where there is no philosophy, there is no knowledge of natural right as such.

—Leo Strauss, *Natural Right and History*

By appealing to an essentially Aristotelian natural-end ethics, we propose to defend the moral claim that individuals have rights. These rights can be described as Lockean and based on the view that there is no higher value than the individual human being. Accordingly, these natural rights reflect the principle that individuals may not be sacrificed or used for attaining ends not of their own choosing. As Nozick has observed, "to use a person . . . does not sufficiently respect and take account of the fact that he is a separate person, that his is the only life he has" and "that there are different individuals with separate lives and so no one may be sacrificed for others".[1] Individuals are inviolable; to act against this principle is, to paraphrase Isaiah Berlin, to sin against the truth that an individual is a human being, a being with a life of his own to live.[2]

Yet the inviolability of the individual cannot be based on simply the difference of persons or the separateness of their lives. Certainly, Marxists would consider these facts inadequate to justify such a claim, for they regard such facts as alterable and as something that ought to be changed. One does not, however, need to subscribe to Marxism to see that these facts in and of themselves provide no normative support for Lockean rights. How do these facts provide a basis for the value of individual autonomy? What is needed is a moral foundation[3] from which the desirability of persons being separate beings, each having and living his own life, can be shown. "One could only sin", Mack notes, "against a person's being a being with a life of his own to live if his having and living his own life is what ought to be".[4] Lockean rights thus require a moral foundation, and we propose to show how an essentially Aristotelian natural-end ethics can provide such a foundation.

THE CLASSIFICATION AND CHARACTERISTICS OF RIGHTS

We could begin our discussion directly with an analysis of natural rights. But within the Aristotelian tradition there is an older, more long-lived concept: natural law. MacIntyre asserts that the concept of rights is not to be found anywhere before about 1400.[5] Strauss claims that the great significance of Hobbes was that he separated the right of nature from the law of nature—a separation that has continued throughout modernity.[6] Finnis places Suarez at the watershed of the move away from speaking in terms of natural law and towards rights;[7] and Villey goes as far back as William of Ockham in locating the origin of the modern conception of rights.[8] In addition, Tuck goes even further back in his sophisticated analysis of the history of rights, arguing that the uses to which *ius* and *dominium* were put in the later Roman Empire have similarities to the modern subjective sense of the term 'rights' without much of the theoretical baggage supplied by modernity.[9]

Whatever scholarly disputes there may be about origins, all commentators are agreed that a shift away from natural law theory took place and that the concept of rights is essentially modern. What this means is that the 'subjective' nature of rights (discussed below) in the modern era stands in contrast to the type of objectivism found in traditional natural-law theory. And as Tuck has noted, this contrast becomes a recurrent theme in the development of natural-rights theories.[10] Further, Alan Gewirth is correct to argue that just because a concept does not explicitly appear in the past in the way we understand it today, it does not follow that the concepts that were used could not imply or implicitly contain the concept in question.[11] However, there is even less agreement on the presence of a modern notion of rights in antiquity than there is with respect to the idea that 'rights' is a peculiarly modern concept. And since our purpose is not primarily historical, we shall be ignoring many of the fine points of historical scholarship for the sake of broad themes. It seems evident to us that, in the main, natural rights and natural law constitute distinct perspectives on social morality, although part of our argument later on will be to show how facets of each perspective can be incorporated into one theory.

The first point to keep in mind is that we hold to the distinction between moral and legal rights. The latter concept is presumably constrained by the former, and the former need not refer to any existing legal system. It is conceivable that one could develop a theory of moral rights based upon the evolution of legal traditions. Here moral rights would not so much constrain what legal institutions could grant as rights, but rather moral rights would function as a community's self-conscious identification of its legal and civic practices. If MacIntyre had a theory of rights (see below), it would probably be of this type. Nevertheless, it is common in the Aristotelian tradition to see law as constrained by morality, and if we can make a case for natural rights, it follows that for us moral rights would be distinct from, and more fundamental than, legal rights. Nevertheless, the distinction between moral and legal rights seems a particularly modern one, because *if* there was a concept of rights in antiquity, it was probably tied to positive law.[12] The morality that acted to constrain positive law in antiquity would have been referred to as 'the right'—a set of objective moral truths that we now capture under the words 'natural law'. Therefore, the possibility of there being moral rights is itself tied to the characteristics of the notion of 'rights' itself; for if 'rights' is a modern concept, then so must 'moral rights' be a modern concept. What then are the main characteristics peculiar to a modern conception of moral rights?

The first characteristic is that moral rights are 'subjective'. The term *subjective* is misleading because one is inclined to tie it to subjectivism. But 'subjective' here means something like 'possessed by the individual' and does not necessarily imply subjectivism or relativism. As many authors have pointed out, the history of rights seems to involve a transition from the objective ('the right' understood as immutable general principles of the good to which behavior ought to conform) to the subjective.[13] Hence the departure from traditional natural-law theory represents a departure from the idea that general principles of justice are alone sufficient to account for the moral basis of legal rights one can claim in virtue of one's individuality, and not simply as a member of a community, nation, or universe. In other words, the 'objectively right' seemed to place too little emphasis upon the importance of the individual (the subject). Early modernity, for example, began speaking of faculties or powers possessed by individuals that grounded their rights. [14] Later modernity emphasized the liberty or choice-making characteristics of individuals. Both, however, grounded rights in the subject. [15]

In addition to the 'subjective' character of rights, there are further characteristics of the concept of rights that must be discussed. For example, another way of putting our preceding problem is to recognize that the term *right* can be used in the adjectival sense, when referring to some action being morally appropriate, and in the substantival sense, when referring to a moral claim or an entitlement of a person. This is, of course, but another way of saying that there is a distinction between what Leo Strauss has called natural *right* and natural *rights*. Yet it is precisely the *connection* between these two senses of right that we will seek to demonstrate in this chapter. To this end, it will be important to distinguish between what it is to be a right from the sort of philosophical justification used for rights claims; for we will be arguing for Lockean rights based on the understanding of a human being's *telos* as presented in Chapter 2 and *not* on the basis of mere natural 'powers' possessed by human beings in some state of nature. Yet in this section we are concerned with classifying and characterizing rights and will thus only be using 'right' in the substantival sense.

Besides the distinction between moral and legal rights, there is also the distinction between general and special rights. General rights are rights that are possessed by all human beings and are not due to any specific reason or circumstance which pertains to a particular person. Since general rights are possessed by all human beings, they are also universal rights. Special rights are not universal. They are rights possessed by particular persons owing to a specific reason or circumstance which pertains only to them. For example, Smith has the special right to play golf at the country club because he is a dues-paying member, but Jones, who has not paid his dues, does not have such a right; or the children of Jones have a right to parental care from Jones, but they do not have such a right from Smith because he is not their father. The rights we are interested in claiming are not due to any special relation to another person; rather, they exist simply because someone is a human being. Our position in this chapter, therefore, will be to defend a theory of general or universal moral rights.

Using Hohfeld's analysis of rights,[16] a right is a three-term relation between someone who is a right-holder, a type of action, and one or more other persons. According to Hohfeld, there are four senses of 'rights'. In each of the following cases, *X* will stand for an action or a forbearance from an action.

1. Jones has a claim-right to Smith's X-ing if and only if Smith has a duty to Jones to do X.

2. Jones has a liberty-right to X relative to Smith if and only if it is not the case that Jones has a duty not to X.

3. Jones has a power-right to X relative to Smith if and only if Smith has a liability to change his legal position through Jones's X-ing.

4. Jones has an immunity-right relative to Smith's X-ing if and only if Smith does not have a power-right to X relative to Jones.

The rights for which we will argue are claim-rights. This is not to say that the claim-rights for which we argue may not also involve what, on a Hohfeldian analysis, are liberty-rights, power-rights, and immunity-rights.[17] Rather, this is just to say that claim-rights are central to our conception of rights, since the correlative duties they entail provide a moral basis for legally constraining certain actions of others.

Claim-rights impose duties or obligations. It is important that the connection between this sort of right and duties be made clear. Duties or obligations have a far wider range of applicability than that of rights. If Jones has a right, then Smith and everyone else has a duty to Jones. Yet if Jones has a right, this does not necessarily mean that Jones has a duty. For example, an infant could have a right to parental care but not have any duties, or one could have a right to eat a 32-ounce steak but not be obligated to perform such a feat. Finally, Smith may have an obligation or duty to Jones, but this does not necessarily mean that Jones has a right to Smith's performance of this obligation. As John Hospers has noted, "Perhaps you ought to help out a friend in need; but does the

friend have a claim on you? Can she claim your help as a right? As a
driver you have a duty to stop at a red traffic light, but who has the right
that corresponds to this duty (especially at an intersection where there
are no pedestrians in sight)?"[18] Smith's obligation or duty to Jones does
not imply that Jones has a right. We shall have need to recall this general relation between rights and duties later on.

Claim-rights impose duties on others. If Jones has a right, other
people must have a duty, but it is the nature of the duty that others have
that determines whether Jones's right is positive or negative. Others are
subject to a positive duty with respect to Jones if and only if they are
morally bound to provide Jones with some good or service. Others are
subject to a negative duty with respect to Jones if and only if they are
morally bound *not* to deprive Jones of some good or morally bound *not*
to inflict some treatment on Jones. [19] For example, if Jones has a positive
right to food, then others have the duty to provide Jones with food or the
means by which Jones can obtain food. If Jones has a negative right to
food, then others have the duty not to take Jones's food or the means by
which he obtains food from him. The rights for which we will argue in
this chapter will be negative rights.

These negative rights are basic and only negative rights are basic.
The logical structure of our moral theory is hierarchical, and the place
accorded negative rights in this theory is basic. By *basic* we mean first
that they are rights which are not derivable from other rights. For example, Jones's right to health care flows from Jones's basic negative
right to act freely and choose to enter a contract to obtain health care, or
the right of the children of Smith to parental care results from Smith's
decision to have children. There is nothing in the conception of basic
negative rights for which we will argue that precludes the creation of
numerous positive rights and duties. All that is required is that the sub-
sequent rights and duties do not contradict basic negative rights.

Secondly, the negative rights for which we will argue are basic in
the sense that they are a type of moral principle which is used to create
a legal system which protects the social and political conditions necessary for the possibility of human flourishing. Negative rights seek to
protect the self-directedness or autonomy of every individual human
being in the political community and thereby protect the condition under
which human flourishing can occur. Negative rights thus do not directly

seek to secure human flourishing, but only the *condition* for the possibility of its social occurrence. As we shall see later, they are 'meta-normative' principles.[20]

These basic negative rights for which we will argue are natural rights. By *natural* we mean that they are rights which exist prior to any convention or agreement, regardless of whether someone is a member of a particular society or community, and are due to the possession of certain natural attributes in virtue of which someone is said to belong to a certain class of beings. Natural rights are, of course, general rights, but not all general rights are natural rights; for someone could hold that all human beings have rights without claiming that there is anything prior to convention or agreement that determines who is or is not a member of the class of beings called human beings. Such is not our view. As argued in Chapter 2, the world of facts is not entirely devoid of values; a notion of human flourishing can be developed from our understanding of human nature. Our argument for natural rights will start from this normative basis. These rights are, as Herbert Morris has noted,

> linked to certain features of a class of beings. Were we fundamentally different than we are now, we would not have [them]. But it is more important than that, for [these rights are] linked to a certain feature of human beings which, were that feature absent—the capacity to reason and choose on the basis of reasons—, profound conceptual changes would be involved in the thought about human beings. [There are rights], then, connected with a feature of men that sets men apart from other natural phenomena.[21]

The basic negative rights for which we will argue are, then, natural in the sense just described.[22]

Rights are the basis upon which a legal system is developed, but if the laws of a legal system are to be equally and universally implemented, then these rights must be a type of moral principle which can be uniformly applied to each and every human being in a social context regardless of that person's particular needs, goals, or circumstance. As Machan notes,

> It is with reference to membership in a community that law has relevance and thus is universal; but it is with reference to living one's life that morality is of utmost significance, even though its application will vary in accordance with enormous differences in people as the individuals they are.[23]

Law pertains to everyone in a specific but universal way, and so the duty legally demanded of others by a right must result from those aspects of human life we all share. Yet the many virtues that constitute an individual human being's fulfillment vary in application from person to person and circumstance to circumstance. For example, one may not have an occasion to demonstrate the virtue of courage in his life, or what courage demands for one person may be something entirely different for another. So the duty which these natural rights demands others to legally fulfill—in other words, the 'meta-normative' obligation that is demanded from all beings in a social and political context—must be (1) something which all human beings are in principle capable of fulfilling; and (2) something which all human beings in a social and political context, regardless of their particular circumstances or specific needs, must have in order to have any possibility of flourishing. Whatever the nature of the duty legally demanded by these natural rights, it must be a duty that is capable of universal and uniform application.

These natural rights are inalienable. This is not yet to say that natural rights are absolute; this feature of rights is discussed below. *Inalienability* means that one cannot, as long as one is a human being, be said not to have a right in a social and political context to the performance of certain legally required duties by others. One can lose or give up a *special* right—for example, Jones has lost his right to play golf at the country club, since he has failed to pay his annual dues— or one can transfer ownership of some property to someone else; but a human being cannot lose or give up what is essentially true about human nature—namely, that a human being has the capacity to reason and choose. Therefore, one cannot lose or give up the rights one has in a social and political context in virtue of this.[24] If one has a natural right to live according to his own choices, then Smith voluntarily giving Jones his watch is not a case of Smith alienating his rights, but is in fact an instance of Smith exercising this right with respect to property. Everyone else in the community would be legally bound to respect Smith's decision. With regard to the right to live according to one's own choices, Herbert Morris has argued that a criminal's choice to violate others' rights ought to be respected and that the criminal ought to experience the implications of the principles exhibited by his choice of that action—namely, being punished. "A person has a right to institutions that respect his choices ".[25]

In other words, when someone is punished for having violated others' rights, it is not the case that the criminal has alienated or otherwise lost his rights; rather, it is the case that the criminal's choice to live in a rights-violating way is being respected. The criminal may not have understood or now may not like what his choice to violate others' rights involved, but, as Machan has noted, "just as changing one's mind about a contract after signing it does not alter its implications, so not desiring to go to jail does not change the objective consequences of one's actions". [26]

Finally, and most controversially, these natural rights are absolute. By *absolute* we do not mean that these rights are unconditional, for they are justified by reference to a human being's natural end. They are not self-evident moral truths. Moreover, we do not claim that there cannot be circumstances in which human social and political life is impossible and therefore circumstances in which it is pointless to apply rights or even situations in which what one may morally do conflicts with what a legal system based on rights requires. (These circumstances and situations are discussed in detail in the next chapter.) Rather, we claim that wherever and whenever political principles are applicable, these natural rights over-ride, 'trump', all other moral considerations in constitutionally determining what matters of morality will be matters of legality and thus one's legal obligations—namely, what one must or must not do. Rights are thus absolute in this sense. [27]

If rights are to have the fundamental role of determining what matters of morality are to be matters of law, and if rights are to be moral principles applicable to human social and political life which determine legal obligations regardless of the consequences, then it is the absoluteness of rights that gives rights the particular normative force they have. As John Hospers has noted, "What value is a right if others can be justified in violating it? It is the absoluteness of rights that makes us secure in claiming them, as we would not be if they were only prima facie". [28] Natural rights simply cannot have the fundamental role assigned to them if they are *all* prima facie.

> If every right can be over-ruled by another right, and if having a fundamental place in a scheme of justice means that whatever occupies that place serves as the court of last resort in settling questions of justice, then natural

rights cannot serve the purpose for which they have been introduced, namely to enable us to identify justice, distinguish it from injustice, and act accordingly in a social context. . . . [This] characterization of the items that have a fundamental place in our scheme of justice would render them systematically *ad hoc* in that each case where one will stop the process of over-ruling cannot have systematic determination.[29]

Instead of claiming that all rights are prima facie, it might just be better to deny that people have rights. Indeed, if our understanding of most of the political theory that stems from the Aristotelian tradition is correct, this is exactly what is done.[30] We disagree with the Aristotelian tradition's negative response to natural rights and think rights play a crucial role in ethics.

One reason that some theorists might deny that natural rights are absolute is that if they are absolute, then there is a conflict between negative and positive rights,[31] and they wish to have a theory of rights that has both. Yet this combination can only be had at the price of depriving rights of their 'absoluteness' and thus their unique ethical function of determining which matters of morality will be matters of law. The conflict between negative and positive rights is real,[32] and showing why negative rights are basic and compossible will be a concern later in this chapter.

One final point needs to be addressed in this section. We intend to continue to use 'natural rights' in this chapter and not 'human rights'. 'Natural rights' is now out of fashion, but in this chapter we believe precision is in order. As J. Roland Pennock has noted, human rights and natural rights are similar to each other in three main respects; (1) both claim universality (applicability to all persons and places); (2) both claim inalienability; and (3) both claim that rights are valid independent of government.[33] But Pennock also notes that the concepts of natural rights and human rights are different, and because they are different, we believe that precision requires us to use 'natural rights'. It more accurately reflects the position we shall be arguing for.

We do not follow Pennock on what these differences are, because in some respects we believe he is mistaken. He claims, for example, that 'natural rights' implies timeless moral knowledge which prevents the discovery of new rights.[34] We do not believe that adopting the natural rights position implies that there is nothing left to discover about morality. In our view, Iredell Jenkins has better identified the main differences between natural and human rights.[35] First of all, human rights are far more positive than natural rights. They tend to take the form of claims *to* or *for* something. This is even the case when liberty is the object of the claim. Secondly, "the doctrine of human rights appeals chiefly to the feelings of men, while that of natural rights spoke more seriously to their minds".[36] Third, human rights are more concerned with providing benefits than with providing protections. And finally, contrary to Pennock's first criterion, human rights attach to special groups or classes of people, whereas natural rights were in the strictest sense universal. While Jenkins himself does not necessarily object to any or all of these differences, we do. It seems only fitting, therefore, that we employ 'natural rights' to signify the position we are arguing for in this chapter.

PART I: THE NATURE OF NATURAL RIGHTS

How to Argue for Rights

In his paper 'The Primacy of Welfare Rights'[37] Martin P. Golding argues for two theses that we believe deserve comment, for they provide a good introduction to our own argument for natural rights. The first is that rights are inherently a social concept. The second is, as the title of Golding's essay implies, that rights are at root claims based upon the promotion of human welfare. Here Golding sees himself as returning to an 'older' tradition as against the liberal tradition which saw rights as 'option' rights, rights concerned with liberties. The first of these theses is endorsed by us. Rights are "inherently interpersonal"[38] because they mark off a moral condition that ought to occur between people.[39] In other words, rights represent *part* of the effort to solve the problem of relations between people. Where others are not present the need for a moral concept about relations vanishes. Since we agree that rights are an inherently social concept, we shall not pursue this thesis but instead focus upon the second of Golding's theses.

If understood in the most general way, we must agree with Golding's second thesis that all rights are essentially welfare rights. For since rights are grounded for us in a natural-end ethics which of necessity looks to human well-being, rights would, in this sense, be a tool of human well-being. But Golding trades on a number of ambiguities inherent in the concept of welfare, and in the end our conception of rights looks quite different from his own. Hence some further analysis of Golding's second thesis is necessary.

Golding's argument centers on an attempt to answer a simple question: why should one person concede that another has a right? Golding notes that this question concerns conceding another has a right as a right and not whether the concession is based upon prudential reasons, kindness, etc. Golding's answer is stated as follows:

> It seems to me that there just is one way in which this concession can come about (aside from its being entailed by another rights claim which he concedes), a way that has two analytically separable steps. The first step consists of the recognition that the object claimed by the other as a matter of right is an element of, or a means to, the other's *personal good*. The second step consists of the acknowledgement that this good is genuinely *a good*, that is, the good-of-[X's] is a good-to-[Y]. By this I, of course, do not mean that it is good for [Y] to acknowledge [X's] personal good or that [X's] good is something that [Y] necessarily has a stake in. [40]

Golding's insight into the process of concession is a crucial one, although we would argue that the order of *conceding* rights is the reverse of the order of the being of rights (to paraphrase analogously Aristotle's claim that the order of knowledge is the reverse of the order of being). We take Golding's point to be that something G is claimed as a good by X for X. Y sees that X values G, that is, that G is a personal good for X. But if G is simply a personal good, Y has no necessary stake in G and may never have one. Even if Y did currently have a stake in G, it does not follow that he will always have one, or that he believes X is due G as a matter of right. To get the right, we need the second step, namely that G is a genuine good for Y.

Golding's discussion is largely formal, so we do not know how he distinguishes genuine good from apparent good or from personal good. Though we certainly agree that G must be an objective or genuine good and as such must be recognized as good by all, we do not accept the reasoning which argues that since G is an objective or genuine good, then it is 'therefore' good for Y and everyone else. If G is an objective good, it can be good for Y and everyone else, but it does not have to be so. Further, we do not accept the reasoning that even if G is a genuine good and good for Y and everyone else—that is, G is universalizable—this implies either that Y has conceded a right to X to G or, more fundamentally, the existence of X's right to G.

It is important to realize that we are not questioning Y's obligation to do good. Although some might mock Aquinas's principle, "Do good and avoid evil", it is fundamental to an ethics of human flourishing.[41] Rather, we are questioning those who would claim (a) that the objectivity of G requires that G be a good that is not always and necessarily related to an individual human being—that is, an impersonal good—and those who would (b) try do reduce entirely the right of X to G to the obligation or duty of Y to do good, namely, respect X's claim to G.

Claim (b) is discussed in the 'Why Rights?' section of this chapter. Claim (a) is discussed now, because it is important to make clear how an Aristotelian natural-end ethics understands the relationship between the genuine or objective good for all human beings—namely, human flourishing—and its individualized and agent-relative character and the principle of universalizability. The following three paragraphs will emphasize and make explicit what was argued in Chapter 2.

1. It should be asked of an Aristotelian natural-end ethics what it really means for there to be one unequivocal interpretation of the human *telos* or unequivocal guidance regarding human wellbeing. If, on the one hand, it means that there is a common set of virtues that all human beings need to possess and follow if they are to find fulfillment, then it should straightforwardly be admitted that there is only one way human beings can flourish. If a natural-end ethics means anything, it is that there are certain virtues with which all human beings, simply because they are human, need to conduct their lives. If, on the other hand, it means that what the virtues which constitute human flourishing call for in terms of concrete action cannot vary in the lives of individual human beings or that certain virtues cannot take a larger role in the lives of some persons than others, then this is saying something which is indeed inconsistent with an Aristotelian natural-end ethics. It has been observed that the whole point of the doctrine of the mean "is that in the very nature of the case it will be related to the particular situation, the principle being that how we feel and

react to a situation should not be a mere uncritical and undisciplined response, but rather the sensible and intelligent reaction
which the particular situation calls for".[42] Further, and as we noted
in Chapter 2, the human *telos* is such that persons cannot actualize
themselves as human beings unless they actualize their unique
potentialities as individuals, and vice versa. We may conceptually
distinguish between the potentialities a human being has in virtue
of *what* and *who* he is, but they are never separate in the individual human being.

2. It should also be asked of an Aristotelian natural-end ethics just
how the objectivity and universalizability of the human good is
understood. The human good is indeed objective and universalizable. Yet, the human good is not some Platonic form. It must
be remembered that the principle of universalizability in a natural-
end ethics does not operate as some a priori principle. This principle is justified only to the extent one can, through an act of abstraction, conceive of human nature and truly predicate this nature
of individual human beings.[43] Though the concept of human nature does have a foundation in reality, that is, it is based on features that all human beings through an act of abstraction can be
seen to share, these features are always and necessarily individualized. Human nature does not exist abstractly or universally, either *ante rem* in a Platonic manner or *in rebus* in a Porphyrian
manner, as the 'universal part' of an individual human being.
Accordingly, when it comes to developing a conception of the
human good based on our knowledge of human nature, it would
be a mistake to treat the human good as if it were something that
was not always and necessarily the individual human being's own
good. Thus, the principle of universalizability pertains to how the
human good is recognized, not to how it exists. It cannot function
in a natural-end ethics in a way that ignores the individualized
character of the human good. It is an error, then, for the principle
of universalizability to be interpreted as implying that one man's
good is another's.

We can quickly see that the Altruistic construction that has been placed on the Principle of Universalizability will not do. For after all, once it is recognized and acknowledged that the actuality of X is but the actuality of X's potentialities, then such a recognition and acknowledgement entail an unmistakable universalizability: if the good of X is indeed but the actuality of X's potentialities, then this is a fact that not just X needs to recognize, but anyone and everyone else as well. And yet the mere fact that a certain good needs to be recognized, and recognized universally, to be the good of X, it by no means follows that X's good must be taken to be Y's good as well, any more than the actuality or perfection or fulfillment of X needs to be recognized as being the actuality or perfection or fulfillment of Y as well. That would be nothing if not downright absurd![44]

To repeat, the human good is always and necessarily individualized.

3. It should finally be noted that the human good in an Aristotelian natural-end ethics is 'agent-relative'. We may say that the human good of any individual is agent-relative if that state of affairs S_1 which constitutes the perfection or fulfillment of A_1 is relative to agent A_1; and this is the case if and only if S_1's distinctive presence in world W_1 is a basis for A_1 ranking W_1 over W_2 even though S_1 may not be a basis for any other agent ranking W_1 over W_2. This does not, however, require that S_1's goodness be merely a function of its being desired or chosen. Rather, it can be an objective good. Further, it can be universalized. Just as the production of A_1's good is a reason for A_1 to act, so the production of A_2's good is a reason for A_2 to act. A_1 cannot claim that his perfection or fulfillment provides him with a legitimate reason to act without acknowledging that A_2's perfection or fulfillment provides him with a legitimate reason to act. Yet this does not mean or imply that A_1's good is A_2's good or even that A_1's good provides A_2 with a reason for action, or vice versa. Even though the human good is agent-relative, the principle of universalizability can be upheld without adopting an impersonalist view of the human good. Objectivity and universalizability of human flourishing are not inconsistent with its being agent-relative.[45]

Though we agree with Golding that rights are justified by reference to human well-being or flourishing, the connection between the two cannot ignore the considerations of the three previous paragraphs. Granted that G must be an objective or genuine good, it must also be the kind of good that is good for both X and Y (and everyone else). Further, G must remain good through any and all circumstances if, that is, G is to be the foundation for a natural right. Also, G must be a good that attaches to X simply in virtue of his humanity; for otherwise, not only will there be no natural right, Y will have no *necessary* stake in G. The good we are searching for must meet these conditions.

But What Is G?

Regarding theories of modern natural right, Leo Strauss has observed that

> Through the shift of emphasis from natural duties or obligations to natural rights, the individual, the ego, had become the center and origin of the moral world, since man—as distinguished from man's end—had become that center or origin.[46]

We uphold the shift of emphasis made by theorists of modern natural right; yet we do not think that arguing for natural rights requires that one reject the natural end of man as the standard for morality. It is not necessary to accept the alternative of either the fulfillment of the individual or the natural end of man as mutually exclusive. Making the individual the moral center of the universe does not require that one accept nominalism, mechanism, or hedonism, nor does accepting essentialism, teleology, and eudaimonism, at least as we have described them in Chapter 2, require rejecting individualism. It is possible for the fulfillment of the individual to be interpreted in terms of the requirements for human well-being. There can be a view of the ego or self that is neither otherworldly nor Hobbesian,[47] but Aristotelian.[48] Further, the achievement of man's natural end need not be interpreted along Platonic lines. There is no such thing as the flourishing of 'man'. There is only the flourishing of individual men. The human good neither exists apart from the choices and actions of individual human beings nor independent of the particular 'mix' of goods that the individual human being must determine as appropriate for his circumstances. Strauss's dichotomy[49] betrays a disturbing tendency, often found among proponents of natural right and natural law, to reify the concept 'natural end' and make it some good that competes with the good of individual human beings.[50] Our argument for natural rights begins, then, with the rejection of the dichotomy between the fulfillment of the individual human being or self and the attainment of man's natural end.

In Chapter 2 it was argued that human flourishing cannot exist unless it is attained by a person's own efforts. Yet the relationship between self-directedness or autonomy and human flourishing described in Chapter 2 is more intimate and vital than may have been realized. To repeat what was said there, self-directedness or autonomy is not merely the necessary means to human well-being. Rather, it is an inherent feature of those activities which constitute the human good that is human flourishing. As Mack states:

> The centrality of autonomy, as a property necessary to any activity's being *constitutive* of living well, allows us to be more specific about the (proper) function of a person's activity, capacities, etc. It is the (proper) function of a person's activities, capacities, etc. to be employed *by that person* (toward the end of) his living well. The function of a person's activities is individualized not only with regard to whose well-being it is the end of the activity (capacity, etc.) to serve but also with regard to who must employ the activity (capacity, etc) for it to fulfill its function. The activity (capacities, etc.) of A must be employed by A if it is to fulfill its function of contributing to the active, ongoing process of A's living well. (And A's activities, capacities, etc. have no "higher" end.)[51]

There is no single human activity that is right that does not involve autonomy or self-directedness. For as argued in Chapter 2, the exercise of human reason or intelligence is the central human virtue, and reason or intelligence does not function automatically. It requires that one exercise the effort to initiate and maintain a conceptual grasp on what one is doing. Human reason (or intelligence) and autonomy (or self-directedness) are not two separate faculties but distinct aspects of the same conscious act.[52] Self-directedness or autonomy makes human flourishing a 'moral good'. That is to say, it differentiates the actualization of potentialities in a human being from those in the rest of nature—for example, an acorn becoming an oak. Self-directedness or autonomy is, therefore, the central feature necessary to any activity being constitutive of a human being's moral good.

As the central feature necessary to any activity being constitutive of a human being's moral good, we know that being self-directed or autonomous is right for human beings from our analysis of the very *character* of human flourishing and not from looking at the results or consequences of self-directed or autonomous actions by human beings. Nor is autonomy or self-directedness right for human beings merely because it is necessary for the performance of virtue. As the activity which must pertain to all other activities for them to be right—namely, as the virtue which must be present in all other virtues[53] if they are to be *virtues*—but which does not itself obtain its rightness (become a virtue) because it contributes to some other end, it is an activity (a virtue) which is an end in itself. It is, however, not merely *an* end in itself. Rather, self-directedness or autonomy is nothing less than the very form, the only form, of *the* natural end of man. Human flourishing is, after all, not a static state, but an activity. An individual human being directing and using his own mind to take actions to achieve ends—living according to his own choices—exhibits the essential core of human flourishing abstractly considered, that is to say, described without specific virtues or concrete goods a particular human being's reason or intelligence determines as needed for the specific circumstances in which he finds himself.

Before ever addressing questions of what someone should think, how someone should act, or what they should do, we know that human beings ought to use their minds, act on their own judgments. This activity is not, to repeat, right for human beings merely because it is conducive to human flourishing or self-perfection. Indeed, we all know of cases in which someone uses his mind, acts on his own judgment, and pursues and keeps values that are not conducive to human well-being. Rather, this activity is right because it is the central necessary feature of human flourishing and as such is a right activity in itself.

We are now in a position to answer the question we have taken from Golding as the title of this section: 'But What Is G?' G must be an objective or genuine good, but G must also be something necessarily good for each and everyone. From what we argued in Chapter 2 and emphasized in the immediately preceding section, we know that G cannot be human flourishing or self-perfection. Even though self-perfection is universalizable, this does not imply that the self-perfection of one person is the self-perfection of another. The individualized character of human flourishing prevents it from being G. Yet, since self-directedness is both a necessary condition for self-perfection and a necessary feature of all self-perfecting acts at whatever level of achievement or development— what we have called the very form in which human flourishing exists— self-directedness just as such is always good for each and every human being. It is the condition under which human flourishing can exist. G is self-directedness.

A world in which human beings are self-directed but fail to do the morally proper thing is better than a world in which human beings are prevented from being self-directed but whose actions conform to what would be right *if* they had chosen those actions themselves. In other words, if I am not the author of the activity, that activity is not good or right for me even if it should nonetheless be true that if I were the author of that activity it would be good or right for me.[54] Nor can a world which compels people to do the 'right' thing be viewed as a morally justifiable means to creating a world in which human beings choose the right thing. The goal is not to maximize human flourishing or acts of self-direction independent and apart from the actual choices of individual human beings in concrete situations. Neither human flourishing nor self-directedness exist in some reified or collectivized form. The goal is to protect the condition under which self-perfection can exist—to protect the possibility of self-directedness.

There may, of course, be circumstances in which it is better that others be in charge of one's life, such as when one undergoes surgery, but this situation would not be a morally good one unless the choice to undergo surgery was one's own.[55] The reason we may say that it is always good that human beings be self-directed or autonomous and never better that human beings not be self-directed or autonomous is the same as why we may say that it is always good that human beings flourish and never better that human beings not flourish—namely, a consideration of the very nature of the natural end for human beings. Self-directedness is both a necessary condition for and an operating condition of the pursuit and achievement of human flourishing. It is necessary for *any* person undertaking *any* right action.[56] And without it, human flourishing would not be human flourishing.

If G—the genuine good for each and every human being—is self-directedness or autonomy, and if self-directedness or autonomy is nothing less than the very form in which human flourishing exists, the condition which must exist if self-perfection is to have any possibility of occurring, then everyone has a necessary stake in being self-directed simply in virtue of being human. Further, and without endorsing an impersonalist conception of human flourishing, it can be noted that Y could not claim that it is right or good for him to have G protected without granting that it is also right or good for X to have G protected. As Mack has claimed:

> The same proposition which a person must invoke (and which it is rational for him to invoke) to justify his pursuit of his own well-being in contrast, say, to his pursuit of the greatest good for the greatest number, viz., that the function of each person's activity, capacities, and so on is to be employed by that person in his living well, shows that a person would be unjustified in bringing it about that another's activity is not directed by that person.[57]

Yet this does not show that X has a right to be self-directed or autonomous. It only shows at best that Y, in virtue of his natural end as a human being, has an obligation to respect X's self-directedness or autonomy. We have not really moved from the adjectival sense of 'right' to the substantival sense of 'right'. We must consider more deeply what a right in the substantival sense involves and whether we even need such a moral concept as a right.

Why Rights?

One question to ask with respect to rights is 'Why use the term at all?' Would it not be sufficient to speak of the duties people owe each other? Could not all rights talk be translated into talk about duties or moral obligations? In part these questions relate to the traditional conflict between the priority of rights and duties, or between philosophical debates over the subjective versus the intrinsic good. The Aristotelian tradition is probably more inclined to believe that the language of rights could be dispensed with than are many contemporary moral theories. A recent case in point seems to be Alasdair MacIntyre's rejection of the concept of natural rights. MacIntyre has said, "There are no natural or human rights and belief in them is one with belief in witches and in unicorns".[58] Not since Bentham declared that natural rights were "nonsense upon stilts" has a more direct dismissal of the concept been offered. Bentham, however, can be overlooked by us as being outside the purview of Aristotelian theory. MacIntyre does not afford us this luxury because he seems to be defending an ethics at least nominally similar to our own.

It is nevertheless not easy to find arguments against natural rights in MacIntyre's work. Only a few brief pages of *After Virtue* are actually devoted to the concept.[59] As we see it, there are two main lines of attack upon the concept.

1. Rights are the product of specific social forms. They possess no asocial characteristics such as one finds in the concept of natural rights which attach to persons simply in virtue of their personhood. Rights "always have a highly specific and socially local character, and . . . the existence of particular types of social institutions or practices is a necessary condition for the notion of a claim to the possession of a right being an intelligible type of human performance".[60]

2. Natural rights do not exist, because all efforts to prove or justify their existence have failed.

We shall label the first argument the 'social argument' and the second the 'justification argument'. The two arguments are connected by MacIntyre's work as a whole, because he seems to be claiming that the Enlightenment has not only failed intellectually, but also socially.

The social argument seems false on the face of it. The Declaration of Independence declares that we have rights to life, liberty, and the pursuit of happiness. Such rights are neither 'highly specific' nor 'socially local'. This declaration of rights is mirrored in other documents in other times and places. What MacIntyre must therefore mean is that a right can only be understood in terms of the *specific* way it is codified and/or exercised in an actual social environment—not by the claim that general statements asserting the presence of such rights cannot be found in actual social and legal documents, or that there are no believers in these rights understood generally. But surely this claim begs all the important questions. The argument either implies a radical social relativism, in which case all moral norms (not just rights) will fall by the argument (for example, 'charity' is no more than what a specific group of people at a specific time and place practice as charity); or the argument fails to understand the traditional relationship the Aristotelian tradition has placed between theory and practice.

With respect to the latter (we shall ignore the former for the moment) horn of the foregoing dilemma, it is instructive to look briefly at the natural-law tradition. There are analogous properties in the relationship between natural and positive law and that between natural rights and their legal protection. The analogy is appropriate here because MacIntyre's argument amounts to the equivalent of claiming that the validity of natural law must be judged in terms of standards applicable to positive law. This in turn means that since positive law differs from society to society, there is no natural law that exists behind it.[61] In classical natural law theory the question was 'How can a stable natural law be rendered consistent with the diversity of political forms?' Aquinas addresses this issue and points out that diversity neither implies the non-existence of natural law nor is inconsistent wih it.[62] The basic idea is that natural law refers to general principles that must be modified to fit specific social situations and the character of the people to whom it will apply. Aquinas even allows for there to be further discoveries about the nature of natural law as well as for societies to be ignorant of the natural law and to adopt valid (in the positive sense) legal principles contrary to it.[63] There is no reason that similar points could not be made with respect to the relationship between natural rights and their instantiation in actual social practice.

Our concern here is not to dredge up the debate on natural law, but rather to point out that MacIntyre has not offered an argument so much as he has simply adopted a certain stance or perspective on the nature of rights. It is a stance we believe runs contrary to the spirit of the Aristotelian position, because it inverts the relationship between universals and particulars. The argument is equivalent to declaring that there is no basis in reality for the universal 'man' because all one sees around one are individual men. This *may* be true, but it cannot be *assumed* to be true in discussing the problem of universals any more than in discussing the existence of natural rights. So to declare that there are no natural rights because all one sees around one are specifically codified legal and customary practices could represent little more than a failure to grasp the relationship between specific practices and general regulatory norms. In addition, given MacIntyre's essentially nominalistic and positivistic approach to rights, we suggest that he would have equal difficulty in proving his favorite abstract concepts: 'society' and 'community'. For if one were to treat society and community as MacIntyre treats 'rights', all one would find would be individuals responding to various stimuli and not "a series of social and political *forms* in and through which the kind of self which can exemplify the virtues can be found".[64]

The Justification Argument is guilty of the fallacy of *argumentum ad ignorantiam* and ignoring the possibility that the failure to establish natural rights might be due to the methods employed in that effort. First, it supposes that because efforts to justify X have failed, X does not exist. Clearly, this is an appeal to ignorance. Secondly, it claims that since the methods of modern philosophy have not been able to justify natural rights, then such rights do not exist. This ignores the possibility that the problem may be due to the epistemological and ontological assumptions upon which these methods were based.

Furthermore, the type of evidence that is lacking for belief in the existence of unicorns and witches is not the same as what can justifiably be used to conclude that natural rights do not exist. We do not believe that unicorns and witches exist not only because no one has been able to verify or otherwise substantiate their existence, but also because no cognitive need is met. But is there no experiential or argumentative basis for a naturalistic moral concept? Is there no cognitive need that is met if natural rights exist? Granted, such concepts are no longer fashionable; yet this hardly argues that the evidence (or lack of it) is analogous to the case of unicorns and witches. Indeed, the entire corpus of Henry Veatch—to give but one example—shows that the case against certain propositions of traditional ethical naturalism is not in the same state as the case against witches and unicorns.

In certain respects our last argument is unfair to MacIntyre. For it may be the case that MacIntyre is not wedded to epistemological nominalism, but rather that he is simply opposed to individualism. Seen in this light natural rights are fictions because individualism is a fiction. MacIntyre, like Marx before him, holds that the fundamental problem with rights is their individualistic character. We, in contrast, hold that it is precisely the individualism of the Enlightenment that represents its greatest moral achievement.[65] *Now*, of course, we have left the realm of rational argument and entered the world of intellectual head butting. But remember, one of our claims about MacIntyre's attack on rights was that it was question begging; and MacIntyre's attack on rights seems more like an argument about what is implied if a certain sort of communitarianism is assumed true than an actual argument against rights.

One way for MacIntyre to dodge our criticisms is to claim that individualism, as we have defined it here and elsewhere, is inconsistent with Aristotelianism. While this might be a forceful point coming from the likes of Maritain or Veatch, it would be a theoretical oddity if offered by MacIntyre. This is because MacIntyre's own approach to moral matters is, in essential respects, outside the Aristotelian tradition in ways not applicable to the other two thinkers. Since MacIntyre rejects Aristotelian naturalism,[66] he has effectively gutted the entire core and substance of Aristotelianism. Without what MacIntyre calls Aristotle's "metaphysical biology", we are left only with the outer shell of Aristotelianism. For it is quite clear that whatever communitarian features exist in Aristotle's political theory, their value and defense is rooted in his "metaphysical biology". It is precisely because of the contribution that community makes to self-perfection, understood in terms of Aristotle's naturalistic teleology, that the political and social forms he recommends are justified. These forms do not 'stand on their own' as they seem to in MacIntyre's work. Their value is determined by the same standard Aristotle uses to evaluate all human practices: our *natural* end. Severed from that naturalistic foundation, one has only another variation on historicism, albeit one with an Aristotelian aftertaste.

We are finally left with what constitutes the major weakness of MacIntyre's attack on natural rights, or, perhaps more accurately, the main explanation for that attack. It seems that it is the *naturalism* of natural rights that is at the root of all MacIntyre's difficulty with the concept. Whatever problems traditional Aristotelian/Thomists have had with modernity's central emphasis upon natural rights, they have seldom attacked the concept broadside, as MacIntyre does, *precisely because of its link to naturalism.* A.P. d'Entrèves, for example, treats the natural rights tradition as akin to the natural-law tradition,[67] lamenting only what MacIntyre favors: the recent de-emphasis of naturalism and the retreat into historicism. Yet without naturalism MacIntyre must *himself* defer to the Enlightenment. For if communitarian standards (rather than naturalistic ones) define our self-perfection, nothing is more evident than the fact that our community is *fundamentally* infused with Enlightenment values and thus that our self-perfection lies in adherence to them. To criticize those values (or any others that dominate the practices of a community) requires a standard or vantage point beyond the community itself. Naturalism can provide that vantage point. Without it, MacIntyre must embrace the values of his community, namely, the values of the Enlightenment, with his own vision of a society grounded in the virtues being relegated to the realm of unicorns and witches. Appealing to *internal* failures of justification will not do either. People may adhere to values despite inconsistencies, and to say they ought to reject such internal inconsistencies presupposes an extra-communal vantage point.

Of course, no one believes that it is in practice possible to dispense with 'rights', since it has become so much a part of our moral discourse. But MacIntyre has at least shown that, at the philosophical level, the question about the value of 'rights' remains. If rephrased for our purposes, the question might become 'Why should we speak in terms of rights instead of the obligation we all have to respect the pursuit of human flourishing?'

The question as last formulated is ambiguous. What would it mean to 'respect the pursuit of human flourishing'? It might mean that we must help or promote the flourishing of others and ourselves. It might also mean that we must not interfere with or hinder another's *pursuit* of his flourishing. This looks like the negative versus positive rights controversy all over again. But in saying that this ambiguity in our question looks like a classic rights controversy, we are saying that 'rights' has not yet conveyed to us its essence; for such a debate could surely occur without recourse to 'rights'. We believe, therefore, that if 'rights' is to have any special significance beyond being a shorthand for what is 'just', 'fair', or 'good', it must meet the following conditions:

1. Deontic Universalism
2. Deontic Irreducibility
3. Individualism
4. Moral Territorialism

If one or more of these conditions are absent, 'rights' talk can be easily translated (without loss of meaning) into alternative moral languages that express moral obligations without the use of 'rights'. We shall first explain the meaning of each of these categories and then show how our theory of rights incorporates them and thus why we believe 'rights' cannot be translated without remainder into other ethical concepts.

First of all, the term *deontic* in the first two categories is not meant to convey a commitment to Kantianism, but rather a commitment to nonconsequentialism. This may seem an odd approach for teleologists like ourselves to be taking, but we did note in the last chapter the way in which we both accept and reject the deontological and teleological traditions as they have been understood in modern times. Certainly, if consequentialism is conceived in traditional utilitarian terms, then no one should have any trouble appreciating our rejection of consequentialism. For our purposes in this chapter, then, *deontic* signifies a commitment to a standard of evaluation for, or constraint upon, the narrowly consequential.

The concept of universalism has been sufficiently explained in the first section of this chapter. The presence of this category implies only that rights, if they exist, are universally possessed and not that all universal rules of moral conduct imply a corresponding right (or that a moral system which possesses universality as a requirement of its rules must therefore employ a conception of rights). Consequently, a right does not *add* anything to a universal moral rule or obligation—it merely *guarantees* it.

In the second category, if rights must be understood in terms of other and more fundamental duties or obligations, such as independent rules of justice, then rights become more a mode of expressing those rules than of adding anything to them. However inconvenient it might be to do without the term *rights*, it would still be in principle possible to abandon it. But what we have just said does not rule out the possibility that rights are *co-extensive* with foundational moral rules or principles.

One need not follow the Dworkinian line that rights are what define the rules themselves. Consequently, it is the last two criteria that are most significant in determining why a concept of rights is morally indispensible. It is probably no accident that the concept of rights arises in the modern era coextensively with the rise of individualism, or that a 'nominalist' such as William of Ockham[68] might have been the first to develop the modern notion of rights. The general, the abstract, the universal, does not seem to capture what is captured by 'rights'. An individualistic component is missing. Apart from the elements of individualism that form a part of the last of our four categories, individualism here is bound up with pluralism. It is precisely owing to the *fact* that individuals are different in their values, circumstances, goals, talents, potentialities, and so forth that a term signifying the *moral* propriety of those differences be available. Lomasky has made this point in the following way:

> Projects clash with impartiality. To be committed to a long-term design, to order ones activities in light of it, to judge one's success or failure as an acting being by reference to its fate; these are inconceivable apart from frankly partial attachment to one's ends. If E_1 is bound up with A's conception of the type of person he is and the kind of life he has chosen to lead, then he cannot regard its attainment as subject to trade-off with B's E_2 simply on the ground that some impersonal standard of value ranks E_2 above E_1. Rather, A will appraise possible courses of action by reference to a personal standard of value. His central and enduring ends provide him reasons for action that are recognized as his own in the sense that no one who is not committed to those very ends will share the reasons for action that he possesses. Practical reason is *essentially differentiated* among project pursuers, not merely contingently differentiated by the unique causal constraints each person confronts from his own distinct spatio-temporal location. That E_1 can be advanced by A might provide A overwhelmingly good reason to act. That B could equally effectively advance E_1 might merit vanishingly little weight in B's moral deliberations. To put it slightly differently, practical reason is inherently and ineliminably indexical. A will regard the assertion, "E_1 is *my* deep concern," as a significant reason in itself for his seeking to advance E_1 rather than some competing end.[69]

A system of abstract and universally categorical rules does not of itself account for the possibility that A and B may give different weight to E_1.

Indeed, if those rules are themselves about various Es, the opportunity for divergence on any E covered by a rule vanishes.

The foregoing leads us to better appreciate the need for a concept like 'rights'. It can now be said that rights attempt to simultaneously blend impartiality and diversity. There is, on the one hand, the need to recognize the plurality of values towards any given E. On the other hand, and simultaneously, there is the need to provide an impartial framework within which that plurality may function. If we abandon the pluralism, the need for a special moral concept like rights disappears, for then all rights claims can be translated without remainder into categorical rules or duties. It is our conviction that one of the inevitable tragedies associated with the multiplication of positive rights is precisely this tendency to render the concept of rights otiose. As positive rights expand, there is a proportionate diminution in permissible individual weightings of any given E with the consequence of a reduction in a pluralism of values.

All this gives us our first step into our concept that basic natural rights are 'meta-normative'. In the language of our present discussion, rights do not define the Es but only the conditions under which the various Es may be pursued. This leads us to our final category of moral territorialism. *Moral territorialism* is roughly equivalent to Nozick's "moral space". It signifies a sphere of moral authority that is completely one's own (what Nozick circumscribes by "borders"). The concept of having moral territory is completely intertwined with the concept of individualism and is a thoroughly modern concept. Natural law, whether in its naturalistic or theological mode, could not find a place for the individual as a *source* of values unique to him or herself. All values were more or less measured by generalized and seemingly impersonal teleological standards. Modernity offered Kantianism and utilitarianism. Kantianism attempted to reconcile itself with individual freedom through its concept of autonomy; but in the end the autonomy a rational individual possesses under Kantianism is indistinguishable from that possessed by any other individual because of the strict demands of universality and categorical rigidity, leaving individualism without any substance. Utilitarianism could offer individuality, but the mathematics of the ethic so collectivized the individual that little moral territory remained—hence worries in utilitarianism about whether there are *really* any private actions not subject to the harm principle. As Lomasky has noted:

> [The utilitarian] has no defenses against utility black holes that suck up aid at prodigious rates. Therefore, he must eschew serious commitment to any end other than the attainment of utility in any guise it may take. A world populated by utilitarians would be one in which everything matters somewhat and nothing very much. It is one in which individuality is neither present nor missed. This, of course, is the world he recommends. [70]

It seems to us to be no surprise that most defenders of liberty have been (and still are) attracted to subjectivism and relativism in ethics. Our point here, of course, is that the individualism which holds that individuals can be a unique source of their own values gives rise to the idea of moral territorialism and would have been difficult to imagine within most classical moral frameworks.[71]

The moral territory we as individuals possess allows us, first of all, to "clash with impartiality" in the sense of ranking a given set of values (or any value) differently from other individuals. It also permits a sphere of freedom which allows both success and failure. Within that moral territory we can call our own, we might achieve our flourishing as a person or fail to, and if we do flourish, the value hierarchy which supports that flourishing may be quite different from that held by other flourishing individuals (as well as equivalent to someone who is not flourishing). In this respect as well, rights are meta-normative: for moral norms, as they are now understood, apply equally in the same way to all. In this post-Kantian world, diversity is either taken to be outside the realm of morality altogether ('prudence') or serves merely as raw data for a utilitarian calculation, again making it morally irrelevant in itself. The concept of rights, therefore, which is necessary to preserve the moral propriety of individualism is also required to guarantee the atmosphere in which that individualism is to flourish. The specific prescriptive rules an individual may employ in his pursuit and value of various Es are themselves dependent upon the 'meta-norms' which give that pursuit space.

We might say that rights are meta-normative because they do not specify the Es—only the conditions under which their pursuit is legitimate. In this sense, the closer one identifies one's rights with what is right, the less need there is to speak of one's rights at all, for rights can

then be identified with particular duties which are just as easily identified by naming the duty itself. If my right to X—where X is a particular
good, service, or condition—can be translated without remainder into an
obligation on your part to either provide me with X or not interfere in
my efforts to obtain X, then we need never speak of rights (except as a
shorthand), but could just as well speak of our specific duties to each
other. On the other hand, if my right to X refers to the boundaries of my
legitimate moral territory, I have not yet said anything about what my
duties to myself are; and with respect to others (or others to myself) I
have not specified any obligations that I owe them other than restraint.
My commitment to restraint is not, contrary to most analyses, merely a
duty I owe to others, but rather an expression of the conditions under
which I will begin to incur obligations through the choices I make within
my own moral territory. It is also an expression of the conditions under
which you, or anyone else, will begin to incur the positive moral obligations that result from choices you make within your own moral territory.
We might say, therefore, that rights define a set of compossible moral
territories.[72]

It is apparent from what we have said that rights and what is right
are not the same, even though the rights we have are held by us because
they are right within the context of the need for a compossible set of
moral territories. Since we admit to a large degree of value pluralism
between moral territories, rights define the basic ways in which that pluralism can express itself in relation to others. But even here rights do not
cover the whole story; for the choices I make within my rights may still
be covered by additional moral rules that govern my own conduct and
my relation to others. I may, for example, have the right to fire an employee 'at will', but it does not follow from that that arbitrary dismissals
are morally proper. We emphasize this point to bring us to a larger one.

In our view, something analogous to a category mistake occurs when
rights respecting restraint is translated into an interpersonal duty. It is
true that one 'ought to respect another's basic right(s)', but the reason
that restraint is due is not because of what I owe you, but because of my
own principled commitment to human flourishing. That commitment
implies standards that define conditions for flourishing in a social and
political context. In other words, one is looking not to what one owes

another, but rather to the objective requirements for producing a compossible set of moral territories consistent with the diversity of value flourishers. The recognition of the validity of these requirements *gives rise* to an expression about my obligation to another (such as to respect another's rights), but is not in the first instance an obligation I owe the other—only an obligation I have which, by the nature of the circumstances (social life), I must direct towards others. This is the Veatchian "third way" we shall speak of shortly. Our point here is that the locution 'One ought to respect another's right(s)' and 'One ought to X to another' do not signify the same moral ontology. Therefore, the common opinion that rights imply duties is true, but fails to identify the significantly different rationale behind the duty implied by rights and those ordinary normative duties we think of when we speak of moral behavior. If rights are to have any special contribution to make to moral discourse, this difference of moral ontology between the two sorts of duties must be maintained.

It should be evident by now why, on our theory, all rights must be negative. The main reason is, of course, that since rights are meta-normative principles defining the conditions under which further norms and actions can be pursued or followed, they are not thereby conceptual directives to specific obligations. Positive obligations are incurred within the moral territories established by the rights claims. And because of our emphasis upon individualism and pluralism, it should be equally obvious that consent will be the main connective for interpersonal obligations (for example, positive rights will be derived from what is implied through voluntary agreement). It is consent that allows one to carry along one's moral territory. We hesitate, however, to claim that *all* positive norms will be a function of consent. The special relationships (such as parent to child) one may have to others may imply certain obligations that are not easily reducible to consent alone. But what was said in the preceding paragraph applies here as well. Rights are negative because they stem, in the first instance, from an obligation to self. At the meta-normative level of moral ontology, it is not what I owe others, but rather what I am obligated to do for myself that grounds rights. Positive rights are fundamentally other-oriented and, as such, describe an obligation towards another.[73] If we are correct, therefore, rights cannot be positive because to make them so would remove the distinctive need for having a concept of rights in the first place—namely, to provide the individual with a context for eudaimonic achievement.

None of this proves that there are rights; only that if the concept is allowed in such a way that it is not reducible to other moral propositions, then it must meet the foregoing conditions. The foregoing conditions in turn put further constraints on what will be allowable as a right, and part of our argument has been and will be that rights must be negative to meet these conditions. For now we need to discuss further how the moral theory we have developed in the last chapter fits with and implies these conditions. In doing so we shall be further clarifying what it means for a right to be meta-normative.

Why We Have Rights

In an effort to avoid having to ground rights on interest-based theories or deontological considerations—ethical frameworks which he rightly rejects—Henry Veatch has posed a novel "third way" of grounding natural rights.[74] Natural rights are not derivative of natural duties we owe to others, nor are they the results of interests manifested through either calculations of personal or social advantage or social contracts. Instead, natural rights are derived from duties one naturally owes to oneself.[75] The argument runs something like this: since we all by nature have obligations or duties of self-perfection (given by the Aristotelian ethic), each of us is bound by nature to fulfill that obligation. To prevent or interfere with a person's effort to fulfill his natural obligation deprives the person of what he and others recognize he ought to do (and so for each of us). Therefore, our duty to self-perfection generates the right not to have the pursuit of our end impeded.

Two important features of this argument, we believe, should be accepted. First, the conclusion is true. No one has the right to interfere with another's pursuit of self-perfection. Secondly, the "third way" is the correct one in the following senses: (1) it appeals to self-perfection rather than to interest or formal deontic duties; (2) it understands self-perfection in such a way that the individual's own pursuit of it is at least of structurally equivalent value to anyone else's pursuit; and (3), perhaps therefore, the argument provides a naturalistic and morally informed basis for saying that whatever rights exist will be universalized across all individuals. After this, however, we part company. In our view, Veatch's argument suffers from a number of defects, not the least of which is its failure to understand the nature of a right. Because the core of Veatch's insight is correct, it was necessary that we first identify the context under which the following criticisms are to take place.

A number of problems stem from Veatch's failure to distinguish a right from what is right. In the foregoing summary of Veatch's argument, it is evident that one possesses the right to freedom from interference only so long as one is pursuing one's self-perfection. But suppose one is not doing this. Suppose one's self-perfection lies in writing philosophical treatises, but one is instead pursuing a life of sloth, or hedonism, or simply sport. Does one now have the right to interfere with this person's path of degradation? We think not. But there is nothing in Veatch's argument that gives one the right to deviate from the path of virtue. The argument does not say we would have the right to interfere with this person either; but if we do not, it cannot be because we would be violating this person's rights. Veatch has correctly seen that having a right is connected to liberty. Yet he has failed to see that having a right has a broader extension than doing (or being in pursuit of) what is right. As we indicated earlier, our rights are not based upon any actual pursuit or achievement of what is right, but upon the *potential* for such achievement. Let us label the failure to clearly distinguish having a right from doing what is right the 'moralist fallacy'.

But suppose the moralist fallacy is no fallacy after all. It still seems to us that Veatch's argument in any case contains a non sequitur. If I have a duty of self-perfection, why are others duty-bound to refrain from interfering with my pursuit of it? Granted I will be prevented from doing something I am obligated to do, and others recognize that I am obligated to do it; but that is some distance away from saying that others are thereby obligated *themselves* not to interfere. One solution might be to claim that by preventing you from achieving your self-perfection I am doing something that prevents me from achieving mine. But in the situation described earlier, my preventing you from degrading yourself may actually *enhance* my own self-perfection, since I have contributed something to another's well-being which may in turn reflect upon my own self-perfection. Yet surely I can keep you from degrading yourself by violating your rights. Therefore, unless one can show without begging the question that a violation of another's rights is always a denial of one's obligation to self-perfection, this attempt to solve the problem will not work.[76] In any case, this approach is not the one Veatch seems to take.

To further indicate the oddity of Veatch's theory, it would seem to follow that if I prevent or interfere with my own achievement of self-perfection (for example, by willfully turning away from the good), then it would be the case that I have violated my own rights. For on Veatch's theory rights are meant to be generated out of the pursuit of an obligation which, when interfered with, constitutes a rights violation. Nothing is said about who is doing the interfering. But surely, although it can be said that I may have rights and either exercise them or fail to, it is absurd to speak of me violating my own rights. What is correct, of course, is to say that I have failed in my obligations. 'Rights' is a relational concept whose applicability applies only with respect to other persons.

It should be evident by now that Veatch's argument fails because he too assumes that the duty expressed by a right is similar in nature to other moral duties one might have, however more or less important some of those duties might be in relation to others. Yet it still might appear that Veatch would not be willing to reduce rights to our usual understanding of duties, for throughout *Human Rights: Fact or Fancy?* he has described himself as offering a justification for the negative, natural *rights* of life, liberty, and property. This suggests that the duties in question are not merely duties owed to others, making the concept of rights something different from the concept of duties. This point presupposes, however, that Veatch's answer to his own question is that human rights are indeed fact. Upon closer examination, we find instead that Veatch considers natural *rights* (as opposed to natural *right*) to be fancy. He believes in duties to self and that there is an objective right, but he does not believe that individual human beings have *rights* in any irreducible sense.[77] Thus, if one engages in conduct that is not perfective of one's nature, then one would not have a right to engage in such conduct. Others would not in virtue of a right possessed by an individual have any duty to refrain from interfering with his nonperfecting behavior.[78]

Clearly, then, when Veatch speaks of a person's right to X-ing, this is but a shorthand for saying two other things: (1) it is right that the person X's, or X-ing is necessary to Y-ing, which is right for the person to do, and (2) in virtue of the rightness of X-ing or X-ing being the means necessary to do what is right, say Y-ing, others (somehow) have the duty not to interfere with a person's X-ing. The concept of natural rights on Veatch's account really is, then, superfluous; the only needed concepts are that of what is right and of the duty of persons to do that.

Since we have compared our conception of negative natural rights to that of Veatch's, we should also at this point briefly compare our understanding of these rights to that of Tibor R. Machan and Ayn Rand. Rand states:

> "Rights" are a moral concept—the concept that provides a logical transition from the principles guiding an individual's actions to the principles guiding his relationship with others—the concept that preserves and protects individual morality in a social context—the link between the moral code of a man and the legal code of a society, between ethics and politics. *Individual rights are the means of subordinating society to moral law.*[79]

This statement is not clear. Are rights normative principles which provide guidance to individuals in the conduct of their daily lives with others? Or are rights meta-normative principles which as such do not provide normative guidance to individuals, but instead provide guidance in the creation of a constitution which will be the basis for a legal system that protects the self-directedness of individual human beings by outlawing actions which use persons for purposes they have not chosen? Rand leaves the exact character of the moral concept of rights ambiguous, for she does not seem to recognize that more than one understanding of her account of rights could be given.

Machan tends, at times, to interpret rights as normative principles which provide guidance to human beings in the conduct of their lives with others. Each person is morally obligated to provide every other human being with the conditions that rights specify.

> Rights specify what social conditions are good or right for people by virtue of their humanity, *and thus what people ought to do, how they should conduct themselves, in a social context.* . . . Rights specify conditions which all of us ought to provide each other.[80]

We, however, regard rights as meta-normative principles. As such, they do not provide normative guidance to individuals in the conduct of their lives. This is, of course, not to say that in the conduct of their lives human beings do not have particular moral obligations to respect the self-directedness of others, but it is to say that rights are not the concept which specifies those moral obligations. Rights are a moral concept which provides the normative basis to law. This concept provides guidance to the creators of a constitution and those who would seek to explain a constitution's meaning or justify its presence.

Though the difference between our conception of negative natural rights and that of Machan's is subtle, it is important. The importance of failing to clearly distinguish between normative principles and metanormative principles can be illustrated by considering what the following argument shows and does not show.

1. If Smith uses Jones for a purpose Jones has not chosen, Jones is not self-directed.
2. Being self-directed is necessary for the possibility of human flourishing.
3. Therefore, Jones is not flourishing when Smith uses him (Jones) for a purpose he has not chosen.

This argument is both valid and sound, but this does not show that Jones may not, in the future, have other self-directed acts and thus flourish to the extent the circumstances allow. It depends on the nature of Smith's initial use of Jones, the nature of the situation in which Jones finds himself as a result of Smith's use of him, and Jones himself. Jones may be like Solzhenitsyn, who turned imprisonment into an opportunity for personal growth and development.[81] Of course, Jones may also *not* be like Solzhenitsyn, and the situation may totally or partially destroy him, physically, mentally, or morally. The effects of coercion vary with each person. Just as good is individualized, so is evil. Determining the effects of coercion on a person is a highly contingent matter that can be assessed only by someone familiar with the particular facts regarding the nature of the coercion, the situation, and the person. Thus, when determining social and political principles—principles which are to be the basis for a constitution upon which a legal system is based and which apply to all persons regardless of their unique situations and needs—one cannot be in the position of trying to determine what the particular effects of Smith's use of Jones will be. Instead, one must be concerned with what is universally and necessarily true and thus must abstract from what is particular and contingent. "Self-directedness is the condition under which human flourishing can occur, and having a principle which protects that condition is of utmost importance." Information of this kind is all one needs to know when creating a constitution for *any* Smith and Jones; for the concern here is not with how conduct turns out (Does it or does it not bring about human flourishing?) but rather with setting the appropriate foundation for conduct.

However, if the distinction between normative principles and meta-normative principles is not clearly made, especially if rights are conflated with principles whose function is to guide personal conduct seeking the end of self-perfection, then rights are subject to application by practical reason and thus may be judged as inappropriate for the person in the situation in which he finds himself. Rights certainly could not be deontically universal or irreducible The justification for rights becomes dependent on trying to assess whether the protection of self-directedness will in every situation promote human flourishing. This becomes an impossible task. It is, therefore, absolutely crucial that rights not be treated as a moral guide to self-perfection. It is disastrous to both prudence and politics when this occurs, not to mention clear thinking.[82]

Does our own account of man's natural end fit with and imply the conditions that must exist if there is to be any point to having natural rights? That is to say, does human flourishing as we have described it require that there be a moral concept which provides for a moral territory that protects individualism and is both deontically universal and irreducible? The answer is unequivocally 'yes'. The natural end is an inclusive end which allows for the morality of an action to be determined by whether an action is an instance of the virtues which constitute it, and not by the calculation of the specific consequences of the action. This is especially true for being self-directed or autonomous, since this is *the* virtue which makes all other virtues possible. As said before, we know that being self-directed is good or right simply from our analysis of the nature of human flourishing. Further, we know that being self-directed or autonomous is good for each and every human being just in virtue of their being human. No matter how different individual human beings or their circumstances may be, we know that it is good or right that they be self-directed. Finally, we know that an individual human being living according to his *own* choices while engaging in the concrete activities that constitute his life among others is the condition necessary for the very possibility of human flourishing and as such is of ultimate value. Without it human flourishing would not be human flourishing.

The account of human flourishing that has been presented does allow for there to be moral concepts that are deontic or nonconsequentialist in character, universal, and foundational (ultimate or basic). Yet the account of human flourishing that has been presented does even more: it shows quite clearly the moral propriety of individualism and pluralism and the need for there being a context in which individual human beings may go about determining, creating, and achieving their own values.

It is vital to note here that the moral propriety of individualism and pluralism and the need for moral space is not tied to the individual human being's actual achievement of human flourishing—namely, to his actually making morally appropriate choices. Rather, the moral propriety of individualism and pluralism and the need for moral space is tied to the fact that each and every human being is (1) a *potential* end in himself who cannot be an *actual* end in himself save through his own self-directed behavior; (2) a being who cannot flourish as a human being (actualize generic potentialities) except through the actualization of those individuative potentialities that make the person the unique person he is; (3) a being whose own insight and judgment is absolutely crucial to knowing what is the right thing for a person to do in a concrete situation; and (4) a being who is a social and political animal, whose very maturation as a human being requires others. Since we have already discussed the 'moralist fallacy', it seems appropriate to require that before beginning the task of determining what individuals should or should not do, there be an acknowledgment of these four facts and thus an acknowledgment of the need for a moral concept whose sole purpose is to protect these basic features of human flourishing—features that apply to all humans regardless of personal differences, circumstances, or particular values. The meta-normative moral concept which protects these by providing for the moral territory in which individuals go about the task of attempting to fashion a fulfilling existence for themselves is that of rights.

In summary, rights are based on the recognition that being self-directed or autonomous is something which is right in itself and that protecting the possibility of self-directedness or autonomy is the objective requirement to be met for producing a compossible set of moral territories consistent with the individualized and self-directed character of human flourishing. Rights are used to create a legal system which defines a set of compossible territories that provides the necessary political condition for the possibility that individuals might carry on a life in accord with virtue. Rights are used to establish the legal limits in which pluralism may express itself in relation to others.

PART II: THE NATURAL RIGHT TO PRIVATE PROPERTY

In the Lockean tradition of negative natural rights, the natural right to private property is arguably its most controversial component. Consequently, we regard it as necessary that we offer some defense or account of this natural right before we leave this chapter. Our purpose here is not to start applying our theory to particular rights that have been traditionally associated with the Lockean tradition. Rather, we seek to outline some implications of our theory in this controversial area to avoid any appearance that we are dodging this controversy and to further indicate the meaning of our foregoing arguments.

Rand has written that "the right to property is a right to action . . . it is not the right to *an object*, but to the action and the consequence of producing or earning that object".[83] We take this statement to be the essence of the correct approach to thinking about property rights. This statement contrasts nicely with the usual understanding reflected in Allan Gibbard's statement that "a property right is, roughly, a right which a person has with respect to a specific thing".[84] Although "thing" is broader than Rand's "object", there is nothing in Gibbard's statement that refers to the essence of a property right as an action. This traditional way of thinking is not completely avoided by those who, like Lawrence Becker, define property in terms of ownership.[85] 'Ownership' is less *object-* or *thing*-oriented than many approaches, but it is still a derivative concept from what must be first said about action. Yet the quasi-legalistic overtones of Becker's approach (not to mention Gibbard's) are not surprising, since for him there is no natural right to property in any meaningful sense.[86]

The relationship people have towards things or objects, whether in terms of possession or ownership, is a function of human action. The central question about property rights, therefore, is how one's theory fits into what one says in general about rights and human action. Our own position can be summarized by noting that human beings are material beings, not disembodied ghosts, and being self-directed or autonomous is not merely some psychic state. Self-directedness or autonomy pertains to actions in the world, actions employing or involving material things taken by flesh-and-blood human beings that occur at some place and at some time. George Mavrodes well expresses the connection between action and autonomy:

> Human life in the world is concerned, to a substantial degree, with the use and manipulation of physical objects. It is there that, in large part, we develop and exercise our creativity and our freedom of choice. And if we do not have a moral freedom here, if it is not morally open to us to decide effectively what use shall be made of many things, then it must also not be morally open to us to decide upon the preservation and development of our lives.[87]

But it is not objects *per se* that the individual needs to have property rights to, as if any random distribution were acceptable.[88] A human being needs to have property rights to things that are the result of his own productive efforts. For individual human beings to flourish, they need to maintain control of what they have produced; human flourishing is, as Mavrodes indicates, not merely intellectual contemplation.

Autonomy, individuality, and rationality, which are pivotal to our conception of human flourishing, are fundamental to our conception of property rights as well. Human actions upon the material world, when understood as a process of production, jointly and necessarily involve autonomy, individuality, and rationality. As David Kelley notes:

> Production is a long-range, rational process. It requires continuous, connected activity, in service of a plan, over lengthy periods of time. It requires technical judgments about the best means to achieve a given end, and economic judgments about the ends best served by a given set of means.

People disagree about such judgments. People differ in the way they value the possible products, they differ in terms of co-operation they find acceptable.[89]

Just as human flourishing is highly individualized and self-directed, so is the process of production. Thus, there need to be private property rights not only in the sense that human beings need to be at liberty to follow their own judgments in creating or producing material goods; they also need to be free to keep, use, and dispose of what they have produced in accordance with their own judgments. Since judgments are themselves not simply psychic states, but most often conclusions about how to interact with the material world, a person's choices and judgments cannot be said to have been respected if the material expression of those judgments is itself divested from the individual.

The notion that production is a highly individualized affair is perhaps our first indication that Locke was mistaken in his contention that God or nature has given mankind a stock of objects (in common or otherwise) from which we must devise a set of rules for just distribution (or even, as we shall see, for original ownership). The most nature offers is the potential opportunity for the transformation of the material world. [90] A theory of property rights will, therefore, concern itself with legitimate exploitation of opportunities not with things or objects. *Ownership* will be the legal expression of the legitimate exploitation of opportunities. Notice that this way of looking at the issue does not rule out ownership in or property rights to that which is not a thing or area of land, such as electromagnetic fields.[91] This way of looking at the issue also does not begin with the essentially collectivist assumption that there is a common stock of goods that everyone must equally regard as 'wealth'. Property, wealth, and any object *qua* object are not beings *in rerum natura*—that is, things which exist 'out there' independently and apart from human cognition and effort. Rather, they are essentially related to the intellectual and physical efforts of individual human beings.

If this individualistic perspective is correct, it seems to follow immediately that we need not consider the mere existential condition or arrangement of material assets as necessarily indicative of any particular moral proposition. In other words, we need not consider, as for example

Becker does,[92] the mere presence of resource depletion or inequity in holdings as indicative of anything of moral interest.[93] More commonly, it is quite illegitimate to regard anything as wealth which is not the product of man's mind or action. Mavrodes finds such a claim "peculiar",[94] and he is not alone. But the claim follows from our general denial of intrinsic value, from our assertion about the primacy of human thought and action in production, and from experience.[95] The relatively impoverished continent of Africa is no less generously endowed with natural assets than is North America; but the former is clearly less wealthy than the latter. We believe that a significant part of the reason for this has to do with encumbrances placed upon the exploitation of opportunity.[96] In any case, wealth is a concept relative to productive acts and interests. In a way reminiscent of Nozick's historical approach, if existential states have no intrinsic moral status prior to legitimate exploitation of opportunities, the existential result would also be morally uninteresting.[97] Each new existential state of the material world is simply a new field of opportunities just as the previous state was. This is true for all existential states considered separately from human action. Our remarks below will indicate that the only difference between existential conditions where questions of 'original acquisition' apply and those where such questions do not has to do with an indeterminancy of appropriate rules—*not* with a difference between 'owned' and 'unowned' objects.

When one thinks of opportunities, one does not think first of objects but rather of actions whose end may be to secure objects. But if we are correct in saying that objects themselves are productions or creations, then even objects cannot be the end of an action but a feature of the actions themselves; and traditional moral wisdom has had plenty to say about the mistake of treating objects as ends. Two points appear to follow from this: (1) the objects or possessions one has must be considered an extension of what one is (assuming no dichotomy between oneself and one's actions) and not as items contingently attached to oneself; and (2) the concept of 'opportunity' must be a function of the general right to action (as specified above) if there is to be a natural right to property. We shall discuss both of the points below, starting with the second one first. Our explanation should help clarify these general remarks and differentiate our approach from the more common approaches taken in the literature.

We have seen that our natural rights consist in a set of meta-normative principles which define a set of compossible moral territories. We also argued that individuals are in a significant sense value creators, each of whose eudaimonic fulfillments is unique to the individual. Rights remain abstract and negative in order to accommodate the truth of individualism. Now since rights define moral territories, they circumscribe areas within which the individual is free to act. Having freedom of action within certain boundaries is nothing less than having an opportunity for action within those same boundaries. Since the extension of the opportunity is equivalent to the extension of the boundaries, the first point we learn about the natural right to property is that it is simply another name for the freedom to act and, hence, live according to one's own choices. To put the point another way, the natural right to property is a natural right and shares the central features of any natural right.

To differentiate a natural right to property from other natural rights we need a differentia. *Opportunity* functions more like a genus because it would be present in all other natural rights as well (for example, free speech being the opportunity to communicate what one wishes within permissible bounds).[98] The differentia for property comes with respect to the concept of exploitation. We understand *exploitation* to be the attempt to transform one's legitimate opportunities into consequences that accord with one's values. Since actions and consequences generally have a material dimension, the act of transformation involved here usually incorporates something tangible. This must certainly be true with respect to drafting positive law in this area; for even intellectual property rights must have a tangible embodiment (such as books, articles, and works of art) if they are to have the protection of law. But at this stage it is enough to note that property rights will concern allowable acts of transformation of the material world. Throughout this discussion, *allowable*, *legitimate*, and similar terms will refer to actions which do not cross the borders of another's moral territory without permission. We shall say something more specific later on about border crossings in this area.

The right to transform the material world is little else than the right to act, since actions occur in the material order. The second component in the natural right to property, therefore, is equivalent to saying that one has the right to act. What becomes controversial is the extent to which one has the right to retain the consequences of one's actions. But how does one go about solving such a problem? The first issue, we believe, concerns a 'burden of proof' argument. With respect to property rights, the burden of proof could go in either of two directions: (1) the individual must show why he must be allowed to keep the consequences of his actions, or (2) others must show grounds for interfering with the retention of those consequences. It is clear from the theory of rights presented in the last section that the burden of proof is the latter. Exercising a natural right is not something one is obligated to justify to others. What *retaining the consequences* means has not yet been examined, especially in light of Nozick's 'tomato juice' example.[99] But even saying this much indicates that discussions of property are off to a wrong start if the central rights question requires that the individual justify retention of the consequences of his actions in the absence of any evidence of a border crossing. Another way of putting the same point is that a discussion of property rights is off to a wrong start if the first question is taken to be 'How much of what a person produces should he or she be allowed to keep?' For us, the question ought to be the reverse: 'When, if ever, can some people interfere with the productive acts of others?'

Secondly, since property is created or produced through an act of transformation, the Lockean Proviso is moot. For there can never be 'enough and as good' left for others if every action issues in a unique transformation. If an action transforms the material order, there can be no other forms of property like it until a similar action accomplishes the same result. Picking an apple from a tree should not be judged in terms of the numbers of apples left, but in terms of the action which transformed the tree into a useful commodity. All this follows, of course, from our claim that there is no such thing as pre-existing (in other words, pretransformed) wealth. One may wish to argue that one is obligated to leave equivalent *opportunities* for others to perform the same act of transformation. But apart from questions of scarcity, it is not clear why one has this obligation. This is because it *is* clear that my act of transformation in no way deprives another of what he had transformed. It might be argued that one has limited another's opportunity; but even if we ignore the question of substitutes, it is unclear how the action has limited an opportunity one had a preexisting right to. Mavrodes[100] claims that the act of transformation deprives another of his rights, because one is acting upon something one had no right to (the unowned object). In this respect Mavrodes fails, as Gibbard does not,[101] to distinguish between depriving another of their rights and depriving them of an opportunity.[102] The former is clearly illegitimate while the latter is not, and acts of transformation under conditions of original acquisition are clearly not rights-violating because (virtually by definition) no one has rights to the pretransformed objects in question.

From all this, it follows that a correct theory of the natural right to property will recognize that no one has a right to the acts of transformation of others, since there can be no pre-existing claims to that which does not yet exist (the transformed entity).[103] Yet, since we are speaking of rights, we are speaking of meta-norms applicable in a social context. The social context requires that the acts of transformation be compossible.[104] Now *compossible* here does not issue simply in 'ambiguity clarification', for any system of rules will clarify ambiguities about who can do what (provided the rules are clear and practicable). *Compossible* here must refer to a set of rules or principles that are consistent with the general theory of natural rights we developed in Part I of this chapter. If we begin first with the issue of original acquisition, we believe that there is a wide latitude of acceptable rules that would satisfy the compossibility requirement. We do not believe, however, that the latitude is completely open.

Since we are at the general level of discussion here, the restrictions upon the latitude of acceptable rules must themselves be general. Here we follow the lead of F.A. Hayek[105] in requiring that the limitations upon the latitude of acceptable rules be universality and negativity. Universality is uncontroversial because all rights are supposed to have this characteristic. We have already argued for the negativity of natural rights. But in this context *negative* means (a) boundary setting in nature and (b) exclusionary; (a) makes (b) possible, and (b) is justified by our previous discussion of the burden of proof and our conception of eudaimonia as requiring moral territories. Both jointly capture the concept of "negative" because natural rights are essentially obligations of restraint, and because there is a lack of a pre-existing obligation not to engage in opportunity deprivation (since no rights are being violated in the process).

Perhaps some examples would help clarify our point. In cases of original acquisition (considered abstractly) a rule which dealt with unowned property on a 'first come, first served' basis would be morally indifferent with respect to a rule which gave all interested parties initial equal shares. Both rules are universal, and both specify boundaries within which one may exclude others from the results of one's acts of transformation. On the other hand, rules which require the divestiture of certain portions of the results of one's transformations or limit action according to some social rule (such as Pareto optimality, or a 'difference' principle), while perhaps universal, are not strictly speaking negative—they are neither completely exclusionary nor limited to mutual restraint. Mavrodes, in his discussion of the original acquisition of a tree, makes a similar point.[106] He claims (as do we) that a number of rules would be possible in such a case and lists the following:

1. Everyone has the right to fell any standing tree, and he who does so thereby becomes the owner of the fallen tree.
2. Everyone has the right to fell any standing tree and to trim off its branches, and he who does so is the owner of the resulting log.
3. Everyone has the right to mark any unmarked tree by painting his initials on it, and he thereby acquires ownership of it.
4. Everyone has the right to claim any unowned tree by marking it and then offering a sacrifice on top of Mt. Cloudpiercer. He who does so owns the tree.
5. Everyone has the right to claim any unowned set of trees by posting, in the village square, a notice of his claim which defines the set, such as 'I claim all of the trees which now stand, and which shall stand in the future, in the valley of the Broad River from its source in the mountains to its mouth at the edge of the sea'. Whoever does so thereby comes to own all of the trees so specified.
6. Everyone has the right to claim any unowned tree by marking it and then giving a feast for all of his fellows. He who does so comes to own the tree.
7. Everyone has the right to claim any unowned tree by marking it and then giving each of his fellows a useful tool, such as an axe or a saw. He who does so comes to own the tree.

Mavrodes argues that since there is no "ready metaphysical principle" to decide which of these is appropriate, they are all possible.[107] We mostly agree. Universality and negativity is a "metaphysical" limitation, but one which does not significantly pare down Mavrodes' list. Specifically, rules 1–5 seem possible on our theory (although we have some ambivalence towards 2 and 4), but 6 and 7 are not acceptable. These two violate our negativity requirement by making one's right contingent upon paying off others (and this is one reason we are ambivalent about 4). As we said, the latitude is wide, but not unlimited.

In specific situations and social settings, how to cash all this out in terms of positive law and rights will be difficult and beyond the purview of abstract moral and social theory. We believe a good deal will be *practically* dependent on actual agreement. Herein, for us, lies the proper, and extremely important, place for social contract theory.[108] What people are willing to agree to will impact significantly on the specific rights structure of a given society, although it will in no way be decisive about the moral quality or character of such a society.[109] Perhaps pouring cans of tomato juice into fluid mediums would be an acceptable procedure for determining boundaries in cases of original acquisition in some strange land of tomato juice fetishists. Similarly, a community of artists might settle upon criteria of visual perspective in their society (for example, you own what you can see) in cases of original acquisition. We find it highly improbable that these criteria would command consensus; but then it is also unlikely that the Puritanical idea that one owns what one can physically labor upon would be the only acceptable principle of original acquisition in all societies either.

Rights of transfer, to use Nozick's phrase, will undoubtedly alter the look of holdings under a given rule of original acquisition as time passes. People will come to discover they have different values than those they may have held at the time of the original acquisition. A would-be artist who gained a large holding under the terms of original acquisition mentioned in the last paragraph may discover he has no talent for art. His own form of flourishing might be best served by divesting himself of part of his land in exchange for other goods (perhaps even rights of use on the lands of others). It is the essence of the individualist position that we cannot settle an appropriate value system for diverse individuals a priori. Within the limits described, rules of original acquisition are less a matter of morality than they are a matter of getting co-operative society off the ground. Beyond that, consistent maintenance of the abstract principles of natural right will be sufficient to protect and encourage individual efforts to flourish.

The Nozickian position (also our own) which allows for the unrestricted voluntary transfer of goods is a feature of property rights that follows from the negativity requirement and the primitive moral proposition that choice is respected through consent in a social context. What we noted in the last section of the chapter is equally applicable to property rights: consent is the means by which the integrity of moral territories is maintained interpersonally. And property is nothing other than the material expression of one's moral territory. In order to be able to carry our moral territories with us across time and in compossible fashion with others, others must restrain themselves from crossing into our territory unless given permission.

Much of what we have said depends upon the validity of the first principle mentioned earlier and to which we promised to return, namely that the 'objects' or 'possessions' that one has must be considered extensions of what one is. An obvious place to begin such a defense is with Samuel Wheeler's article, 'Natural Property Rights as Body Rights'.[110] In this article, Wheeler argues that if we have natural rights to our own bodies, then there are natural rights to property, because property rights can be derived directly from the natural right to our bodies. Although we cannot discuss the details of this argument, it seems appropriate to mention Wheeler's thesis here, since he links property to personhood and argues that interferences with a person's property are direct interferences with that person. The thrust of the argument is that there is no nonarbitrary way to distinguish what is ordinarily thought of as property from things that are parts (by extension) of a person's body. Thus if we have the natural right to our bodies, we would also have the natural right to that which we make a part of our bodies. We cannot make something a part of our bodies in violation of the rights of others; but short of that, Wheeler claims there is no upper limit to what one can have a natural right to on the basis of his argument.

While we would support Wheeler's basic contention that property is part of personhood in a way that is much stronger than a Lockean "mixing of labor" thesis, we are unpersuaded by his effort to regard objects to which we might have property rights as extensions of our body parts.[111]

In the first place, Wheeler begins the defense of his thesis by direct reference to our bodies. By the end of his article, however, he begins referring to a person's "agenthood".[112] This suggests that it is not our bodies at all that ground the natural right to property, but rather the fact that we have status as moral agents—our bodies themselves being extensions of our 'agenthood'. Furthermore, Wheeler fails to use 'body' in a consistent fashion throughout the article. At one point, for example, he argues that clothing is "artificial fur", and that therefore clothing is an artificial body part to which we would have the same rights as we might to an artificial limb.[113] Similarly, a house is like a turtle shell. But the problem is that our bodies do not have either fur or shells, and therefore Wheeler has not shown how these things (unlike artificial limbs) are extensions of our actual bodies, but only of some imaginary body we might have possessed. We believe it would have been better to claim that the natural right to property is a direct function of our right to moral agency rather than our bodies. This would have saved him from having to make somewhat ludicrous comparisons between objects and body parts or functions.

In any case, we need to explain why property is a feature of one's self or 'agenthood' rather than one's body; for the use of one's body is also an exercise of one's agency. Since we have already shown that persons have natural rights to their pursuit of eudaimonia, if we can show that property is simply an extension of self, we would have the natural right to property as well; for then, the natural right to property—appropriate to a certain context—is essentially a restatement of the basic natural rights for which we have already argued. Therefore, a few things need to be recalled regarding what we have claimed a human being is and what human flourishing involves.

Two-substance dualism is false. Human beings are not isolated, lifeless atoms occupying space in a mechanistic universe, nor are they simply a disembodied mind or consciousness. Neither is a human being an 'incarnate spirit' that inhabits a body for a period of time, nor is a human being some unique combination of mind and body. The conception of a human being that has been advanced by us rejects dualism in toto. Instead, a human being is a living, material thing with the power to engage in self-directed activity through the exercise of his own reason and intelligence in order to meet the needs of his life. Self-directedness or autonomy pertains, then, to actions which occur at some place and at some time and that constitute the lives of flesh-and-blood human creatures.

Human beings are not isolated beings that can exist separate and apart from the world like some Cartesian ego. As living things, human beings are constantly interacting with their environment, and as living things with the power of conceptual awareness, human beings are directing and determining the nature of their relationships with their environment. In fact, human existence is constituted by relationships. This might not, however, seem unique. It might be objected that a rock is related to its environment; yet a rock does not exist in such a relation through any action of its own. It does not relate itself to its environment. *Human* existence, on the other hand, is relational.

The classic expression in Aristotelian realist thought of the relational character of human existence is found in the claim that human awareness is intentional or inherently relational. It is primarily through conceptual awareness that human beings avoid being isolated from the rest of the cosmos. There are two senses in which human awareness may be said to be an intentional activity.

1. It is impossible for someone to be aware and not be aware *of*. The very character of human awareness is such that it cannot be or exist unless it is ultimately of or about something other than itself. The exercise of reason or intelligence (self-directedness or autonomy) is not and cannot be something entirely private, a mere process of *inspectio mentis*. Human beings must exist as related to something other than themselves. This is the primary and metaphysically fundamental sense in which human awareness may be said to be intentional.

2. Human awareness is purposeful or goal-directed. Our interests and needs direct the use we make of our conceptual capacity. The use we make of our conceptual powers depends on the ends we seek in trying to attain our natural end. We use our intellectual capacities to gain control over our environment. This is the secondary sense in which human awareness may be said to be intentional and one that is important for our purposes. It should be noted that even actions taken for no other end than knowledge, namely, for

so-called speculative knowledge, are only ultimately taken because knowing the what's and why's of things is one of the final ends which constitutes human flourishing. Human reason or intelligence is exercised in the service of life, not vice versa.

As living things, human beings have no choice about being related to other things in existence. Yet human beings do have much to say about what they will be related to and the manner by which they will be related. Further, human beings have the responsibility for creating relationships that will enable them to flourish. We are beings that create relationships, and these relationships—be they logical, loving, or productive—are the means by which humans know, care for, and control their environment. They are both the means and the constituents of human flourishing.

Once one recognizes that human life is constituted by relationships and abandons the traditional atomistic individualism that is usually associated with the natural right to private property; once one considers the fact that human beings relate themselves to the world through their conceptual powers; and finally, once one abandons the picture of human thought (i.e. concepts) as some 'spiritual' or ghostlike event that occurs mysteriously inside our bodies, then human actions which transform the material world—whether it be planting a field of corn or performing a piano concerto—can be seen to be nothing less than extensions of self. They make up the life of the person. As a being whose conceptual powers allow it to create, control, and use relationships, the exploitation of opportunities in the world is a fundamental expression of what and who an individual human being is.

Taking control of another's property against their wishes can now be seen to be nothing less than taking control of one of the central relationships that constitute a human being's life. Human beings are individuals who are necessarily related to other beings, but they have the unique power to create and control these relationships, to fashion a worthwhile existence for themselves. When human beings no longer have control of one of the central ways they live, they cannot be said to have their natural right to live according to their own judgments respected. There is and can be no dichotomy between a human being's natural right to live according to his own choices and a human being's natural right to private property. The latter is the expression of the metaphysical fact that human beings are material things who flourish through the exploitation of opportunities in the material world.

The acceptance of this basic natural right does not preclude the possibility that what one does within the legitimate boundaries of one's moral territory has 'undesirable' neighborhood effects upon others. Such effects may be of interest to moralists, but they do not necessarily imply unethical action and certainly do not imply the presence of a rights violation. If A produces a better product than B, then the consequences to B will be 'undesirable'; but A has not necessarily done anything 'wrong' and has not violated B's natural rights. One is not by nature obligated to provide others with a stream of favorable consequences.[114] One is only obligated to restrain one's actions in such a way that the moral territories of others are not penetrated without permission. But this brings us back full circle to our initial thesis about the concept of natural rights.

CONCLUSION

In this second part of this chapter we have not dealt with the myriad of problematic issues surrounding the establishment and maintenance of a positive legal environment for the protection of our natural right to property. We recognize fully that there are many thorny problems here and that there would be such problems even if our conception of property rights became the norm. We are also not adherents of the position that would claim that such a complete positive system could be deduced from a general theory of property—or any natural right—independent of social circumstances, history, and attitudes. We are, nonetheless, convinced that general principles are necessary signposts. No society has or will be able to function without a general conception of itself; and which general conception is justifiable remains a viable and necessary task.

We believe that when it comes to property rights, more than the discipline of philosophy is required for a workable social order. We believe our task has been to provide a defensible general framework. Others with more specialized competencies can apply or speculate about the viability of general philosophical theses in particular circumstances.[115] But if the general framework is wrong, the application will be skewed. We have therefore tried to show not only how our conception of the natural right to property flows from the more general theses we have been advancing throughout this book, but also how the usual general conceptions of what property is are off the mark.

It is nevertheless the general character of a natural right that has been our main concern in this chapter. We have argued that natural rights—specifically basic negative rights, what we have called Lockean rights—can be justified by reference to a human being's *telos*. We maintained from the start that these rights implied duties (namely, they were claim-rights) and not mere liberties or powers. This justification did not, however, argue that these natural rights were justified because they were simply a means to human flourishing. Nor did this justification argue that rights claims could, without remainder, be translated into duty claims that every human being owes every other human being.

It was instead argued that Lockean rights were the social and political expression of the claim that there is no higher moral purpose, no other end to be served, than the individual human being's self-initiated and self-maintained achievement of his individuative and generic potentialities. We argued that Lockean rights are the only meta-normative principles that can provide for a compossible set of moral territories that the highly individualized and self-directed character of human flourishing demands. These rights were, therefore, not merely the result of a consideration of what some general principles of justice required, but came from the recognition that human beings are individuals who cannot be ends-in-themselves save through their own self-directed behavior.

4

LIBERTY AND THE
COMMON GOOD

Nothing great is accomplished in the world save through a heroic
fidelity to some truth which a man who says "I" sees and proclaims; a
heroic fidelity to some mission which he, himself, a human person,
must fulfill; of which, perhaps, he alone is aware and for which he lays
down his life.

—Jacques Maritain, *The Person and the Common Good*

In the preceding chapter we argued that the Lockean claim that men
have a natural right to liberty can be justified by appealing to an essentially Aristotelian conception of man and ethics. Yet two central concepts that emerge from an Aristotelian account of human beings and
morality are that 'man is by his very nature a social and political animal'
and that 'the good of the individual human being is intimately bound up
with the common good of the political community'. These concepts are
often used to contrast liberalism's approach to politics with that of
Aristotelianism, but they are most frequently used in opposition to the
Hobbesian atomism and egotism that some, such as Leo Strauss and
C.B. Macpherson, claim underlie the Lockean approach to political and
social theory. Thus, it remains to be seen if our attempt to give liberalism a foundation in an ancient source can succeed, for there seems to be
two fundamental questions regarding compatibility: (1) Can the Lockean
claim that the function of the state is to protect and implement the natural right to liberty (in all its forms[1]) be rendered consistent with the Aristotelian claim that the function of the state is the promotion of the
common good of the political community? (2) Can the individualism
which has been so strongly emphasized in the account of human flour-

ishing and in the justification of the natural right to liberty be reconciled with the Aristotelian claim that human beings are by nature social and political animals?

We contend that an affirmative answer can be given both of these questions. We believe (1) that the implementation and protection of the natural right to liberty is just what the common good of the political community is and (2) that the natural sociality of human beings not only does not conflict with the emphasis given to individualism, but is crucial in explaining why there needs to be such a 'meta-normative' concept as a right. Our purpose, then, is not to deny the natural sociality of human beings or remove the concept of the common good from the vocabulary of political and social theory. Instead, our purpose is to indicate how two traditions—often thought incompatible—can merge and benefit from each other's strengths.

It is certainly the case that most political theorists in the Aristotelian tradition do not cash out the common good of the political community along Lockean lines. Given our broad use of *Aristotelian*, we shall examine the views of some rather different representatives of this tradition in the course of presenting our position. The alternative theories discussed next will range from the virtually theological account given by Maritain to the individualistic ethics of David Norton. We thus intend to argue for our own account of the common good, as well as our own view of human sociality, both by way of contrast with other views and by way of direct exposition.

INDIVIDUALITY, SOCIALITY, AND THE COMMON GOOD

Human beings are social and political animals. In terms of natural origins, human beings are certainly not isolated entities in a state of nature. Rather, we are always born into a society or community, and thus it is fundamentally erroneous to attempt to conceive of man as an entity who initially takes it upon himself to join society. We have no option to join society; we already belong. Furthermore, we can be said to possess by nature certain potentialities which cannot be actualized in isolation. We need association and companionship with others if we are to have any chance of flourishing. It is only through co-operation and collaboration with others that human beings come to adequately provide for their basic needs and highest aspirations. Our fulfillment and well-being must involve life in society—that is, the attainment of goods that only a community or association of individuals could ever provide. Thus, we are social and political animals in the sense that we naturally need to associate and co-operate with others to succeed at being human and in the sense that our natural origin is within society, not some state of nature.

Nevertheless, the fact that human beings are social and political animals does not require that one be regarded as no more than a part within the greater social whole. Aristotle's claim in the *Politics*, for example, that the polis is 'by nature' prior to the individual and that it is a whole of which the individual is a part does not mean that the *polis* is ontologically prior to the individual. Rather, it means that community life is a whole in which a person naturally moves in order to actualize his potential and in which he is a part.[2] Our need for others does not mean that we are no longer individual substances. On the contrary, individual human beings are ontologically fundamental to their community. They constitute it and serve as the foundation of its being. Human communities or societies[3] are not substances in their own right and have no ontological priority over their members.

We do not mean to imply, however, that there cannot be human groups which possess a kind of unity which cannot be explained by the mere physical existence of the individuals who compose them. Human groups in this sense can exist, but only as an accident of individual human substances, and only as the result of shared beliefs and goals of the individual members that compose the group. As D. J. Allan has put the matter:

> Men have capacities which can only be developed to the full within the *polis*. But there is a reverse side to this, namely that the State is only as real as a community of individual men whose capacities have been thus developed. Man is a social animal in an even higher degree than the bee. But then he is also not a social animal in the same way as the bee: he possesses the power of speech, which permits, and is naturally designed for, consultation about mutual advantage.[4]

The unity that a human group possesses results only if the members judge that common action is needed to attain an end and only if they decide to pursue that end—nothing else. John Wild, for example, defined a human group as "a set of diverse, individual activities made one by reference to a single end, rationally held in mind by the different members".[5] Under this definition a human group is a noetic and moral entity, not a substance or 'organic' whole. Furthermore, simply because there can be groups in the sense described, namely, human groups, does not mean that any and every set of ordered relationships among persons constitutes a human group.

The fact that man is a social and political animal and thus needs others to attain greater knowledge and material well-being, not to mention love and friendship, does not in any way make the attainment of well-being anything less than something the individual must do for himself. One can, of course, be told truths, endowed with wealth, and given affection; but these will not in themselves lead to fulfillment. A person must still use his own intelligence and choice to fashion a worthwhile existence. Presence in a community does not remove the necessary connection between self-fulfillment and individual responsibility. As Veatch maintains:

> [N]ever can a human being possibly be what he ought to be, or make of himself what he ought to, without doing so fully by his own deliberate choice and in light of his own understanding of his natural end, and what that end calls for in the way of day-by-day conduct and behavior. [6]

Man's fundamental need for social and political life does not come from what he can receive from others, but rather from what he can do *with* others. It is the greater possibility for growth and achievement that social and political life affords that constitutes its extreme importance for man. Thus, community life not only does not change the need to be the author of one's own actions, it intensifies it.

Clarifying the exact relationship between individual and community has always been something of a problem within the Aristotelian tradition. The problem stems from the attempt to steer the middle course between atomistic individualism on the one hand, and organic collectivism on the other. Some thinkers, to avoid the 'atomism', 'atheism', 'mechanism' and 'materialism'[7] of liberal individualism, have pursued lines of argument that are more problematic than the 'defects' of liberalism they wish to avoid. A case in point is Maritain's discussion of the person in his now classic *The Person and the Common Good*.[8] The main problems with Maritain's conception of 'the person and the common good' begin in Chapter 3, where he draws a distinction between 'individuality' and 'true personality'.[9] The term *individuality* is meant to characterize the material side of our nature. This side of our nature is described as having "no determination", since it derives all determinateness from form, and as having an "avidity for being", since in and of itself matter is potentiality.[10] Moreover, because matter is divisible, individuality is particularized. Personality, on the other hand, deals with our spiritual side.[11] Personality is the unifying feature of ourselves and is described in various places as knowing, loving, growing, creative, inexhaustible, and so on. Personality is superior to individuality. Indeed, "evil arises when, in our action, we give preponderance to the individual aspect of our being."[12] Thus the goal in life is to move away from individuality and towards personality.

Although Maritain emphatically denies it, the distinction between individuality and personality as he constructs it constitutes a bifurcation of human nature.[13] All the activities attributed to persons, such as loving and knowing, are attributed to personality. Individuality serves no other purpose than to individuate. Yet even Aquinas argues that it is Socrates who knows and not merely Socrates's spirit or 'personality' that knows.[14] Man's unified nature demands that care be taken in describing his mode of being. Our so-called 'material' side is every bit as constitutive of what we are as the 'spiritual' side. Indeed, Aquinas also notes that the very nature of reason itself cannot be understood apart from our materiality.[15] It is thus more than misleading to attribute such processes as knowing and loving to one side of our nature, while leaving the other side to do no more than locate us in space.

The claim that the pursuit of individuality leads to all evil is quite false. Indeed, just the opposite may be true. As David Norton argues:

> Our consideration of "personal truth" reveals that the great enemy of integrity is not falsehood as such but—ironically—the attractiveness of foreign truths, truths that belong to others.[16]

Maritain could have chosen to make his point in terms of the pursuit of some potentialities being more conducive (or destructive) to human well-being than others. Instead, his dualistic account of human nature tends to reify abstractions while ignoring the existential component of individual human living. For example, knowing and loving for Maritain are less the product of individual effort than they are general properties attached to some aspect of our being. The result, as one might expect, is a tendency to see persons as instantiations of abstractions rather than the abstractions as concepts growing out of the actual pursuits of individuals. Once this mistake has been made, it is no surprise that any liberal political theory will look anarchistic and materialistic.

If the temptation to bifurcate human nature is not avoided, human life will tend to be viewed as a composite of partitionable functions or activities. This in turn will tend to generate a conception of our natural end as being something outside of ourselves—something that we seek, but which is not a part of our individuality prior to attainment. If, on the other hand, the various aspects and dimensions of a person's life are seen as extensions of a single process of self-development, our natural end will be, as Aristotle put it, more of an *activity* than simply an attainment. Under this latter conception, the presumption must be that no portion of an individual's life can be 'partitioned off' without jeopardizing the very integrity of that life. Thus a society that takes from the individual the product of his effort, or enslaves him, or attempts to limit the freedom of his mind, or compels him to act against his own judgment, prevents a person's attainment of his natural end.

To remain faithful to personal integrity, the benefits of social cooperation must be obtained by rational means—that is, by discussion, persuasion, and voluntary, uncoerced agreement. In a moral human community, physical force or the threat thereof may be used only in retaliation and defense, and only against those who initiate (or threaten to initiate) its use. The individual human being's natural right to liberty must be the fundamental principle of the community's laws, for it indicates the fundamental precondition to be met if his life among others is to indeed be one that will have any possibility of self-actualization.

> The choice to learn, to judge, to evaluate, to appraise, to decide what he ought to do in order to live his life must be each person's own, otherwise he simply has no opportunity to excel or fail at the task. His moral aspirations

cannot be fulfilled (or left unfulfilled) if he is not the source of his own actions, if they are imposed or forced upon him by others. [17]

Since the requirements for human fulfillment are at least partially determined by the nature of man, and since this must be understood as applying to every man—past, present, and future—the good for man has to include a consideration of abstract principles covering a wide variety of concretes.

It is up to every individual to apply these principles to the particular goals and problems of his own life. It is only such principles that can provide a proper common bond among all men; men can agree on a principle without necessarily agreeing on the choice of concretes. For instance, men can agree that one should work, without prescribing any man's particular choice of work.

It is only with abstract principles that a social system may properly be concerned. A social system cannot force a particular good on a man nor can it force him to seek the good: it can only maintain conditions of existence which leave him free to seek it. A government cannot live a man's life, it can only protect his freedom. It cannot prescribe concretes, it cannot tell a man how to work, what to produce, what to buy, what to say, what to write, what values to seek, what form of happiness to pursue—it can only uphold the principle of his right to make such choices.

It is in this sense that "the common good". . . lies not in *what* men do when they are free, but in the fact *that* they are free.[18]

There is a difference between treating abstract moral principles as extensions of the lives and choices of individuals—where individuals are the fundamental realities and adherence to principles is the guide to successful living—and the reification of abstractions—where the abstractions take on an existence of their own and individuals are treated as mere placeholders or receptacles for the abstract moral principles.

The preceding distinction can best be illuminated by way of criticism of Maritain's conception of the common good. For Maritain seems to commit precisely the error described in the last paragraph. Consider the following:

The common good is common because it is *received* in persons, each one of whom is as a mirror of the whole.[19]

In addition, Maritain describes the common good as "the end of the social whole".[20] Maritain asks us to conceive that the common good has some sort of substantial ontological status which we as individuals receive. The separate ontological status of the common good is, of course, not supposed to require the treatment of individuals as a mere means to the good of the whole. Obviously this conception would mean that the common good is not a mere collection of private goods. The common good is instead a communicable good among persons and thus neither ignores them nor is defined by them. Nevertheless, it is a good that is received by persons which, upon reception, can be communicated. And since one does not receive that which is not independent of oneself, the common good has its own ontological integrity.

Among the reified abstractions we are to receive are: material prosperity, spiritual riches, hereditary wisdom, moral rectitude, justice, friendship, happiness, virtue, and heroism.[21] Notice that these goods are received rather than achieved. Had Maritain presented his case in the language of achievement, he would have noticed that only individuals achieve and that common goods are common because the individuals who take the responsibility to achieve them will have realized a generally similar achievement. And because only individuals achieve, the concrete specification of the goods in question will differ from person to person and circumstance to circumstance. There is no such thing as happiness or friendship or material prosperity for society as a whole, for any attempt to specify the nature of these goods necessarily averages and consequently glosses over the particularities involved. Given Maritain's view of individuality, however, this may be just what he desires. But there are no good reasons to accept Maritain's way of looking at this issue and a number of good reasons for not ignoring individuality. Chief among these reasons is that holistic conceptions of social ends tend to locate responsibility in society rather than in individuals. But since society is not an individual and can therefore have no responsibilities as such, the practical effect of a conception like Maritain's must be (at best) that goods concretely appropriate to some persons will be authoritatively imposed on other members of the community.

We do not wish to give the impression that friendship, happiness, virtue, and the like are purely subjective goods. We have argued the contrary position in earlier chapters. Nevertheless, the flexible and indeterminate nature of these goods, when stated in the abstract, leaves only two avenues of responsibility open for their more concrete specification: (1) the individual must bear the final responsibility for the achievement of these goods (in voluntary consort with others), or (2) someone else (such as a political authority) must dictate the courses of action that will be taken to achieve these goods and also set the standards for what will count as a realization of them. As our arguments in Chapters 2 and 3 indicate, we believe the second alternative to show a disrespect for persons. Here our point is that there is no way to translate Maritain's abstractions (within his own framework) into action without adopting (2). And if (2) is the course we must take, then the individual person is, despite all denials to the contrary, a mere part in the good of the whole. [22]

It is, perhaps, Maritain's hierarchical outlook that contributes to the problem here. He seems to believe that there must be something whose good stands between the good of individuals and God's good. This good is the good of the whole community, which is itself made up of wholes (persons). The good of the whole community is something different from goods individuals may realize and is superior to any goods they may realize. Yet we find it difficult to understand how the Aristotelian categories of act and potency, form and matter, could be applied to this whole made of wholes. What part of the whole of wholes is characterized by form and what part by matter? Can the whole of wholes be analyzed in terms of a distinction between personality and individuality? Is it not the case that the only concrete examples of a whole of wholes that we have are living organisms, thus making Maritain's claim that he wishes to avoid an organismic conception of society suspect? When called upon to explain what this whole made of wholes is like, Maritain can only draw an analogy to the mystery of the Trinity and to the "deficiency of our language'.[23] We, on the other hand, see no reason to posit an intermediary between us and God. Indeed, we find it more reasonable to suppose the opposite, since each of us is saved or damned as an individual. Furthermore, a sense of community does not seem to require a whole of wholes for its realization. All that is necessary is a commitment on the part of individuals to (a) the fundamental principles of social order (such as natural rights) and (b) the more particularized purposes of the various groups of which one is a member. Actions which respect the rights of others and which accord with the purposes of groups to which one naturally or by choice belongs are sufficient to generate a meaningful notion of the common good in both a general and a particular sense.

The misleading nature of the personality/individuality dichotomy mentioned earlier gives rise to a Platonic conception of the common good of the political community and hence an impossible one. Since individuality is materiality, the whole object of our existence is to shed our materiality as far as possible.[24] Reminiscent of Plato's *Phaedo*, our materiality or individuality is the repository of all negative qualities. Thus the degree to which we shed these qualities is the degree to which we have a chance for attainment of perfection and the true common good. However, since we cannot attain perfection due to the fact that we are "a poor material individual",[25] a society of 'pure persons' is impossible. We are thus faced with a choice between transcendent perfection, which is desirable but impossible, and base sensuality, which is possible but undesirable. We have already noted our objection to Maritain's conception of individuality. Here our objection is to the impossibility of the standard in question due to the false nature of the choice he gives us. Paradoxically, it is the false nature of this choice that causes the very problems Maritain is trying to solve. For since perfection is impossible, cynicism about the improvement of man seems the most plausible reaction to failed efforts to achieve the impossible. The Hobbesian conception of man is thus given the status of being 'realistic', because it remains the only other alternative offered. The person who claims that 'everybody has his price' is simply the alter ego of the person who sees our material being as the source of all evil.

Our objections to Maritain's conception of man and the common good do not necessarily require the rejection of a transcendent order any more than they require a rejection of community. These objections do, however, presuppose a more adequate conception of man's materiality— one that allows for materiality to make a positive contribution to man's final end. Furthermore, these objections indicate the value of pluralism, diversity, and individuality and their role in formulating a correct conception of the common good. Holistic abstractions may be useful in categorizing the *kinds* of goods people should pursue, but without the limiting factor and value of individuality, persons tend to lose their *personal* identity. Finally, these objections require that a conception of the common good take into account the realities of acting in and through a material world. Our next chapter on the commercial society will indicate more fully the nature of this last point.

The Lockean claim that the function of the state is to implement and protect the natural right to liberty can thus be regarded as nothing more nor less than the promotion of the common good of the political community. In other words, the common good of the political community is a set of legal conditions which are determined by individuals' natural rights and thus govern the procedures that individuals use in fashioning a worthwhile existence for themselves. When understood in this way, the common good of the political community concerns procedures in social living and not what should be the specific results of those procedures. The common good of the political community is thus not to be substituted for the individual's natural end. Though they are not in conflict, at least when correctly construed, they are not the same and should not be conflated. Living a good human life remains something an individual must do for himself. Government should only provide the conditions in which this possibility might occur. And when one sees the individual as an integrated whole rather than as a composite, the individualism of the liberal political tradition can be justified without recourse to atomism.

UNITY, CO-OPERATION, AND THE COMMON GOOD

According to the Aristotelian political tradition, the function of the state is to promote the common good of the the political community. Yet, since the political community is not an entity in its own right, there can be no good for it just *as such*. So what does it mean to speak of the common good of the political community? John Finnis claims that the notion of the common good for the political community is one that

> neither asserts nor entails that the members of the community have the same values (or set of values or objectives); it implies only that there be some set (or set of sets) of conditions which needs to obtain if each member is to attain his own objectives. [26]

The common good of the political community need not be a single goal that all men must strive to attain. Rather, the common good of a political community need only be that set of conditions that allows for the well-being and self-actualization of the community's members.

The common good of the political community must be in accord with the well-being of "each and all".[27] It cannot be in conflict with any requirement of an individual human being's fulfillment. Furthermore, it is important to note that the locution 'each and all' provides the key to a proper understanding of the common good. The 'each' provides a check on all and the 'all' provides a check on each. The good of an individual human being cannot be sacrificed for the sake of the community good, and the community good cannot be made subservient to the good of some individual. The central problem of the common good is, therefore, discovering a principle that neither sacrifices the individual to the good of the whole nor defines the good of all in terms of some individual's good. To solve this problem, any principle that characterizes the common good must be very general, abstract, and minimalistic. It must also be, as we shall show below, a procedural principle rather than an end-state principle. At this stage it is enough to note that Lockean and Aristotelian conceptions can be synthesized if the common good of the political community is seen to be just the general condition of that community which would allow for the possibility of the flourishing of the individual community members. Given this conception of the common good, the function of political action would be to ensure those political conditions that allow for the possibility of the achievement of human excellence by individuals within the community.

The crucial question is how we determine what political conditions ought to exist in a human community so as to allow for the possible flourishing of individuals, and it is with the answer to this question that reconciling Lockean political conclusions with the Aristotelian concern for the common good concretely appears. For what is the claim that men have a natural right to liberty but a claim about what political conditions ought to exist in a human community so as to allow for the possibility that each and every human being might flourish? Although human flourishing is certainly not defined in terms of individual rights when considered apart from social and political life, and although the claim that individuals have the basic, negative, natural right to liberty is not a self-evident moral truth but must be justified by reference to the human *telos*, there is a sense in which human flourishing can be understood as being defined in terms of respect for this right. Human beings are indeed social and political animals, and the natural right to liberty is *the* social and political expression of the fundamental insight of an ethics of human flourishing. Just as there is no higher moral purpose than an individual human being's *self*-perfection, so the natural right to liberty is the ethical standard employed in developing a constitution whose legal system creates the general condition of liberty that is necessary for the possibility that individuals might choose to conduct their lives in self-perfecting ways. In a social and political context, one cannot speak of human flourishing apart from respect for the natural right to liberty, and in this sense the former is 'defined' by the latter. Implementing and protecting the natural right to liberty throughout the community is, then, just the sort of condition that characterizes the common good.[28]

Yet, no sooner is it said that implementing and protecting the natural right to liberty is the common good of the political community, but comes the objection that this proposed reconciliation of Lockean and Aristotelian political traditions regarding the function of the state is an oversimplification. Though the state may have the function of protecting individual rights and though the protection of these rights promotes the common good, there is more to promoting the common good than protecting rights, and so there is something more for the state to do. Before considering what this 'something more' could be, there are two points that should be noted.

First, the common good of the political community must be something which is good for each and every member of the political community. So whatever is claimed to belong to the common good must not only be good, it must be sufficiently universal. As we have argued at great length throughout this book, protected self-directedness is truly good for each person, so liberty fulfills this requirement. Anything else that allegedly belongs to the common good of the political community must fulfill this requirement also. Second, even if the common good of the political community can be shown to consist of something more than protecting the right to liberty, it cannot be claimed to be something *supra*-ordinate to this right; for this right, as already stated, determines whether a political community preserves that condition that is absolutely essential to the possibility that a human being might flourish when he lives with others. If the natural right to liberty is not protected, self-directedness—the condition for the possibility of human flourishing—is destroyed. This right, as noted in Chapter 3, provides the social and political context in which individuals apply the normative principles (virtues) required by human flourishing. Thus, the means or procedures employed to achieve any alleged additional feature of the common good ought not to be inconsistent with the protection of this basic right. If the notion of the common good for the political community should prove to contain, as a matter of principle, contradictory features, then its attainment in a political community would be impossible and would, therefore, no longer be something the state should attempt to achieve.

At this point, it is necessary to consider the following question: Is it possible for there to be situations in which the social and political expression of human flourishing and the normative requirements of that very same end conflict—conflict not because of some moral failure on the part of someone, but conflict simply because the situation is such that it is impossible for the social and political expression of the human *telos* (natural rights) and the virtues called for by that end both to be met? Another way of putting this is: Is social and political life always possible? This is a very important and difficult question. It is important because it asks what the purpose of social and political life is, and it is difficult because it will require a careful explanation of the sense in which rights are 'absolute'. We thus need to deal with this issue before considering whether the common good can be interpreted as requiring that the state do more than protect and implement Lockean rights.

THE LIMITS OF SOCIAL AND POLITICAL LIFE

The Aristotelian view holds that the purpose of social and political life is to secure the common good, but this good is an intermediate good and is for the sake of the human flourishing of each and every person. Thus, we may say that the purpose of the social and political community is the moral well-being—the human flourishing—of each and every person. Accordingly, natural rights apply, have a point, whenever human social and political life is possible, and the social and political community is possible, then, whenever it can secure its purpose—namely provide a context in which people might live among each other *and* pursue their highly individualized and self-directed well-being. Now clearly, there can be situations in which social and political life is not possible. Disasters, such as earthquakes, fires, floods, shipwrecks, and famines do occur, and it would be ludicrous not to acknowledge that this makes a difference to the applicability of ethical principles which seek to establish the social and political context that protects the self-directed and highly individualized character of human flourishing for *each and every member* of society.

Yet, it is here that we have to be very precise about just what it means for social and political life not to be possible. Exactly how do earthquakes, fires, floods, famines, shipwrecks, and so forth make social and political life impossible and natural rights inapplicable? What is it about such disasters or emergencies that change the situation from a social and political one to a situation which is asocial and apolitical? The answer, we believe, is found by distinguishing between an emergency situation and a normal situation.

> An emergency is an unchosen, unexpected event, limited in time, that creates conditions under which human survival is impossible—such as a flood, an earthquake, a fire, a shipwreck. In an emergency situation, men's primary goal is to combat the disaster, escape the danger and restore normal conditions (to reach dry land, to put out the fire, etc.). . . By normal I mean metaphysically normal, normal in the nature of things and appropriate to human existence. Men can live on land, but not in water or in a raging fire. Since men are not omnipotent it is metaphysically possible for unforeseeable disasters to strike them, in which case their only task is to return to those conditions under which their lives can continue. By its nature, an emergency is temporary; if it were to last man would perish.[29]

People who are caught in an emergency can and ought to have only one concern: to return to those conditions where it is at least possible for them to flourish. A normal situation, at least, does not make it impossible for persons to flourish. The proverbial example of two men who, through no fault of their own, find themselves in the ocean fighting for possession of a plank which can only support one of them comes readily to mind.[30] This case illustrates most vividly how an emergency can make social and political life impossible. Without attempting to determine what the ethically proper course of action would be in such a situation, if there is one, this is a situation in which the flourishing of both parties cannot be attained—*social and political life is impossible*—and individual rights, the very social and political principles which exist to guarantee the possibility that each and every person might flourish, have no point. Such a situation by its very nature precludes the possibility that both parties will flourish.

We may say, then, that when social and political life is not possible, when it is in principle impossible for human beings to live among each other and pursue their well-being, consideration of individual rights is out of place; they do not apply. We cannot properly speak of someone's individual rights being violated, for that would be a category mistake.

It has been objected, however, that those who do not have sufficient resources to meet their basic nutritional needs are in the midst of their own disaster and thus have no obligation to respect the rights of those who wish to keep more than what they need to meet their basic nutritional needs.[31] Yet it should be observed that poverty, ignorance, and illness are not metaphysical emergencies. Wealth and knowledge are not automatically given, like manna from heaven. The nature of human life and existence is such that every person has to use his own reason and intelligence to create wealth and knowledge. Poverty, ignorance, and illness have and can be combatted by human beings. This presupposes, of course, that individual rights are respected so that people are free to be as creative as possible to meet life's problems and needs. The existence of people in desperate need does not by itself, however, make social and political life impossible or individual rights inapplicable.

Yet the objection of the last paragraph can be made more forcefully. Suppose, for example, there is a man who through no fault of his own is starving in the street and after repeated but unsuccessful requests for assistance and work finds himself with no alternative at this time but either to take the bread of the rich man, without asking his consent, or to die.[32] This objection raises the following questions: (a) Is not this situation analogous to the emergency situation? (b) Is this not a situation in which social and political life is impossible and thus individual rights would have no point? (c) And if so, would it not be inappropriate to say that the poor man violates the rich man's rights when he takes his bread without the rich man's consent? (d) Therefore, could not this Aristotelian justification of Lockean rights be turned around and used as a basis for redistribution of the wealth, and then would not a classical liberal's suspicions of the Aristotelian approach to ethics and politics be justified after all?

All of these questions can be dispensed with if we will but distinguish carefully between questions (a) and (b). Regarding question (a), it must be admitted that the starving man in the street is in a situation which is very similar to the emergency situation described earlier; for he finds himself in dire straits through no fault of his own, as were our two men in the ocean after the shipwreck. Yes, *this* man is in an emergency situation. From his perspective what he ought to do is to attempt to flourish, and if this means that he takes the rich man's bread, so be it. In fact, he is in such an emergency that it would be reasonable to presume people sufficiently benevolent that if the rich man knew the poor man's full story, he would indeed have consented to the poor man taking his bread.

Yet this is not to say that the poor man has a free hand and could not be taken to court and legally and rightfully charged with stealing the rich man's bread. This is because of what one must consider when thinking of question (b): it must be noted that the situation of the man starving in the street is different from the two men fighting over a plank in the ocean. In that situation *both* men were in dire straits, the starving man in the street is alone in his distress. The rich man and presumably many other members of the community are not in an emergency. Social and political life is clearly possible and operative. Further, taking the poor man to court provides a way to determine whether the man was indeed in the extreme situation in which we have supposed him to be. Moreover, it is also important to distinguish between a situation which is still governed by the principles of a legal system (individual rights) and the particular judgment that a judge would have to render in an emergency case of this kind. What the judge should rule the poor man's punishment to be, assuming that the rich man is not benevolently inclined, is not something that can be determined from the philosopher's armchair, and this is but another reason for insisting that the situation be viewed as a social and political one. What philosophers often suppose to be the case has to be determined by the facts in the real world, and this is again why the situation should be treated as a social and political one where consideration of individual rights apply. Questions (c) and (d) are, then, answered negatively.

There are, however, two possible rejoinders to the foregoing response to the starving-man-in-the-street example to which we need to reply.

1. Are we not guilty of giving the starving man incoherent moral advice? It seems that this man is being told: 'You ought to try to flourish (that is, take the rich man's bread)', and 'You ought not to violate individual rights (that is, *not* take the rich man's bread and perish)'. After all, the man can be legally charged with stealing bread! This objection conflates, however, the dual moral function of the human *telos*: this ultimate end provides the basis for the principles (the virtues) individuals need to possess to flourish and the principles (individual rights) a legal system needs to make social and political life possible. The starving-man-in-the-street example shows that one can be in a situation where what one morally ought to do and what a legal system requires are not the same. Contradictory moral advice has not been given. Rather, the moral advice that has been given, namely, 'You ought to flourish, take the rich man's bread', conflicts with what the law requires, and even though the legal system has an ethical grounding in the natural right to liberty—it provides the basis for a constitution that would be the foundation for the laws which a judge would need to apply to this particular case—the relationship between the law and ethics is neither direct nor isomorphic. Law, politics, and ethics can only be concerned with what is for the most part, and so there can be conflicts between what one is morally allowed to do and what an ethically legitimate legal system requires.

In fact, as stated in Chapter 3, individual rights do not provide moral guidance the way other moral principles do. This was one of the things we meant when we described individual rights as being 'meta-normative'; they apply primarily to the creation of a morally legitimate constitutional and legal order.[33] Rights provide a link between morality and legality; they do not, as already stated, provide a *direct* or *isomorphic* link between the two. If a legal system is based on natural rights, then its laws have a normative basis. But this is not to say, as the starving-man-in-the-street example shows, that there cannot be situations in which one morally ought not to obey the law of an ethically legitimate legal system and also suffer the legal consequences, whatever they might be. Thus, not only do individual rights not apply in asocial and apolitical contexts, they also do not provide moral guidance for an individual person in a social and political context even though they are nonetheless applicable.

2. How many people must be starving in the street through no fault of their own for social and political life no longer to be possible? It is not, however, merely a matter of numbers; it is also a matter of time and opportunity. People fighting for a plank in the middle of an ocean or running for their lives during an earthquake have no time or opportunity to do anything other than try to escape the situation. For social and political life to be impossible, it must be *in principle* impossible for people to live together and flourish—that is to say, there must be neither time nor opportunity to do anything other than attempt to escape from the desperate situation. No other moral consideration is possible. The number of people who are in a desperate situation is an important consideration only because this affects whether there is any time or opportunity available to do anything other than what literally amounts to fighting for one's life. Such questions as 'Is relief help on the way?' 'Can it be provided?' 'Is it possible to leave the devastated area?' 'How much time do I have?' are relevant to determining if social and political life is possible. As already implied, this is not a matter that can be determined a priori. Politics is not mathematics. Yet the fact that some people are in dire situations and might not survive, let alone flourish, is not sufficient to show that social and political life is impossible and individual rights inapplicable.

Next, let us suppose that a famine occurs and people through no fault of their own are starving, and let us further suppose that there is neither time nor opportunity for anything to be done except for the starving to break into the grain silos of the rich, who have foolishly and immorally refused to render *any* assistance. Have the rights of the rich been violated, or is this situation more like the two men fighting for the plank in the ocean and thus not a social and political situation in which individual rights have any applicability? After the famine, how would a court of law, based on a legal system committed to the principles of individual rights, rule? Even though there might have been a few rich people not in distress during the famine, it seems reasonable to say that under such conditions social and political life was indeed not possible and thus talk of individual rights in that situation would be inappropriate. The rich could not claim to have had their rights violated in such a situation.[34]

This is not to say, however, that the starving had a right in any sense to the grain in the silos of the rich. Rather, this is just to say that the situation cannot be judged in social and political terms—rights of any kind do not apply.[35] Further, this is not to say that there cannot be some very difficult 'borderline cases' and room for judicial discretion.

It might still be replied that all this discussion of what it means for social and political life to be possible is fine and good, but it does not change what has been admitted—namely, that the obligation to respect individual rights is merely a matter of whether the consequences of such conduct serve the well-being of a person. Not so. What has been admitted are two things: (1) there can be situations in which social and political life is impossible and thus situations where individual rights have no applicability; and (2) there can be situations in which what a person ought to do and what an ethically legitimate legal system requires him to do may conflict. These admissions do not show that individual rights can be 'trumped' if the consequences for following them are bad enough. Rather, they show that we live in a universe where *moral* tragedy is possible.[36]

It can be objected that to make the foregoing admissions is to put forth a theory of absolute rights in name only; for if an ethical principle is to be absolute, then the principle must hold under all conceivable circumstances.[37] This is true, but we must be careful in how this is interpreted. Is the ethical principle 'One should never do evil that good may come of it' an absolute principle in literally all conceivable circumstances? People who endorse this principle would certainly consider it an absolute principle. Yet would they not admit that there are situations in which even this principle does not apply? For instance, one would not counsel the mentally incapacitated that they should never do evil that good may come of it. It would make no sense to attempt to apply this principle to the actions of those who are not responsible for what they do. Or imagine someone counseling rocks that they should never do evil that good may come of it. Moral concepts have a limited range of applicability, but this does not affect whether they are absolute.

Now, if such considerations apply to the precept 'One should never do evil so that good may come of it', then certainly there is nothing peculiar or inconsistent about our claiming that not all situations can be approached in terms of social and political principles and nonetheless claim that rights are absolute in the context to which they apply. What should be emphasized here is that unless one is speaking of what Aquinas would call a transcendental concept like 'being', which cannot be applied in the same sense to all its referents, concepts must have a limited range of applicability if they are to convey a definite meaning.

It is simply silly to suggest the term *absolute* be interpreted as requiring that a concept or principle not have limitations on its range of applicability. A principle is absolute if it holds in all situations to which principles of its sort or kind apply, and natural rights are absolute as long as social and political life is possible.[38]

COMMON ENTERPRISES

We claim, then, that the natural right to liberty can indeed be understood as an absolute right and that the common good of the political community can be understood as being constituted by a legal system dedicated to the protection and implementation of this basic right. Yet many times it is claimed that the state is needed as an authority to supervise those co-operative endeavors that characterize community life. The argument for this claim can be summarized as follows: it is impossible for man to attain his natural end independently of community life. Community life by its very nature requires that man co-operate and collaborate in common enterprises. Yet common enterprises require that there be someone in authority to make sure everyone 'pulls his own weight'—otherwise there will be shirkers and the aim of the common enterprise will not be achieved. Thus, the state is needed as an authority who will make sure that everyone 'pulls his own weight' in the common enterprise of the community as a whole. As Yves Simon points out:

> [U]nity of action depends on unity of judgment, and unity of judgment can be procured either by way of unanimity or by way of authority; no third possibility is conceivable. Either we all think that we should act in a certain way, or it is understood among us that, no matter how diverse our

preferences, we shall all assent to one judgment and follow the line of action it prescribes. . . . But to submit myself to a judgment which does not, or at least may not, express my own view of what should be done is to obey authority. Thus, authority is needed to assure unity of action, if and only if, unanimity is uncertain.[39]

The common enterprise of society, Simon claims, would seldom if ever take place if one had to achieve unanimity.[40] So there must be authority whose judgment is final, and in the political community this must be the state.

It is true that if common enterprises are to succeed, there must be co-operation and co-ordination among participants. However, it by no means follows from this that there must be directors or planners for all forms of human co-operation. Co-operation and co-ordination of activities in a common enterprise can arise out of the voluntary interaction of the participants in accordance with how they perceive their well-being. Co-ordination of action does not necessarily imply unity of judgment about ends. As we noted earlier, all ordered relations among persons do not constitute human groups. It is what Hayek calls "the constructivist fallacy"[41] to assume that all common enterprises require directors or central planners. Indeed, the entire system of division of labor, specialization, and market exchange is an example of a common enterprise that is highly co-ordinated but has no planner. In fact, the entire system is so co-ordinated that it is doubtful that such co-ordination of activities could be achieved by some director or even a group of directors.

We are not saying that there are no common enterprises that require directors, authoritative co-ordination, or planners. One need only consider such activities as playing in an orchestra or on an athletic team to recognize the need for some authority and planning. We *are* saying, however, that if social life is a common enterprise, it may be neither necessary nor appropriate that social co-operation be planned or authoritatively directed. Moreover, examples such as the ones just mentioned do not show that the *kind* of authority necessary for common enterprises is that which comes from the state. Indeed, the very examples of an orchestra and an athletic team indicate that common enterprises can have authorities that do not involve the state. So the argument which attempts to show that the state is needed as an authority to co-ordinate and supervise common enterprises is not persuasive.

The examples of an orchestra and team are, nevertheless, often used to suggest an analogy between them and the political community. Just as orchestras and teams require that there be someone in charge, some authority, so does a human community. Thus, the state's function is to direct and co-ordinate activities within the community in order to attain those social/political goods that constitute the flourishing of individual human beings. Now it can be admitted that there is a sense in which this analogy could be rendered consistent with the Lockean political tradition. If the purpose of the analogy is to indicate the necessity for authoritative adjudication of the rules, then it is comparable to claiming that a human community needs law—namely, a system of rights and duties that allows each and every member of the community to seek fulfillment. The necessity for authority in this sense is admitted by Lockean political principles. But if the analogy is designed to show that the use of resources (material or otherwise) must be authoritatively directed, then the analogy can and should be rejected.[42]

Still, some would insist that common sense dictates that people often have to be forced to do things they do not want to do for the benefit of all.[43] Our arguments do not ignore this point, since those prone to rights-violating activities will not be allowed to do what *they* want to do. But presumably the objection is more significant than this. The real objection seems to be that given people's ignorance they will often be inclined towards courses of action that contribute less to their own well-being and that of others than some other course of action. For example, forcing all parents to educate their children is said to be for the common good, because some would save their money and not do so if given the choice. However, by requiring education and by providing public schools, the children, their parents, and society are benefited in the long run.

Although we believe that the currently dismal condition of today's public schools is due to their public nature, we shall ignore this tack and speak only to the concepts involved. It is true that if everyone educated their children properly, we would all be better off. But it does not follow from this that the end justifies the means, nor that the means suggested (coercive public schooling) will achieve the end in question. If coercive measures, rather than other forms of social influence, are used to secure an end contrary to what people would choose to do voluntarily, then coercive measures tend to increase and perpetuate themselves. The evidence for this is the growing number of state-controlled programs, increasing taxation, and continued lack of parental control over curriculum. It is more than doubtful that the common good (rather than the good of professional educators) is being served here.

Nevertheless, it could still be argued that these practical problems do not detract from the fact that the populace is being habituated to the value of education as well as gaining increased knowledge. Surely these advantages contribute more to society than the problems detract from it. This last assertion, however, is by no means evident, and what started out as 'common sense' is no longer so obvious. What people have been habituated towards is probably less the value of education (which was generally valued before public schools anyway) than the steps one must take to 'get by' in the current system. In short, the commonsense maxims that may be applicable for advancing the goals of specific organizations with defined goals and purposes are not appropriate to the political community in general.

Regrettably, the foregoing arguments are not clearly recognized in the Aristotelian political tradition. This lack of recognition is due, at least in part, to a failure to come to grips with an ambiguity in the use of the term *polis*. *Polis* can be understood in a broad or narrow fashion. Broadly, it means "a community, a complex system of human relationships, voluntary as well as coercive, personal as well as public".[44] Narrowly, it means "an association of citizens in a constitution".[45] In other words, the *polis* can be understood as either a human community or a state.

The failure to note this difference is also responsible for the claim advanced by some Aristotelians that the essential function of the state is one of co-ordination, rather than the use of coercion to enforce laws designed for the purpose of protecting individual rights. This is perhaps the most significant thesis posited by the Aristotelian tradition against the liberal implications of the Lockean tradition. Given the importance of the claim that co-ordination is the essential function of state activities directed towards the common good, it is worth a detailed look at one such theory—the conception of the common good offered by Finnis. An examination of Finnis should be especially helpful, since the passage from his work cited earlier was one with which we claimed agreement.

FINNIS AND THE COMMON GOOD

For Finnis the foundation of the common good depends primarily on a conception of order and unity. He offers us four types of order (or unity), the last of which is most significantly related to the common good: (1) 'the order which we can understand but which we do not ourselves bring about' (such as physical processes in nature), (2) the unity or order we can bring into our own understanding (such as logic, epistemology), (3) the unity or order we impose upon that which is subject to our power (such as art, technology), and (4) 'the unity or order which we bring into our own actions and dispositions by intelligently deliberating and choosing'.[46] Given this fourfold classification and the primacy of the fourth type of order, the common good will be an order that is deliberately planned and chosen for the community as a whole.

Finnis's classificatory scheme requires him to see all human orders as, to use Hayek's terminology, a "taxis" rather than a "cosmos".[47] A taxis is an order that is deliberately planned and structured. A cosmos is also an order, but this order is an evolved or spontaneous order that is not the product of anyone's design. Finnis is committed to a design theory of human institutions precisely because he does not see that there is a fifth type of order. This fifth order is something of a combination between order 1 and order 4 above. It is an order that is not deliberately brought about (*qua* order), but is nevertheless the result of deliberate and purposeful actions on the part of individual human beings—a cosmos and not a taxis. Without this fifth type of order, one must see all human institutions, even market phenomena, as essentially the product of deliberate design, and Finnis does tend to view social processes in just this way.[48] It is thus our purpose to show that social order need not be of the type envisioned by Finnis and that his account represents just another version of the constructivist fallacy. We shall show this by looking at some of the particulars of Finnis's system. Our conclusion will be that our version of the common good does not suffer from the defects to which Finnis's account is subject.

There are ambiguities and obscurities in Finnis's account of the common good that call for at least brief examination. Let us begin with his conception of a group:

> a group. . . whether team, club, society, enterprise, corporation, or commu-
> nity, is to be said to exist wherever there is, over an appreciable span of
> time, a *co-ordination* of activity by a number of persons, in the form of
> interactions, and *with a view to a shared objective.* [49]

Our emphasis indicates that the two key terms here are *co-ordination* and *shared objective*. Finnis indicates shortly after this passage that by *shared objective* he means having some idea "of the point of continuing co-operation".[50] (Note the use of the term *co-operation.*) This conception of shared objective does not seem to conflict with our own procedural conception of the common good. Indeed, Finnis goes so far as to say that

> there is no reason to suppose that the members of a political community
> each have, or ought to have, any one such aim or determinable set of aims
> which political community does or should seek to support.[51]

So far, so good. With the possible exception of the term *co-ordination*, which we shall speak of shortly, Finnis's account remains essentially unobjectionable.

We begin to part company, however, when it comes to Finnis's actual definition of the common good. Here is how Finnis defines the common good:

> a set of conditions which enables the members of a community to attain for
> themselves reasonable objectives, or to realize reasonably for themselves
> the value(s), for the sake of which they have reason to collaborate with each
> other (positively and/or negatively) in a community.[52]

This definition implies that if social conditions make possible the pursuit of *un*reasonable values or objectives, then those conditions must be changed so that people only pursue reasonable objectives. However, the protection of individual rights, as we have defined them, necessarily leaves open the possibility that some will pursue unreasonable values and objectives—such is the very nature of freedom. Finnis's definition, on the other hand, closes off a necessary feature of human freedom. Thus it is clear that what he means by "a set of conditions" is not what we would mean, however close the two theories may appear on the surface. Finnis may wish to claim that the pursuit of reasonable values contributes to the well-being of all whereas the pursuit of unreasonable values do not. *Ceteris paribus* such a claim is unobjectionable. Yet here is a place to recall a point made earlier in this chapter—namely, that conflicting or contradictory principles cannot constitute a conception of the common good. The requirement that only those conditions be allowed that lead to the pursuit of reasonable values conflicts with the conditions that provide for freedom of action. We have argued that the latter condition is the more fundamental and that all other principles must accord with it. Thus the definition of the common good cannot be defined in terms of reasonable action alone.

Our next area of concern centers around the use of the term *co-ordination*. In and of itself the term is not troublesome, but it may have connotations of someone doing the co-ordinating (such as the government). The constructivist connotations of 'co-ordination' are not necessarily evident in Finnis's chapter on the common good. It is clear from our citations above that Finnis also uses 'co-operation' and 'collaboration' as more or less synonymous with 'co-ordination.' However in the chapters on justice and authority, which Finnis claims are integrally connected to his conception of the common good, 'co-ordination' is used almost exclusively. And it is in these chapters that Finnis's most collectivist elements emerge.

It cannot be part of our purpose here to examine in detail Finnis's theory of justice. Instead, we shall look at some of the key elements of his theory of distributive justice, since distributive justice represents one of the most concrete examples of the 'co-ordination problem'. Consider the following:

> A distribution is *distributively just*, . . . if it is a reasonable resolution of a problem of allocating some subject-matter that is essentially common but that needs. . . to be appropriated to individuals.[53]

Obviously the key concept here is 'essentially common'. Finnis leaves us no doubt about the meaning of this phrase:

> A subject-matter is common, . . . if it is part of no individual person and has not been created by anybody, but is apt for use for the benefit of anyone and everyone: for example, solar energy and light, the sea, its bed and its contents, land and its contents, rivers, air and airspace, the moon. . . .[54]

Once we know what constitutes a common subject-matter, the problem then becomes one of 'appropriating' it to particular individuals.

We believe that all the basic assumptions of Finnis's analysis can be denied. In the first place, it is by no means evident that the state (or the legal system, or the council of economic advisors) should be the one that determines to whom these 'common' resources should go. It might be the case that the market should allocate all of these goods. Since Finnis makes no distinction between market and command forms of allocation, his theory culminates in a command assumption—one that is not even required by his own principles. Unlike Finnis's approach of deciding to whom resources are to flow, the market mechanism requires from the state only the enforcement of a set of procedural rules. Moreover, Finnis begs the whole question in his definition of a 'just' distribution by never spelling out what the "problem of allocating some subject-matter" is supposed to be. If the problem to be solved is one of economic efficiency and increased material wealth, Finnis's command approach lacks a historical precedent for success.

Secondly, Finnis's list of common goods leaves little that would not be common and operates on the status quo assumption that what is called common now *must* therefore be a common good (for instance, water and air). The 'fact' that these goods are essentially common is, however, refuted by Finnis's own list; for "the land and its contents" are in large measure private, at least in this country. Moreover, we fail to understand the rationale for communizing the list of resources Finnis presents but not their products. Surely the reason cannot be that these resources are not in fact subject to privatization, for too much work to the contrary has been done of late.[55] If the reason is that markets in consumer goods better serve the common good than markets in resources, then Finnis has not made this argument, and it is dubious anyway. Finally, it is difficult to understand how the state could control all the resources that go into production and not the production process itself.

Thirdly, we would simply deny that there are any *scarce* resources that are "part of no individual person and [have] not been created by anybody". There is, for example, no such thing as solar energy apart from the individuals who employ their intelligence towards producing it from the generally non-scarce resource of sunlight. Even on Finnis's own principles we can see no difference between the person who creates a new photo-electric cell and the person who manufactures a toaster, the latter of which is presumably allowed to be controlled privately. Our objection, of course, cuts deeper than this, since we are saying that natural resources in some degree of scarcity simply are not human goods until some individual has turned those resources into something others can use. If, on the other hand, the resource is not scarce, there would be no problem of co-ordination anyway.

It seems then that Finnis's list of essentially common material goods is either arbitrary or begs the whole question about whether such "subject-matters" are the proper province of the state. Indeed, a further unquestioned (and unargued for) assumption is that legislators, when given the power of distributing goods and designing the laws to do so, are inclined to consider the common good, and that it is a perversion of the natural course of things when they do otherwise. Human history does not lend such an assumption much credence, and unless one has an idealistic vision of legislators, all the incentives of such power are to the contrary of impartiality and justice. Nevertheless, given Finnis's assumption, one would expect that the value of a market order is strictly instrumental. All biases are to be towards community control unless the market can establish unequivocally, on a case-by-case basis, that its mechanism is superior. Consider the following:

> private ownership will be a requirement of justice, provided that the increased stock of goods yielded by such a regime is not hoarded by a class of successful private owners but is made available by appropriate mechanisms. . . to all members of the community, in due measure.[56]

And furthermore:

> Where owners will not perform these duties [providing employment, grants and loans for hospitals, schools, cultural centers, orphanages, etc.]. . . then public authority may rightly help them to perform them by devising and implementing schemes of distribution, e.g., by 'redistributive' taxation for purposes of 'social welfare', or by a measure of expropriation.[57]

It is not only clear from these remarks that private ownership is of instrumental value only, but also that this kind of extensive state monitoring of productive activities hardly qualifies as a system of private ownership. We would maintain, on the contrary, that (were a choice desirable) the biases on such matters ought to be reversed—that is, unless public ownership or control can be shown to be unequivocally superior to the market, the market ought to be preferred.

It is the state which has only instrumental value. The market, we would argue, has both instrumental value and 'intrinsic' value, since the market is based upon the principle of a respect for individual rights. Despite Finnis's comments on the purpose of the state being the enhancement of individual flourishing, his interpretation of his own remarks actually issues in a theory where the individual exists for the sake of the community and not in his own right. This charge can best be substantiated by examining his brief critique of Nozick. In response to Nozick's argument that redistribution schemes based on coercive taxation are unjust, Finnis counters by denying Nozick's basic principle: he denies that voluntary transfers of goods to which one is entitled confer entitlement, which would make coercive interference with the transfer unjust. Finnis denies this principle by claiming that what one is entitled to in the *first* place includes the obligation to contribute to redistribution schemes if called for by the common good. Thus Nozick cannot complain about interference, since such interference actually constitutes the enforcement of property rights.[58]

Finnis's argument only 'works' at the expense of entitlement itself or on a view of entitlement that regards entitlements as conferred by the community. Of course, if the community can confer entitlements it can also revoke them, meaning that individuals are trustees of resources and not entitled to them. On such a view, any individual's success is continually subject to expropriation whenever the community feels it would enhance the common good. Finnis's principle thus seems to be that one owes the community the products of one's efforts even before they have been produced, for to build into the notion of 'entitlement' an obligation for redistribution is to place the lives of individuals in perpetual mortgage to the community.

Presumably we have the obligation to submit to redistribution because of the benefits we enjoy through community life.[59] However, being the recipient of benefits does not necessarily produce an obligation. For example, there are quite often positive externalities produced by corporations that we are recipients of. No one argues, though, that we are thereby obligated to part with some of our resources as payment to those corporations. We submit, then, that we have satisfied our obligation to the common good by respecting the rights of others. The positive neighborhood effects of respecting rights may be a reason for respecting them, but they do not generate additional obligations on our part. Finnis's system, on the other hand, is grounded in the view that an individual's life is conferred to him by the permission of others.

It should be no surprise, then, that *co-ordination* is the dominant term in Finnis's theory of justice. Given Finnis's collectivistic outlook, there would indeed be a lot for the state to co-ordinate. There is even a quasi-Marxist strain in Finnis's thought to the effect that the more successful and complex a society becomes, the more need there is for authoritative control. Consider the following:

> it is also true that the greater the intelligence and skill of a group's members. . . the *more* authority and regulation may be required, to enable that group to achieve its common purpose, common good.[60]

Market processes are immediately ruled out of court as an appropriate means for dealing with increasing complexity. For Finnis (following Simon) there are only two ways of co-ordinating action: unanimity and authority.[61] Since the "exchange of promises" falls under the first way, market processes must be a species of unanimity. But "unanimity is particularly far beyond the bounds of practical possibility in the political community".[62] Thus rule by authority is our only choice. We would argue, following Hayek, that market principles are more necessary as society becomes more complex, because no authority can manage the complexity. It is not possible to pursue this line of argument here. Our purpose at this stage is to simply substantiate our earlier claim that Finnis's doctrine is authoritarian.

We have argued that Finnis's theory of the common good, although appearing to conform to our own in essentials, is deceptive. Unlike our theory, Finnis's rests on the constructivist fallacy, is collectivistic, and is authoritarian. It is, however, fair to say that Finnis's theory does accord with the Aristotelian/Thomistic tradition as it is most commonly presented. Our purpose in this book is to show that this tradition can be seen as compatible with free, productive, and pluralistic societies. The effect of a theory like Finnis's, however, is to mold modern societies according to conceptions better suited to closed and homogeneous societies. This too accords with the usual way the tradition has been presented. Yet we have already seen that it is not necessary that co-operation and co-ordination of common enterprises be the result of some planner or authority, and it is certainly not the case that co-ordination of common enterprises is a unique function of the state. Human beings throughout the community work in concert through voluntary association without the direction of state authorities. Though it is true that the state can be an authority, what differentiates state authority from other forms is that the state possesses a *legal* monopoly on the use of coercion. The unique character of state authority will not be noted, and indeed cannot be, if one fails to differentiate between the community and the state.

ENDS, PLURALISM, AND THE COMMON GOOD

The difficulties with the Aristotelian political tradition discussed above rest on the failure to recognize a basic distinction—one that explains the tradition's inability to fully account for the difference between state authority and other forms of authority. The need for the distinction becomes apparent when one asks: 'How could there be some single end for a society as large and as diverse as the United States? What single end could constitute the United States' common good? What single end could be envisioned by every member of this society?' It is one thing for the Society for the Prevention of Cruelty to Animals or even the Society of Jesus to have a specific end that each of their members seek, but it is quite another thing for a society as large and as diverse as the United States to have such an end.

It should be realized that this difficulty is not *merely* a problem of size. Human beings are very different. Though they are indeed alike in possessing the capacity to reason and choose, their humanity is manifested in numerous ways. Each person's life plan is so different that it is hard to see how there could be a single end everyone could aim to achieve. Moreover, everyone striving to achieve one single end does not seem to be something desirable, for self-actualization is a process that is accomplished in many ways. The common good of political community just cannot be construed as a single end and remain consistent with the self-actualization of each and every person.

The political community is not, despite the insistence of some Aristotelian political theorists, necessarily a human group. As we noted earlier, a human group can exist if and only if there is a single end rationally held in mind by the members of that group. This condition is not met by a political community. Furthermore, it would be neither desirable nor possible for the state with its legal monopoly on the use of physical force to attempt to establish a single end (nor even a limited set of ends) for all. To achieve sufficient universality regarding a single end, it would require creating a society along Orwellian lines, and even then it would fail. A human group is a *noetic* and *moral* entity, and these are the very things that state coercion would destroy. The state is most ill-suited as an institution for the fostering of human groups, since its mode of operation is coercion and not persuasion, discussion, or voluntary agreement. Just as the attempt by the state to coerce virtue in the individual is self-defeating,[63] so too are its efforts in attempting to create human groups.

It might be objected that securing the protection of the right to liberty constitutes a single end, thus contradicting the foregoing argument. If anything that is the object of human purposes qualifies as an end, then obviously protecting liberty is an end. But such a broad conception of 'end' in this context is more misleading than helpful. For surely there is a difference between those conditions that make the pursuit of ends possible and the ends themselves. Nevertheless, it might be argued that it is equally misleading to deny that the protection and promotion of individual rights is an end.

Since there are indeed ambiguities here, we wish to draw a distinction between procedural and determinate ends. A procedural end is the object of a human purpose, the function of which is to define the conditions under which the pursuit of other (determinate) ends will occur but which does not specify what those ends will be or when and how they will be realized. A determinate end, on the other hand, is the object of a human purpose with identifiable characteristics which can be used to help specify appropriate and inappropriate courses of action for the realization of that end. The procedural ends that characterize a political community represent the conditions under which any and all specific forms of human activity can take place. They must, therefore, be as open as possible with respect to the determinate ends they will allow.[64]

Thus, when we deny that there is an end for society as a whole and that a society like the United States does not constitute a human group, we mean to say that there is, in fact, no one determinate conception of human well-being held in the minds of all members of the political community *and* that it would be contrary to the pluralism and freedom necessary for the realization of human well-being if there were such a conception. The value of modern pluralistic societies is that determinate ends are not the object of the sociopolitical structure itself, but are located *within* that structure where they belong. It is not our intention, however, to argue that a common commitment to procedural ends is unnecessary and/or inappropriate. Indeed, since our purpose here is not to reject the Aristotelian tradition, but to retain at least some of its central features, the common pursuit of human well-being gives rise to the necessity for a common commitment to procedural ends.

We believe that the argument presented above does not force us into the kind of atomism so often (and sometimes falsely) associated with liberal political orders. It could be argued, for example, that without some determinate end towards which all members of the political community are working, there would be nothing to unify those members and thus create a sense of community spirit. And without a sense of community spirit, the very principles that serve as the foundation of the political community will be forgotten and thus threaten the existence of the community itself. It is here that the Aristotelian tradition has something to offer. Nevertheless, if this sense of community is not to be an empty ideal, the common bond must be something that *can* be shared by a pluralistic society. The most likely candidate here is a common commitment to a set of procedural principles that promote diversity and encourage individual achievement. There is nothing in the nature of such principles that precludes a common commitment to them accompanied by a communal or shared sense of their worth and value. Indeed, a shared sense of commitment to the protection of individual rights is vital to their maintenance, since that sense of commitment helps in the protection of those rights and keeps those in power from expropriating them.

Nevertheless, Aristotelian political theorists must recognize that a political community is not a human group in the sense that clubs, fraternal organizations, corporations, and the like are human groups. There is no determinate end functioning as a goal that defines the roles of the members in society, and it is inappropriate to try to organize a political community along such lines. For as we have already noted, the coercive efforts to create such an organization tend to destroy the very sense of commitment that is desired. And once Aristotelians recognize these points, the desire to construe the promotion of the common good of the political community along lines other than simply protecting the natural right to liberty will lessen.

NORTON AND THE COMMON GOOD

Despite our foregoing criticisms of 'the tradition', our conception of that tradition is broadly enough defined to allow us to conclude this chapter with an examination of a position much closer to our own. In *Personal Destinies*,[65] David Norton also has a theory of distributive justice, but that theory is not grounded in the effective rejection of the importance of individualism as is Maritain's theory, nor is it a species of the legalistic collectivism we found in Finnis. Indeed, it is perhaps significant that Norton does not talk in terms of the common good at all. Given the individualist character of Norton's version of telelogical eudaimonism, to talk of a good that is defined in terms of the collective rather than in terms of individuals could be more misleading than helpful. Nevertheless, there are values common to all which serve as the foundation of justice and thus make Norton suitable for inclusion here.

Norton claims that the foundation of justice is the following:

> The foundation of justice is the presupposition of the unique, irreplaceable, potential worth of every person, and forms of sociality that neglect or contradict this presupposition . . . deal justice a mortal wound at the outset.[66]

From this conception of the common potential worth of every individual Norton develops a theory of entitlement. At the lower limit each person is entitled to what is necessary for self-actualization, including food, shelter, and decent treatment. "At the upper limit [one] is entitled to those *commensurate* goods whose potential worth [one] can maximally actualize in accordance with his destiny. . . "[67] It is the "upper limit" that is the focal point in Norton's discussion. His basic claim is that since not all goods are suitable (commensurate) with what one is, one will only be entitled to those goods consistent with one's personal calling. Philosophers are not entitled to Ferraris (even if they could afford them), although a person who could utilize the potentialities of that machine without sacrifice to his basic life's work might be so entitled. Thus the following passage offers a good summary of Norton's position:

> According to normative individualism, all persons possess an equal but limited entitlement in virtue of equivalence of potential worth, while differential entitlements accrue among individuals according to differences in degree of self-actualization. [68]

The first question one is likely to have about such a theory is: Who is to decide whether a good is or is not commensurate with the pursuit of one's personal excellence? Norton's answer to this question is that individuals will decide for themselves. Unfortunately this answer is qualified in a way that opens the door for continual interference in people's lives:

> Under normative individualism the final ground of the distinction between true and false desires is the nature of the individual himself, and he himself is the final authority. But by the emergent nature of individualism the exercise of this final authority by the individual is deferred until true individuation is attained, and meanwhile others must share with him the responsibility for the determination of his true interests. [69]

The implication of this passage is that others can specify one's entitlements if the person in question has not yet reached a stage of "true individuation". Although the door is here opened for massive amounts of control and/or snooping from one's neighbors, Norton does not pursue such a line of argument. Indeed, he goes out of his way to argue for almost the opposite conclusion.

It is important to recognize that Norton feels compelled to avoid the subjectivist conclusion that whatever one desires is what is good for one. He therefore believes that there are objective goods commensurate in different ways with different individuals, and this seems to require more than letting everyone decide for themselves (through voluntary trade) what they are entitled to. We believe, however, that Norton has pursued a line of reasoning that is (a) not required by his principles, and (b) actually contrary to or subversive of those principles. Our main objection centers on the fact that Norton's theory of justice (as he interprets it) seems to abandon the developmental quality of the pursuit of individual excellence in favor of a theory with static or legalistic qualities.

Suppose we begin our analysis with Norton's own example. A

philosopher has appropriated for himself a Ferrari. Since Ferraris are incommensurate with the nature of being a philosopher, this philosopher is not entitled to the car. In fact, the philosopher has committed an act of injustice, for "injustice consists in deprivation of what is claimed with entitlement, and in advancement of unentitled claims".[70] Assuming that there is no race car enthusiast going without a Ferrari, the injustice here consists in advancing an unentitled claim. Surely, however, this conception of injustice and unentitlement is much too strong. If the philosopher bought the car in a voluntary transaction, no matter how ill-suited he may be for using the car, he would still *own* the car and thus be entitled to it in some sense. We have no reason to believe that Norton is advancing a theory of ownership which holds that legitimate ownership occurs only when the good is commensurate with one's calling. We are unclear, however, whether Norton would call for the forcible expropriation of the car by the state. (In fact, we doubt it.) It would seem, then, that Norton is using *injustice* here in a moral sense and not necessarily in a political one. If so, he leaves the reader hanging on the difference between the two.

Perhaps we could grant, for the moment, that the philosopher who spends his (limited) time and resources on the Ferrari is being untrue to himself and is thus committing an injustice. If we make this assumption, it does not follow that the philosopher should have the car expropriated. A further argument is required, and this argument is presumably given in the first clause of the definition of injustice. The philosopher who cannot use the car properly is presumably depriving someone else of the car who could use it properly. However, this argument is plausible only if a static zero-sum model of resource acquisition is assumed. And it seems to us that Norton does adhere to this model in his argument. That is to say, he seems to assume that the purchase of the Ferrari by the philosopher is at the expense of someone else who could use the car properly.

When confronted with the question of resource acquisition and wealth, there are only two models to choose from: the exploitation model and the creationist model. The former holds that all wealth is gained at the expense of someone else; the goods one person receives are essentially depriving someone else of those goods. The second model holds that wealth is created. Thus, one person's gain is not necessarily another's loss, and the acquisition of a good by one person does not imply the loss of that good to another. The exploitation model conceives of goods and services as baked in a finite pie waiting to be 'distributed'. The creationist theory holds that the size of the pie can expand or contract depending on the creative energies of market participants. The exploitation model is static; the creationist model is developmental. It is beyond the scope of this chapter to argue for one of these models over the other. It should be clear from all our remarks to this point that we would adhere to the creationist model. Most Aristotelians, however, seem to favor the exploitation model, perhaps because Aristotle's own social situation, and most of human history, have been structured along such lines. Capitalist economic systems, nevertheless, have shown that the exploitation model is not a necessary feature of social life.

But apart from the economics, one would have thought that Norton's own principles would have led him in the direction of the creationist position. A major theme of his book is the creative power of individuals and the limitless diversity of potential goods they have to offer. Had Norton seen that the creationist model better fits with his own argument, he might have noted that the illiterate's possession of 'too many' books need not be in any sense a deprivation of the philosopher who could always use more books. Thus the philosopher is not unentitled to the Ferrari because of what he has done to others, but only because of what he is doing to himself. And even with respect to what the philosopher is doing to himself, Norton has not shown that anyone else has the right to expropriate the car from the philosopher.

We have, however, moved too quickly and conceded too much. Being a philosopher does not preclude the possibility of being an enthusiast for Ferraris any more than it precludes skill as a golfer. Since individuals are a composite of numerous potentialities for Norton, there can be no a priori incompatibility between Ferraris and philosophy (although common sense would render their compatibility less probable than others). Indeed, Norton himself argues that such determinations of commensurability must be done a posteriori.[71] Yet Norton also argues throughout his book that eudaimonia is a continuing (and continual) activity and not a plateau of cessation. Thus, even a posteriori, it is not clear that the philosopher is not 'entitled' to the Ferrari, for maybe he believes he can handle it properly and still be a philosopher, or maybe he simply wants to *find out* if he and the Ferrari are compatible. Perhaps the philosopher simply wants to hold out that possibility for himself in the future. To argue that the philosopher must *prove* his competence with the Ferrari before he can purchase one is to stifle exploration and turn the a posteriori into the a priori. Norton's own earlier arguments for the complexity and diversity of individual achievement are so convincing that the only practical and sensible solution is to allow the individual complete freedom of choice and to have an entitlement theory that is minimalist and procedural. This may court subjectivism, but that is a price worth paying given that the alternative is to stifle individual achievement.

Norton's response to our preceding remarks might be to rely on his concept of authority. Consider the following:

> How much food is too much? How much sex is too much? How much conviviality, or fame, or influence? The true authority resides within the individual himself, and were self-knowledge perfect no other authority would be necessary or desirable. Because self-knowledge is imperfect and in many cases non-existent, however, claims must be susceptible of objective validation.[72]

In cases in which the individual does not have complete self-knowledge, some authority is presumably supposed to step in and correctly organize entitlements. The practical difficulties of this approach are obvious and insurmountable, and that can be said without giving up the claim that such authorities can exist from time to time, or without abandoning the claim that individuals do not always know what is good for them. Yet the real issue here is not practical but theoretical. Does being in a position of knowing what is good for someone else confer the authority to restructure the other's use of his resources? In some cases (for example parents and children) the answer is yes, although it is unclear whether the affirmative answer is given because of the knowledge possessed or the special relationship involved. In any case, Norton never spells out exactly why such authority would be conferred, and in most cases we do not believe that authority is conferred in this way. We may know, for example, that a colleague of ours should give up the afternoon soap operas and read more philosophy, but that does not confer upon us the authority to confiscate his television.

It seems to us that conversation, peer pressure, economic sanctions, and other forms of gentle and not so gentle persuasion are more in order in response to incommensurate uses of material goods than is coercive interference. Because many (or most) of us are imperfect with respect to self-knowledge, Norton's proposal seems to amount to a vision of the citizenry as being in perpetual adolescence; this vision violates his opening principle of the potential worth of all individuals. If respect for potential worth of all individuals really is the foundation of justice, it can only be respected by allowing the individual to be entitled to his *mistakes* as well as his successes. A conception of authority which allows individual self-determination only when there is perfect self-knowledge removes a necessary feature of what individuals are entitled to. It may seem a paradox to claim that respect for the individual is shown just as much by granting them entitlement to incommensurate goods as to commensurate ones, but reflection will indicate that persons of integrity would wish nothing else for themselves. And the only way to encourage that kind of integrity in others is to treat others according to the same principle. Norton's principle would only foster dependency and retard development.

Minimalist and procedural entitlements that encourage marketlike social structures also encourage individual flourishing. This claim is not utopian, for numerous examples can be cited of people who continually thwart their own best interests under such an arrangement. But the operative principle is nevertheless that the individual is responsible for his or her own life and that he or she is both entitled to the consequences of choices made (favorable or unfavorable) and also not entitled to interfere in the lives of others without their consent. This form of treating others with respect *is* the common good; and even if we are wrong in some of the details of our analysis, our basic point is that all forms of the common good must be derivative from this principle.

It is interesting to conclude by noticing that Norton bases justice in love. This is not the sentimental love of the guitar mass, but rather an "aspiration to higher value".[73] Moreover, this love is based upon "the presupposition that within every person is the regulatory principle of justice, to be manifested in that self-love that is the foundation of love of others".[74] Norton teaches that narrow self-love (what he calls egoism) must be expanded and deepened into a true-form of eudaimonic individualism. It is our contention that the market encourages this by setting the appropriate conditions for human flourishing. But in the end, neither the market nor any other social arrangement can replace the individual's own responsibility for the quality of his life. Herein lies the basis for rejecting those conceptions of the common good that posit an end outside the individual and for society as a whole.

5

COMMERCIALISM, FRIENDSHIP, AND LIBERTY

Simplicity and truth of character are not produced by the constraint of laws, nor by the authority of the state, and absolutely no one can be forced or legislated into a state of blessedness; the means required are faithful and brotherly admonition, sound education, and, above all, free use of the individual judgment.

— Spinoza, *Tractatus Theologico-Politicus*

COMMERCE AND FRIENDSHIP

By now it is a familiar ploy of critics of liberal social orders to point to Aristotle as an alternative to liberalism. Liberalism is said to be rooted in individualistic calculative self-interest, whereas Aristotle is thought to posit the priority of the community over the individual, co-operation, and even friendship. But we agree with Bernard Yack when he claims that these critics of liberalism have over-romanticized and overcollectivized Aristotle's own views on the nature of political and social life.[1] Our argument, like Yack's, will not be that Aristotle is somehow *really* a liberal political theorist in disguise. Instead, our argument is that some of the central elements of Aristotle's social theory are not incompatible with, or can be modified to support, the kind of liberalism we have been advancing.

To accomplish our end, we shall concentrate mainly on the concept of Aristotelian friendship. As Cooper points out, nearly one-fifth of the *Nicomachean Ethics* is devoted to the issue of friendship.[2] Moreover, friendship forms a significant part of Aristotle's political theory through the concept of civic friendship. It seems to us, therefore, that if a case for liberalism can be made on Aristotelian grounds, friendship must be examined. To some extent we have already discussed this concept in Chapter 2. But there our focus was primarily on 'character-friendships'. In this chapter, on the other hand, we intend to concentrate mainly on 'friendships of utility', or what Cooper more properly calls "advantage-friendships". We shall argue that advantage-friendships are the basis of commercial orders, and properly so. Moreover, efforts to model social orders on any other form of friendship are bound to fail and are contrary to the implications, and often the text, of Aristotle's social theory. Our examination of advantage friendships should not only vindicate liberalism from the charge of being incompatible with Aristotelianism, but also indicate the proper place of such relationships within an Aristotelian natural-rights perspective.

Advantage-Friendships

Aristotle clearly takes character-friendships to be the paradigm case of friendship. This raises the question of whether, and in what sense, advantage-friendships are really forms of friendship. In this connection we believe it is most instructive to look at Cooper who, on the one hand, takes relationships of utility or advantage to be a form of friendship under certain conditions, while on the other hand eschews most commercial transactions as qualifying as advantage-friendships.[3] In Cooper's interpretation of Aristotle, friendships exist only when "the friend will wish his friend whatever is good, for his own sake, and it will be mutually known to them that this well-wishing is reciprocated".[4] In friendships of utility or advantage-friendships, the good wished is to be benefited. This is a lower order good from the one wished for in character-friendships. Thus the type of good involved, rather than the character of the personal relation, demarcates the type of friendship. This is because all forms of friendship, according to Cooper, must wish another good for *his own sake*. Personal relations that treat the other as means to one's own good do not qualify as friendships of any type.

Although Cooper claims that Aristotle emphasizes the altruistic ingredient of friendship, Cooper more properly and commonly employs *unself-interested* to refer to the wish that one's friend achieve a type of good for his own sake. Therefore, to form a friendship there must be an unself-interested concern for the other person's good. This would seem to preclude all advantage-friendships (certainly commercial ones), because one person's concern for another seems to be purely instrumental—that is, one takes an interest in the other for one's own sake and not for the sake of the other. It should be noted that Cooper does not require that the unself-interested concern for the other be the only concern, nor apparently the primary one. Nevertheless, such a concern must be present for a relationship to qualify as a friendship.

Although commercial relationships seem to be precluded by Cooper's insistence on the presence of unself-interested goodwill, he allows that certain forms of commercial relationships do qualify as advantage-friendships. Consider the following:

> Friends of all three types . . . wish for their friend's well-being out of concern for the friend himself. This is as true of a businessman who, through frequent profitable association, becomes friends with a regular customer, as it is of a husband and wife or two intimate companions who love one another for their characters. Such a businessman looks first for mutual profit from his friendship, but that does not mean that he always calculates his services to his customer by the standard of profit. Finding the relationship on the whole profitable, he likes this customer and is willing to do him services otherwise than as a means to his own ultimate profit. So long as the general context of profitability remains, the well-wishing can proceed unchecked; the profitability to the well-wisher that is assumed in the well-wishing is not that of the *particular* service rendered (the particular action done in the other person's interest) but that of the overall fabric of the relationship. Here, then, one has a complex and subtle mixture of self-seeking and unself-interested well-wishing and well-doing.[5]

This passage is instructive because it shows (a) that merely having an advantageous relationship with someone does not thereby produce an advantage-friendship, and (b) that commercial relationships can carry with them a mutually unself-interested concern for the other provided the context of profitability remains. Notice, however, that commercial transactions which do not possess the 'regular-customer' feature would not qualify as advantage-friendships.

It is our view that Cooper's interpretation of Aristotle on advantage-friendships is mistaken both as an interpretation of Aristotle and as a theory of advantage-friendships in general. First, Cooper's interpretation fails to explain the phenomena. Consider the case of the businessman cited above. In this case the businessman, after repeated associations, comes to *like* his customer (or vice versa) and may occasionally go out of his way to do something special for him, even though that special favor may not have been necessary. Notice, however, that it is not advantage that matters here, but rather the personal qualities of the parties involved. Presumably on Cooper's account there would be no friendship if the businessman had decided, as a matter of good business practice, to give regular customers special treatment simply to keep them as regulars. Consequently, the advantages involved become a contingent factor in the relationship this businessman now has to his customer. Cooper has described not what advantage-friendships are, but how a higher form of friendship can grow out of contexts that originated for mutual advantage.[6] In essence, Cooper treats all forms of friendship as more or less complete versions of character-friendships. The advantages being received are incidental (or becoming so) to what is essential about the friendship (namely, the unself-interested relationship now being formed).

It is our view that Cooper has gotten the matter entirely backwards. Advantage-friendships are only incidentally character-friendships, but are essentially defined by the advantage each person self-interestedly seeks to gain by the association. Under Cooper's interpretation the reverse is the case. In this connection Aquinas saw the matter correctly:

> [O]f those who love one another for the sake of utility, one does not love the other for the sake of the other but inasmuch as he receives from the other some good for himself. . . . Thus they do not love their friend for what he is in himself but for what is incidental to him, his utility or pleasantness. Therefore, friendships of this sort plainly are not friendships essentially but incidentally, ...[7]

If Aquinas is correct, the door is open to seeing advantage-friendships as a type of co-operative association, but one which lacks the essential ingredient of a true friendship. Since our purpose here is not to examine character-friendships, we will allow Cooper that wishing another good for their own sake is that essential ingredient. The other types of friendships would involve ingredients found in the essential kind, but would lack the essential component in its full sense (see below).

It is also our contention that commercial relations can be considered paradigmatic forms of advantage-friendships, and in this connection

Cooper has a most interesting footnote.[8] In that footnote he discusses Aristotle's contention that there are two types of advantage friendships: one governed by explicitly agreed-upon exchanges, and the other by the characters of the two parties to the exchange. An example of the former might be a signed contract. An example of the latter might be a hand-shake. We need not dwell on this distinction here because we bring it up again below. Cooper's thesis is that the former type of friendship (call it an 'L-friendship', for legal friendship) is a purely commercial transaction and thus no friendship at all, "not even an advantage-friendship". L-friendships lack the element of mutual unself-interested good will. The second type (call them 'C-friendships') can have elements of good will and be a type of friendship. The *Nicomachean Ethics*, therefore, removes essentially commercial transactions from the realm of friendships.

The *Eudemian Ethics*, on the other hand, offers a different conclusion. Consider these remarks by Cooper:

> The EE begin by marking off the same two types of advantage-friendship (1242b31–32), . . . But as the argument proceeds it becomes apparent . . . that this division is provisional only; the latter type is really a confused relationship, in which the parties cannot decide whether to treat one another as *real* friends or as advantage-friends . . . Thus, in this passage Aristotle actually implies that it is only where an association *is* purely commercial that it can count as an advantage-friendship . . . .[9]

Cooper goes on to suggest that the *Nicomachean Ethics* (*NE*) and not the *Eudemian Ethics* (*EE*) should be taken as the final word on the subject; but even Cooper admits that Aristotle "refuses to abandon completely the earlier ideas which are causing the trouble."[10]

If Cooper is correct in noting a shift of doctrine between the two treatises, we believe Aristotle got it right in the *EE*. We are not, however, persuaded that the differences between the two treatises amount to anything other than a slightly more ambiguous treatment in the *NE*—not a substantive shift of doctrine. The *EE* is more forthright in proclaiming that there is no single or defining element that pervades all three forms of friendship. Consider, for example, the following passage.

> Therefore to confine the use of the term friend to primary friendship [i.e. character-friendships] is to do violence to observed facts, and compels one

to talk paradoxes; though it is not possible to bring all friendship under one definition. The only remaining alternative, therefore, is, that in a sense the primary sort of friendship alone is friendship, but in a sense all sorts are, not as having a common name by accident and standing in a merely chance relationship to one another, nor yet as falling under one species, but rather as related to one thing. (*EE*, 1236b20–27.)

What Aristotle means by "related to one thing" is that all forms of friendship have a relationship to the primary form (character-friendships) but are not reducible to it. In other words, the other forms of friendship cannot be *defined* in terms of the primary form, nor do they stand to it as instances to their species; rather, the different forms of friendship stand in different relationships to the primary form while exhibiting one or more of the attributes of that primary form. Yet, since the relationship between the the various types of friendships is not "accidental' or by 'chance', we would also expect there to be a general conceptual frame-work for the term *friendship*. It is somewhat difficult to know for certain, given the ambiguity of the texts, what that framework might be. But we would suggest that Martin Ostwald's rendering of *philia* is closest to correct, provided it too is not understood in the mistaken way of attempt-ing to define all forms of friendship in terms of the primary one: *philia* "designates the relationship between a person and any other person(s) or being(s) which that person regards as peculiarly his own and to which he has a peculiar attachment".[11]

It seems to us that the attempt to define all forms of friendships in terms of unself-interested good will restricts the range of friendships and logically functions in a genus-to-species form. This violates the message of the preceding passage from the *EE*. However, we also admit that Aristotle's discussion, especially when both treatises are considered, is not without ambiguity. In the end, therefore, the logical and textual am-biguities in Aristotle open the way for alternative interpretations. Given what we have argued above, our approach will be to consider commer-cial transactions as paradigm forms of advantage-friendships. We believe this interpretation, especially in light of Ostwalds interpretation of *philia*, can be adopted without doing an injustice to the spirit of Aristotle's doctrine.

Commerce and Advantage-Friendship

Part of the problem in regarding commercial transactions as forms of friendship, however attenuated they may be, is that such relationships are clearly self-interested. In our culture, as Websters shows, *self-interested* means "selfish" which in turn means "without consideration for others". We shall argue that selfish behavior is possible in commercial transactions, but not essential. What is essential for commercial relationships is described in the following passage from Adam Smith.

> Man has almost constant occasion for the help of his brethren, and it is in vain for him to expect it from their benevolence only. He will be more likely to prevail if he can interest their self-love in his favor, and shew them that it is for their own advantage to do for him what he requires of them . . . and it is in this manner that we obtain from one another the far greater part of those good offices which we stand in need of.[12]

What this passage shows is that market transactions require an interest in others. It is true that this interest is a means to satisfying one's own interest, but it is an interest in others nonetheless. Suppose then, following Ostwald, that what all friendships have in common is an interest in others. Some of these (the highest types) have this interest in an unself-interested sense. Other types, however, carry a genuine interest in others, but not for their own sake. Market exchanges require a genuine interest in others, because one's own success depends upon getting others to see one's own interest as their interest; in other words, sharing an interest.

Oddly enough, command economies do not require an interest in others, for obedience, and not persuasion, is their mode of eliciting co-operation. Command structures can, and often do, embody selfishness (understood as lack of concern for the interests of others) in a pure form, since those issuing the commands need pay no heed to anyone's interests but their own. Voluntary market transactions, on the other hand, will not occur if both parties do not see the relationship as mutually advantageous.[13] This shared interest and advantage, at least for the duration of the transaction, embodies several features that can be found in higher forms of friendship: mutual advantage, mutual interest, co-operation, unity of purpose, and even good will.

If we take the simple case of a two-person, two-commodity, voluntary exchange, all the features of friendship just mentioned can be found. Mutual advantage is obvious, and mutual interest is demonstrated by what Smith rightly perceived to be necessary for voluntary exchange to occur. Co-operation is manifested by the conclusion of the exchange. Only unity of purpose and good will remain. The first is more easily understood if we posit a third-party interference in the transaction. If we assume that the third party wishes to prevent the transaction by force and not by offering a more advantageous trade to one of the parties, then it is evident that both the original parties share a unity of purpose in their desire to complete the transaction. Both would see the third party as a threat to what the two of them wish to jointly accomplish (the trade), and it is this sense of joint accomplishment that expresses their unity of purpose.

The case of 'good will' is more problematic than the other characteristics—hence our use of scare quotes. For example, Aristotle claims that mutually recognized good will is necessary for friendship. (*NE*, 1156a5) However, he also claims that advantage-friendships do not contain good will. (*NE*, 1167a12) Cooper's arguments demonstrate that good will (understood as wishing the other well for his own sake) can be part of advantage friendships, but our argument implies that this kind of good will is not essential to advantage friendships and does not characterize the most common feature of such friendships. In this connection, two avenues of discussion are open to us: (1) refrain from using the concept of good will in advantage-friendships, but employ a more rudimentary form of the term; and (2) recognize that there is an abstract sense ot the term that underlies advantage-friendships but which factors in only obliquely in any specific case. The second of these will be discussed during our discussion of civic friendship below.

If we cannot characterize advantage-friendships as possessing good will because each party does not wish for the other's good for the other's own sake, then perhaps there is something *like* good will present here. We believe that what is present is simply 'wishing the other's good'. In any voluntary trade, one wants the other to obtain what he believes good because it is the means to achieving what one desires for oneself. This is the means by which, at least during the specific transaction, one comes to regard the other as 'peculiarly his own and to which he has a peculiar attachment'. If this wishing for the other's good is mutually recognized, as it would be if the trade occurs, then an advantage-friendship is present. What is absent here is the wishing for good *for the sake of* the other. Nevertheless, it is the wishing for another's good that forms the basis of good will proper. Furthermore, we believe that it is this idea of merely wishing another good that is tacitly understood by Aristotle to keep relations of mutual advantage in accord with the 'friendliness' exhibited by the primary form of friendship. And just as good will by itself does not imply a friendship (because one might have good will towards someone who does not know of it), neither does merely wishing for another's good imply an advantage-friendship, for we can also wish for the good of someone we do not know. Therefore, advantage-friendships, like the primary form, do depend upon mutually recognized wishing for the other's good. A wants B to get what he wants so A can get what A wants. This explains the incentive businesspeople have to get *satisfied* customers.

In many respects, then, advantage-friendships share components found in character-friendships. Of course, as Aristotle points out these friendships are prone to disputes (*NE*, 1162b5-20) and break down easily because utilities change. (*NE*, 1156a22) But they belong in the category of friendships because of the similarities to the highest form just mentioned. In addition to what we have argued above, we would add that advantage-friendships have a range of forms that more or less approximate character-friendships. At the top of the range are transactions like those described in Cooper's example of the regular customer. Here one is not sure whether it is real friendship or advantage-friendship that binds the two together. (*EE*, 1242b35–40) At the lowest end of the scale would be those transactions in which one party plays upon the weaknesses of the other to gain a quick trade. Here the high-pressure salesperson comes to mind and the transaction exists on the border of co-operation and exploitation. At the center, however, are the normal voluntary transactions that result in mutually recognized 'gains from trade' for both the parties. These central cases are the essence of commercial relationships, for too much of the high end of the scale would lower trading volume and too much of the low end would breed distrust and destroy the conditions of trade themselves.

As a final distinction under the current heading, we would like to argue that advantage-friendships fall into two basic categories: formal and personal. This distinction is founded upon Aristotle's distinction between moral and legal friendships of utility (i.e., 'C-friendships' and 'L-friendships' mentioned earlier). (*NE*, ll62b23–37) In the legal type of friendship the terms are made explicit, whereas the moral type relies on some element of trust. For Aristotle, trust in a commercial setting means that an advantage would be returned at some future time rather than immediately upon receipt. The one party therefore trusts the other to return the favor. Aristotle seems to associate the legal form more directly with commercial transactions where payment is given at the time the benefit is received. Yet Aristotle's limited experience with types of commercial relationships, when compared to our own, somewhat restricts the usefulness of his discussion of his own distinction.[14] We have therefore chosen to use different terms which bear a resemblance to Aristotle's own terms, but which do not require an adherence to Aristotle's own discussion.

Formal friendships of advantage are those relationships governed by clearly understood legal, contractual, or customary rules.[15] One's contractual relationship with one's employer would be an example, as would most shopping trips to the local mall (since prices are marked and both parties know reasonably well what their roles are). Personal friendships of advantage, on the other hand, are transactions not grounded essentially upon explicit formal rules. Attending a garage sale or swapping collector's items might be examples here. Many small businesses, when they first get started, are grounded in personal friendships of advantage among the founding partners. In our society, although most noncommercial friendships of advantage would fall under the category of personal, most commercial transactions come under the category of formal.

Even though Aristotle correctly identifies an important distinction, he fails to draw a connection between them and seems to place a higher value on the moral (personal) types of advantage-friendships. Nevertheless, the connection between the two can be accounted for within Aristotle's theory, and this connection considerably lessens the reasons for giving a higher value to the personal form. What Aristotle fails to realize is that the personal forms of advantage-friendships inevitably transform themselves into the formal variety if they are sustained over a period of time. Aristotle notes that advantage-friendships are prone to dispute and misunderstanding. There are strong incentives, therefore, to formalize the transaction so that both parties know what to expect and what their responsibilities are. Moreover, economists are correct to note that the increased certainty and clarity of responsibility makes transactions more efficient, leading to increasing gains and advantages for all.[16] In other words, it is simply more advantageous for all concerned if trading for mutual advantage is predominantly formal. A further important incentive to formalize advantage-friendships must also be noted: since, as Aristotle points out (*NE*, 1157a17), bad people can form advantage-friendships as well as good, and since it is often difficult to determine the character of someone else, formalized transactions reduce the risk and information costs characteristic of dealings with relatively unknown persons.

It might be argued that Aristotle is right to attach a higher value to personal friendships of advantage, since these are more like true friendships by possessing more human and 'friendly' qualities. Yet formal friendships of advantage are like true friendships also: they are more stable and less prone to dispute than their personal counterparts.[17] In addition, the explicit terms allow for future planning and co-operation that is difficult with purely personal forms of advantage-friendships. The problem with holding that personal friendships of advantage are more friendly—truer friendships—than formal friendships of advantage is that it assumes that character-friendships are a species (a universal notion) and that advantage-friendships are but instances of this kind of relationship. Consequently, all advantage-friendships turn out to be little more than poor cases of the primary sort. Such an assumption misconstrues the way Aristotle understands *friendship*. As *EE* 1236b20–27 has shown, there is no way to bring all cases of friendship under one definition, and so there is no theoretical reason to attach a higher value to personal friendships of advantage than formal ones. And clearly the evolution of commercial systems indicates that people find it more advantageous to associate on explicit terms.[18] Saying this in no way implies that the human qualities more evident in personal advantage-friendships are not to be valued. Rather, it is to say only that since it is advantage that is being sought, formal relationships more effectively secure that advantage.

Civic Friendship

Aristotle claims that lawgivers are more concerned to foster friendship among their citizens than they are with promoting justice. (*NE*, 1155a23–24) This claim raises the question of the kind of friendship Aristotle is speaking of here. *Civic friendship* is the term used by Aristotle, but is this form of friendship a fourth kind or a version of one of the three main types? As we shall see, Aristotle considers civic friendship as falling under one of the three main types—friendships of advantage. Locating civic friendship under the category of advantage-friendships implies that civic associations are not, and cannot be, associations of character-friendships. There is a temptation to interpret Aristotle's political writings as requiring, in an ideal sense, a community where all are friends of virtue. After all, Aristotle says that although states may be founded out of need, they continue "in existence for the sake of the good life" (*Politics*, 1252b30). And he also states that "the same things are best both for individuals and for states, and these are the things which the legislator ought to implant in the minds of his citizens". (*Politics*, 1333b36-37.) Therefore, if character-friendships are at least part of what it means to live a good life, then the best states will be those whose citizens associate for the sake of virtue.

It seems to us quite mistaken to try to read Aristotle as holding that citizens should hope to associate with one another as friends of virtue. As Aristotle himself notes, (*EE*, 1245b20–25) it is neither possible nor desirable to have many friends of this type. True friendships must occur in circles much smaller than those which characterize a state. In any case, our purpose here is not strictly exegetical. We wish to explain civic friendship as a form of friendship of advantage and then allow our previous chapters on the common good and rights to explain the connection between civic friendship and the good life proper. In essence, civic friendship is connected to the good life through the 'common good' as we interpreted it earlier. The common good serves to continue the association for mutual advantage as well as provide the necessary social and political conditions that make living the good life possible. It is thus neither advantage without principle nor principle beyond advantage that characterizes the nature of the civic life.

In both the *Nicomachean* and *Eudemian Ethics* Aristotle claims that civic friendships are versions of friendships of advantage. (*NE*, 1159b25–

1160a30; *EE,* 1241a32–1243b35 passim) In many respects, however, the *Eudemian* ethics is clearer on this question than the *Nicomachean.* Consider the following passages:

> Civic friendship on the other hand is constituted in the fullest degree on the principle of utility, for it seems to be the individual's lack of self-sufficiency that makes these unions permanent—since they would have been formed in any case merely for the sake of society. (*EE,* 1242a5–9.)
> Civic friendship is, it is true, based on utility, and fellow-citizens are one another's friends in the same way as different cities are, . . . nor similarly do citizens know one another, when they are not useful to one another. (*EE,* 1242b23–26.)
> Civic friendship looks to equality and to the object, as buyers and sellers do. . . . When, therefore, [friendship] is based on definite agreement, this is civic and legal friendship. (*EE,* 1242b33–36.)

Notice that these passages clearly see civic friendships as friendships of advantage. Furthermore, these passages suggest a more accurate understanding of the relationship between individuals and groups in society than would a theory modeled after character-friendships

Modern readers balk at the idea that civic orders can be founded and maintained on advantage because their understanding of this is informed by Enlightenment social-contract theory. In such theories advantage is understood as a form of self-interest defined as the unprincipled gratification of desire. If the civic association does not satisfy enough of one's personal desires, one will seek to abandon it unless kept in check by Leviathan. The alternative seems to be using character-friendships as the central concept and then judging societies in terms of their conformity to that model. All highly pluralistic and commercial cultures fail to live up to this standard because the overwhelming percentage of one's dealings with others are on an advantage basis. Moreover, the institutions that arise in such cultures are predominantly formal (some would say 'impersonal'), further removing people from the 'personal' qualities that seem to be necessary for friendships. The result, then, is a choice between hard-headed Hobbesian egotism or pollyannish hopes for citizens who love and care for each other as good friends do.

There is, however, an Aristotelian mean between these extremes. In the first place, our arguments coupled with some recent insights by

Bernard Yack indicate that Aristotle may not be so far removed from the liberal tradition as some commentators would like. These passages from Yack suggest this and the appropriate context for finding the mean.

> The key to Aristotle's political teleology lies in his suggestion that the capacity for reasoned speech leads man to argue about "the advantageous and the harmful", and *therefore also* the just and unjust. . . . Political communities would then be based on sharing in argument about general standards of justice and goodness, shared standards brought to light and registered in some way in what Aristotle calls the *politeia*, the political regime.[19] (Emphasis added by Yack.)
>
> The political community forms out of the shared interest of individuals seeking a self-sufficient community. A group of individuals can serve each other's interest because of the variety of their skills and their proximity to each other. No special virtues qualify them to be members of that community. But those individuals can form a community of shared interest only through forming a community of argument around standards of political justice. They thus come to share standards of justice and expect their fellow citizens to live up to these standards.[20]

These passages suggest that if individuals can see their advantage in terms of general rules that make those advantages possible, then the mean between Hobbesian atomism and character-friendships is found. Just as two traders can mutually value the context of profitability that makes their trade possible, so too can citizens who associate with one another come to value the principles of justice that give rise to and regulate their mutually advantageous association. We need not suppose that the association for mutual advantage is devoid of an appreciation of how the advantages themselves depend upon the existence of rules designed to secure those advantages. Nor must we suppose that the parties involved can only co-operate with one another if they will another's good for his own sake.

As economist James Buchanan has shown, the existence of formalized rules themselves is advantageous,[21] and this truth is undoubtedly appreciated by most members of a relatively stable community. The only question remaining is whether these rules are truly just. We have discussed our own views on this in other chapters. Here it is enough to realize that the link between civic friendships and character-friendships is through the goodness of the rules themselves and not through the form of friendship or through transforming one form of friendship into another. Civic friends are linked by virtue only if the rules they see as mutually advantageous are just ones. They are not, and will never be, friends of virtue in the sense of having a selfless interest in the good of other citizens.[22] This explains why theories of right and justice are more philosophically significant than theories of political organization or friendship. It also confirms our view, not always or necessarily shared by Aristotle himself, that the attainment of the good life is an individual quest.

By this time it has perhaps occurred to the reader that our argument in favor of an Aristotelian foundation for commercial societies has ignored what is most significant about Aristotle's works—his criticism of those features most common in commercial societies: unlimited acquisition, usury, industrialism and technocracy,[23] and the undisciplined pursuit of the satisfaction of desires. These are common themes used by opponents of liberal capitalistic cultures to criticize such societies. These 'Aristotelian' critics are numerous: recent attacks on market societies can be found in such articles as T. J. Lewis's 'Acquisition and Anxiety: Aristotle's Case Against the Market',[24] and Scott Meikle's 'Aristotle and the Political Economy of the Polis'.[25]

Lewis, following Karl Polanyi, argues for the thesis that Aristotle understood market systems (contrary to the assertions of many economists), but Aristotle consciously rejected them on both normative and economic grounds. Instead, using a model founded upon the household as the central unit of economic analysis (rather than the individual), Lewis claims that Aristotle sought an economic system which produced goods, but only to the limited extent that such goods were necessary for living the good life. The good life *precludes* anxiety about one's material well-being and acquiring wealth for its own sake, and it *includes* character-friendships among citizens as well as redistributing material surpluses so that self-sufficient heads of households may participate in civic activities which are central for living the good life.

Lewis takes Aristotle to be advocating a form of civic friendship modelled after character-friendships. We have already argued above that such an interpretation is mistaken and that even if correct as an interpretation of Aristotle, it would not be worthy of support. But further, Lewis interprets the marketlike discussion of exchange in Book V of the

Nicomachean Ethics as characteristic of, and appropriate for, lower classes, such as craftsmen and laborers. Heads of households, who will be the true citizens of the polis, must restrict the excesses of these inferiors and direct the social product for use by those whose sensibilities and self-control are of a superior order. Given a small enough community, the heads of household can participate in political activity and associate with one another on the basis of character-friendships. As Lewis himself notes, this conception of political life depends upon the validity of the concept of natural slavery,[26] and we would add it also depends upon the idea of fixed and natural classes existing to serve the lives of the highest class.

This elitist conception of political order raises questions that go beyond our present analysis. For example, whether such an interpretation is an accurate account of Aristotle's views on political economy is, we suspect, open to serious question. And if the interpretation were correct, such a theory ought to be rejected on both moral and economic grounds. Since our primary purpose here is not exegetical, the degree to which Aristotle does or does not advocate market structures will have to be determined by scholars of the period. But even if Aristotle himself should turn out to be antithetical to the market order, rejection of that aspect of his thought in no way entails the rejection of the central themes of Aristotelian ethics upon which our preceding account of friendships of advantage rests.

Meikle, like Lewis, also believes that Aristotle understood the basic nature of a market economy and rejected it on normative and economic grounds. Moreover, Meikle also believes that the key to the appropriate economic order lies in Aristotle's theory of friendship. However, unlike Lewis, he does not specify exactly what the theory of friendship is supposed to contribute to the discussion. Instead, a significant portion of Meikle's analysis is devoted to the commensurability problem that is said to exist when goods are traded.[27] According to Meikle, Aristotle is searching for a way to analyze the applicability of justice to exchange relationships in Book V of the *NE* and in the *Politics*. To do this Aristotle must find some standard that will establish a "proportionate equality" between the goods exchanged, since this approach accords with the rest of his theory of justice. Aristotle must, in other words, find some standard by which different goods can be made *commensurable* with one another. Without some means of establishing a standard for commensurability, equality (a necessary ingredient of justice) will not be established either. Meikle argues that Aristotle tries both money and need (*chreia* usually translated as 'demand') to solve the problem, and he concludes that Aristotle himself recognized that neither approach was satisfactory.

Since need is not often associated with commercial orders, we shall ignore Meikle's discussion of it here and consider money. Money is an attractive option because it seems to render the incommensurable commensurate by being a universal medium of exchange. But Meikle argues, probably correctly, that Aristotle came to realize that money would not solve the commensurability problem. In the first place, money is itself a commodity and therefore cannot serve as the standard for rendering commensurable all commodities. Secondly, money cannot create commensurability, because proportionate exchange existed before money did. Money can, however, serve as a *measure* of a common standard or value; but that still leaves open what that standard might be. Here Aristotle introduces need to help solve the problem. Perhaps money can come to measure the need people place on such dissimilar items as beds and houses that might be exchanged for one another. This, however, seems to suffice for 'practical' purposes without showing what it is about beds and houses that makes them commensurable. Thus, "at the end of it all, he has succeeded only in formulating profound and original problems to which he can find no solutions".[28] Aristotle's problem can be solved, Meikle speculates, with a Marxian theory of value.

Assuming Meikle's interpretation of Aristotle is correct, Aristotle fails to arrive at a solution to his problem because he is seeking the wrong kind of answer. Aristotle appears to want to discover some intrinsic characteristic in the goods themselves that will inform us about the ways in which they are or are not commensurable. It is only natural, therefore, that Meikle would posit the Marxian theory of value as the solution, since it also attempts to offer a universal intrinsic standard for the evaluation of exchange relationships. It is our view, on the other hand, that goods have no intrinsic value that can be culled from their nature and used to evaluate commensurability; and this claim is quite consistent with the theory of property we argued for in the last chapter and our general theory of value found in Chapter 2. Yet Meikle (and

Aristotle) are quite correct to recognize that money does not render goods commensurable either. The solution, we believe, lies in the *essence* of marginal utility theory—a theory we do not believe Aristotle could have appreciated and which was not shown to be so appreciated by him by either Lewis or Meikle.[29]

The essence of marginal utility theory lies in its claim that people have preferences which they rank within a context of scarce resources and opportunity costs. Assuming the absence of fraud or coercion, what is presumably uniform in any exchange relationship is the fact that both parties (given the background conditions just mentioned) rank the good(s) to be received through exchange highest in their order of preferences at the time of the exchange. This remains true throughout all exchange relationships, whether they be prior to the introduction of money (barter) or with respect to speculations in currency. The relationship between the parties to the exchange is thus one of equality, since both parties, within the confines of their own subjectively determined opportunity costs, rank the good in question equally, that is, highest in their order of preferences. This is also to say that the equality is in some sense proportionate. That is, although both equally rank the good(s) highest in their order of preferences, that ranking is relative to, and a function of, their *different* opportunity costs. So the good(s) in question is not given equal value by one individual relative to the other, but proportionately equal value.[30] Indeed, it is this relative equality in the ranking of preferences that makes the good(s) commensurable. Goods, *in se*, are neither commensurable nor incommensurable, but acommensurable. This is why the same two goods which A and B might be willing to exchange will not necessarily facilitate an exchange between C and D, even if C and D possess identical commodities; the goods for C and D do not stand in the same equal proportionate relationship as they do for A and B.

We claim that the foregoing represents the essence of marginal utility theory because we believe that nothing in the foregoing account requires a commitment to such meta-ethical propositions as the subjective theory of value. In other words, the truth about the ranking of preferences can be admitted without having to buy into the whole package of theories often associated with marginal utility analysis. But the rendering of goods commensurable through equality of preference ranking does, interestingly enough, commit one to the proposition that advantage-friendships are possible between any two people at virtually any time in a commercial society. Since goods are not intrinsically valuable, the possibilities for their standing in the requisite position on one's preference function to facilitate exchange are virtually limitless. Only commercial orders offer this possibility, since they do not predefine the relationships individuals must have with respect to interpersonal exchanges.

Of most significance for our purposes, however, is the fact that exchange relationships or friendships of advantage pose no obstacle to the main thrust of Aristotle's views on justice and ethics. Indeed, perhaps commercial societies offer us insights into the solutions to problems Aristotle's own social order could not have provided him with, although no doubt commercial societies raise their own sorts of difficulties. That Aristotle was not an advocate of many of the features characteristic of commercial orders does not, in itself, prevent the possibility of a defense of commercial societies on Aristotelian grounds. Indeed, the main point of our analysis in this section of the chapter has been to claim that commercial relations are paradigmatic of advantage-friendships in the Aristotelian sense.

FRIENDSHIP AND CONTRACTARIANISM

Do the principles which apply within a commercial framework also apply to the framework itself? In other words, if the free pursuit of advantage-friendships is permissible in commercial exchange relationships, should a similar model be used to understand the political institutions which ground the commercial order? These questions naturally lead one to the place, if any, of contractarian considerations within an Aristotelian framework. It has been argued that the two approaches are entirely incompatible[31]—the Aristotelian has no room for contractarian perspectives. We shall remind ourselves in a moment why there is truth to this claim; but for now we must realize why the door is opened to contractarian considerations.

Part of the reason for taking contractarianism seriously within an Aristotelian framework stems from Aristotle himself. Consider the following passages:

> [F]riendship would seem to hold cities together, and legislators would seem to be more concerned about it than about justice. For concord would seem to be similar to friendship and they aim at concord above all, while they try above all to expel civil conflict, which is enmity. (*NE* 1155a23–27)

And

> [T]he political community seems both to have been originally formed and to endure for advantage; for legislators also aim at advantage, and the common advantage is said to be just. (*NE* 1160a11–15)

It is clear that Aristotle is speaking of advantage-friendships in these passages. It is equally clear that he is making a practical, not a theoretical, point about the organization of civil society. Friendships can take priority over justice because there is a practical necessity in achieving a peaceful social order. Citizens need to 'get along' with one another, for if they do not, the attainment of higher virtues is an impossibility. The first step in achieving a peaceful social order is to get the members of society to see the political framework as being to their mutual advantage: "a city is said to be in concord when [its citizens] agree about what is advantageous. . . . "(*NE* 1167a27-29) This, of course, raises the question of whether it is their real or perceived advantage that should be secured; but it seems evident from these passages that perceived advantage is certainly a necessary condition for peaceful co-operation or concord.

The last point indicates that it was not just Hobbes, Spinoza, and Locke who first looked at politics 'realistically' and saw the primary importance of peace or concord—Aristotle did so as well. Political realism demands that peace or concord take at least practical precedence over justice and virtue. It would seem to follow, then, that a methodology which did not begin from a specific moral commitment, but considered only perceived advantage would be useful in determining the prospects for peace or concord. Contractarianism in general considers the question of what people are likely to agree to. Since advantage-friendships are not, per se, in violation of the demands of justice, such information about the prospects for agreement would be of value to the Aristotelian 'legislator'. Some contractarians take the further step of using what people are likely to agree to as a basis for making claims about what they ought to agree to or what people are predominantly like as rational agents. As we shall see in a moment, these additional features of contractarianism can and must be rejected by the Aristotelian. Nevertheless, the ever-impending demand for concord renders the central features of the contractarian methodology useful to the Aristotelian social theorist.

Making Use of Procedural Social Contract Theory

No matter what its purpose may be, no matter what specific form it may take, a social contract theory is based on what people actually or hypothetically consent to. Regardless of what theory of human nature or human motivation is used, consent is the *sine gua non* of social contract theory. From the standpoint of an Aristotelian legislator who is interested in the practical problem of organizing civil society, social contract theory is of interest because getting people to consent to a political authority is the primary problem he faces. It is for this reason that we think that there is something 'modernity' can offer the 'ancients' regarding this problem. As already noted, however, the idea that social contract theory could be of use to an Aristotelian legislator has long been viewed an impossibility. To see how an Aristotelian legislator could possibly benefit from the insights of social contract theory we must first note an important distinction.

Jeffrey Paul[32] has distinguished between two forms of social contract theory: 'substantive' and 'procedural'. A social contract theory is said to be substantive if it seeks to establish the ethical principles by which the ends and policies of social and political institutions are evaluated or the ethical principles by which the goals and actions of persons are judged. This may take the form of a theory of justice, or this may result in a general theory of ethics. The social contract may be actual or hypothetical. Regardless of the specific form, a social contract theory is 'substantive' in character when an effort is made to provide a basis for the ethical legitimation of social and political institutions, or a standard by which human conduct can be ethically justified. We have criticized such theories in Chapter 1 and elsewhere.[33]

On the other hand, a 'procedural' social contract theory does not provide a basis for the ethical legitimation of social and political institutions or a moral standard for evaluating human conduct. Normative principles, if they are employed at all, are supplied through some other theoretical source. The discovery of the moral knowledge by which to evaluate social and political institutions or persons is in no crucial way tied to the processes of creating a contract, bargaining, strategizing, consenting, or promising.[34] A social contract theory is said to be procedural only if it seeks to *explain* how the structures of political authority (for example, adjudicative, executive, and legislative) and society in general (for example, commercial institutions and practices) might be created. *Explain* refers here to a conceptual account of how human beings might create a social and political order based on a certain set of assumptions about human conduct, not how, according to historical records, people have created social and political orders. Such an account could describe what actually occurred, but it does not concern itself with whether it in fact does.

Since a procedural social contract theory does not attempt to develop either a theory of justice or a general theory of ethics, such a theory need not be tied to a hedonistic theory of value, ethical subjectivism, relativism, or special vantage points from which the theory is constructed—be they that of an 'impartial spectator' or from behind a 'veil of ignorance'. It is perfectly possible for a procedural social contract theory to be linked to an ethical theory that is based on the existence of a human *telos* which proposes a theory of basic, natural, negative rights as the standard by which social and political authority is legitimated. It is this possibility we seek to exploit in dealing with the problem of organizing civil society.

Since the Aristotelian legislator by definition already has the theoretical knowledge necessary to morally evaluate social and political institutions, he has no need for substantive social contract theory. Only social contract theory that is procedural in character can assist the Aristotelian legislator. Procedural social contract theory is of assistance as primarily a heuristic device. It allows the Aristotelian legislator to understand how people might come to regard their political institutions as mutually advantageous. An understanding of this gives the Aristotelian legislator the necessary elements in an overall theoretical account of what would make institutions required for the protection and implementation of natural rights possible.

Generally, a procedural social contract theory views human conduct in terms of no other motivational consideration than *perceived* advantage, and though this is not by any means an adequate account of human conduct, it does explain a sufficient amount of human behavior to be heuristically useful. A good example of a social contract theory adaptable to this proceduralist outlook is James Buchanan's account of what he has called a "constitutional contract". [35] We will discuss Buchanan's theory in greater detail later.

There are two basic reasons why procedural social contract theory is useful to the Aristotelian legislator as a heuristic device: (1) procedural social contract theory allows the Aristotelian legislator to reject political elitism—it opens up the door to liberalism; and (2) it does not prevent the Aristotelian legislator from providing liberalism with a moral foundation. The first reason allows the Aristotelian legislator to show that a social and political order that protects natural rights is a real possibility and does not require a commitment to political idealism. By stressing the explanatory power of any social and political theory which acknowledges that much human conduct can be understood in terms of *perceived* advantage, the first reason provides a basis for rejecting the tendency of the 'ancients' to let political authority reside in only those who really know what virtue and justice is. Indeed, the problem with ancient political theory is that the rule of virtue and wisdom is not sufficiently attentive to the requirements of co-operation and consent.

The second reason allows the Aristotelian legislator to show that a social and political order whose primary concerns are co-operation, peace, and concord (as contrasted with justice and virtue) does not require a commitment to political cynicism. By noting that the practical social and political expression of human flourishing amounts to a society which allows humans to interact on the basis of their own *perceived* advantage, the second reason provides a basis for rejecting the tendency of the 'moderns' to interpret liberalism as entailing ethical subjectivism or relativism. Indeed, modernity (specifically substantive social contract theory) has failed to legitimate political authority largely because of its reliance upon subjectivism and relativism. Co-operation and consent based upon perceived advantage are not, by themselves, sufficient to guarantee legitimacy.

These two reasons for adopting the proceduralist approach to social contract theory need, however, to be explained in greater detail.

1. The first reason can be illustrated by considering the pointed ex-

change between Cardinal Wolsey (the hardened political cynic) and Sir Thomas More (the political idealist) in Robert Bolt's *A Man For All Seasons.* Wolsey asks More, "You'd like that, wouldn't you? To govern the country by prayers?" More responds, "Yes, I should," and Wolsey replies, "I'd like to be there when you try." Analogously, is the social and political order that expresses the natural rights for which we have argued only to be achieved when we live in a world in which virtue and love characterize the lives of most people? Our point is not to say that human beings cannot live virtuously or be motivated by love; Hobbesian man has been rejected and replaced by Aristotelian man. Rather, it is to say that it would be dubious to assume that the social and political order for which we have been arguing is likely to ever exist if it depends on most human beings most of the time living virtuously or being motivated by love. Politics is not mathematics, and it is concerned with what is for the most part. So, given that we do indeed have some idea as to what the proper social and political order for man is to be, is there a way we can steer a course between the Scylla of political cynicism and the Charybdis of political idealism? We think so. We believe the contractarian literature in general, and Buchanan in particular, go some distance towards describing those institutional elements which are necessary for the development of the type of political order for which we have been arguing.

In trying to explain how it is really possible for a political order which protects basic, negative natural rights to be based on a secure foundation, we want to employ a theory which uses as little 'moral capital' as possible. We must avoid the Charybdis of political idealism. We agree with James Buchanan's endorsement of Sir Dennis Robertson's description of the economist's task as that of showing how to minimize the use of the scarcest of all resources, love.[36] We would only add that virtue is certainly second in the list of scarcest resources. In other words, we endorse a methodology which considers human beings, who, although capable of love and virtue, would in terms of only their *perceived* well-being (which may or may not be well-informed) consent to a type of 'social contract' which could be made into a constitution that protects and provides the means for implementing basic, negative, natural rights.

2. When it comes to organizing a civil society, the previously cited quotations from Aristotle regarding the priority of advantage-friendships

over justice provides us with the second reason why procedural social contract theory is useful as a heuristic device to the Aristotelian legislator. Considering the highly individualized character of human flourishing and the central role of autonomy in making human flourishing what it is, the only way one can adequately explain the process by which authentic interests of individuals play their role in the achievement of social co-operation and the creation of political peace and concord is by appealing to a methodology that uses perceived advantage as the motivational force. The point here, however, is not that we wish to save on our use of 'moral capital' in explaining how political authority is created. Rather, it is just the opposite. Procedural social contract theory, better than traditional Aristotelian theory (such as Yves Simon's account of political authority), allows us to see how the highly individualized, self-directed nature of human flourishing would actually function in bringing about social co-operation. Indeed, in the practical, everyday world in which one can know very little about the real (as opposed to apparent) good of others, mutual toleration of the pursuit of individual interests is just what a social and political order dedicated to preserving the possibility that all community members might flourish requires!

Procedural social contract theory expresses in practical terms what a commitment to natural rights requires—namely, mutual accommodation to individual pursuits of goals and interests and mutual consent to the rules that are to govern those pursuits. It thus has as its central methodological assumption what we have argued is the only morally legitimate way for human beings to interact—that is, consent based on each person's judgment as to what his well-being consists. Even though social contract theory cannot legitimate its central methodological assumption (the legitimacy of consent itself), it can nonetheless be used. Indeed, Locke, Jefferson, and many of the Founding Fathers are examples of theorists who appeal to consent as the way to implement moral principles that have an extra-contractual foundation. Despite current fashion, social contract theory need not be Hobbesian in character. Thus, it is precisely the nonmoral character of procedural social contract theory that makes it so useful to the Aristotelian legislator, for it allows him to use his extra-contractual moral knowledge to justify consent while still taking advantage of the explanatory powers of social contract theory.

It should be noted that there is nothing self-contradictory in there being procedural social contract theories which permit human beings to be motivated by something more than *perceived* advantage. Indeed, we have insisted and will insist that there is 'something more' to human conduct. Yet since the most powerful explanatory accounts we have in the social sciences are those found in economics, and since a society which allows people to interact on the basis of their own perceived advantage is the practical social and political expression of human flourishing, there is not only nothing lost in using an economic model of human conduct, there is something gained.

The Procedural Constitutional Contract

We noted earlier that Buchanan's explanation of a 'constitutional contract' could be used as an example of a procedural social contract theory. There are, however, two important qualifications that need to be made. The first is for Buchanan's intellectual protection; the second is for our own.

1. In all fairness to Buchanan, we should make it clear that he would not approve of the use we would make of his theory of 'constitutional contract.' In *Freedom in Constitutional Contract* he characterizes the attempt to ground the principles of justice in nature, science, reason, or God as "transcendentalism". Buchanan states: "To the transcendentalist that law is legitimate, and just, which meets the external ethical criteria chosen for him by the *witch doctors*", and "I find the rejection of any rule more congenial than the claim of any man to have discovered the 'truth' in values on his own. . . ."[37] A few pages later, he states: "'Fairness,' as an attribute of rules, is defined by agreement; it is not, and cannot be, defined independently of agreement, or at least of conceptual agreement."[38] Certainly, Buchanan has no use for the type of theorizing we have conducted throughout this book.

We would only note that he, like many other advocates of individualism and contractarianism, assumes that ethical knowledge and tolerance of divergent beliefs and practices are not compatible. He also assumes that accepting the existence of ethical truths commits him to a Platonic or what we have called an intrinsic view of the good. We certainly hope to have shown by now that such assumptions are not true and that the protection of individualism, pluralism, and diversity that Buchanan holds so dear has really no leg to stand on if there is no ethical truth. We will, however, comment futher on this issue later and in Chapter 6. With apologies to Buchanan, we shall employ his theory of constitutional contract for our own purposes. Our use of social contract theory is, then, procedural and confined to explaining the process of creating a political constitution.

As already stated, we seek to use the type of explanation that an economist would use to conceptually account for how people would come to consent to a constitution, that is, create a legal system. It should, however, be made clear that we do not seek to explain how a constitution would evolve out of market processes by means of some 'invisible hand' or process of 'spontaneous order'.[39] Even though many of our social, and indeed legal, institutions have developed independently of our design and intent, we agree with Buchanan when he states:

> Man must look on *all* institutions as potentially improvable. Man must adopt the attitude that he can control his fate. He must accept the necessity of choosing. He must look on himself as man, not another animal, and upon civilization as if it is of his own making. . . . The American cannot, and should not, neglect the fact that his own heritage of freedom, although owing much to its European antecedents, was deliberately constructed in large part by James Madison and his compatriots. Theirs were no invisible hands. They set out to construct a constitutional framework for the "good society," which they defined implicitly as "free relations among free men".[40]

We thus seek by means of economic theory to show that people will not only come to recognize and accept the need for political institutions, but create and consent to them.

2. The following needs to be said about our use of Buchanan's theory of constitutional contract: (a) Our use of Buchanan's theory is for purposes of illustration only, we do not wish to commit ourselves to the idea that only Buchanan's account of how a constitutional contract might be created could be used by an Aristotelian legislator. There may be other acceptable social contract theories. (b) We have chosen to use Buchanan's account of how people might come to recognize the need for political institutions precisely because Buchanan makes no claim to be using social contract theory for substantive purposes. Generally, "Buchanan does not succumb to the temptation to imagine some idealized or *efficient* state of affairs that *ought* to be realized independent of

the current rights structure".[41] His theory is the closest we have encountered to the type of procedural social contract we have described. Yet it does not always seem that Buchanan keeps the distinction between substantive and procedural social contracts clear in his own work or even recognizes such a distinction. (c) We do not believe that Buchanan's theory of how a constitutional contract is created can, without assistance from normative theory and a wider theory of human motivation, explain how the constitutional contract can be sustained.[42] As said earlier, however, we view procedural social contract theory as providing only the *first* step or the necessary elements in an overall theoretical account of how an Aristotelian legislator would obtain a mutually advantageous political order.

Buchanan's Theory of Constitutional Contract

According to Buchanan's theory, people will come to recognize and create political institutions by simply considering what their own *perceived* advantage requires. By only using the type of considerations an economist would employ to explain human conduct, Buchanan shows how a movement from 'anarchy' to 'Leviathan' would take place. The details of Buchanan's account need not concern us; but the general thrust of the analysis does. Two key concepts need to be kept in mind. First, in a state of anarchy an equilibrium will be reached among the participants with respect to how much further defense and predation they are willing to expend towards their neighbor's goods. Buchanan calls this a state of "natural anarchistic equilibrium". It, for him, is the initial condition from which the social contract will be made, for this condition represents the *actual* endowments individuals would bring to the contracting process. This is a significant concept for the Aristotelian legislator, because such a legislator must promote concord and consent on the basis of real (rather than ideal) endowments if actual consent is the desired end.[43]

Secondly, the movement away from anarchy and to Leviathan marks an advantageous move for all participants. The process here includes overcoming certain 'prisoner's dilemma' problems, but in the end the participants are better off with the state than without it. Implied in this move to more optimal circumstances is the idea that a rule-governed order is preferable to one that is not. Rules help define the legitimate boundaries between persons that are absent in a condition of anarchy. It follows as well that the rules adopted will meet consent conditions because they flow from the actual endowments of anarchistic equilibrium. The Aristotelian legislator is again instructed, for by imagining the circumstances under which a set of agreed-upon rules based upon the actual conditions of the consenting parties would be established, that legislator will have a better understanding of the means to social concord than by looking to the requirements of virtue alone. And since the pluralistic nature of human flourishing requires the presence of meta-normative conditions for such flourishing to occur, the practical expression of this would be a concern for protection against possible predation by one's neighbor.

What kind of state, however, have the parties to this constitutional contract consented? Buchanan explains:

> At the constitutional stage, the state emerges as the enforcing agency or institution, conceptually external to the contracting parties and charged with the single responsibility of enforcing agreed-upon rights and claims along with contracts which involve voluntary negotiated exchanges of such claims. In this "protective" role, the state is not involved in producing "good" or "justice" as such, other than that which is embodied indirectly through a regime of contract enforcement. . . . Because of each person's interest in the security of agreed-on-rights, the legal and protective state must be characterized by *precepts of neutrality*. . . . "The law" enforced by the state is not necessarily that set of results which best represents some balance of opposing interests, some compromise, some median judgment. Properly interpreted, "the law" which is enforced is that which is specified to be enforced by the initial contract, whatever this might be.[44]

Such a state is clearly not interested in producing justice and virtue. It will not attempt to enforce any conception of the good life on its citizens. Rather, it is concerned with establishing peace and concord among its citizens. Here we find that first step or set of necessary conditions from which an Aristotelian legislator would work and could approve. For as D.J. Allan has observed, Aristotle does not "credit the politician, in his capacity as lawgiver, with the power of manufacturing happiness or virtue, but represents him as *establishing the framework* within which happiness clan be attained".[45] Our contention is that 'framework' is best understood along contractarian lines.

On the other hand, it should be clearly understood that to say people will come to recognize the need for political authority in terms of their own *perceived* well-being is not to say that *all* we need to consider when discussing the creation of political authority is the economist's view of human nature and values. The very "precepts of neutrality" by which Buchanan's "protective state" is supposed to be characterized cannot be understood, defended, or long maintained apart from a much wider view of human nature and appeal to moral philosophy. Buchanan's account of the creation of a constitutional contract cannot, by definition, explain what it really means to "establish peace and concord among its citizens", for 'peace' and 'concord' are ultimately normative notions.[46] The Aristotelian legislator, however, can interpret the protective role of the state as something more than merely the implementation of rules that result from anarchistic equilibrium in which all interests have equal normative worth. "Precepts of neutrality" can be easily transformed from their amoral status to the moral purpose of protecting and implementing natural rights. In other words, natural rights can provide normative content to what it means to consent to a constitution which "establishes peace and concord among its citizens".

Buchanan seems, at least at times, to have recognized the deficiencies of the economist's view of human nature and values.

> To the extent that existing rights are held to be subject to continuous redefinition by the state, no one has any incentive to organize and to initiate trades or agreements. This amounts to saying that once the body politic begins to get overly concerned about the distribution of the pie under existing property-rights assignments and legal rules, once we begin to think either about personal gains from law-breaking, privately or publicly, or the disparities between existing imputations and those estimated to be forthcoming from idealized anarchy, we are necessarily precluding and forestalling the achievement of potential structural changes that might increase the size of the pie for *all* . Too much concern for [distributive] "justice" acts to insure that "growth" will not take place, and *for reasons more basic than the familiar economic incentives argument. . . .*
>
> At issue here, of course, is the whole conception of the State, or of collective action. I am far less sanguine than I once was concerning the possible acceptance of a reasonably well-defined constitutional-legal framework. . . .
>
> We may be witnessing the disintegration of our effective constitutional rights, regardless of the prattle about "the constitution" as seen by our judicial tyrants from their own visions of the entrails of their sacrificial beast.

I do not know what might be done about all this, even by those who recognize what is happening. How do rights re-emerge and come to command respect? How do "laws" emerge that carry with them general respect for their "legitimacy"? [47]

In other words, failing to realize that the behavior of citizens in general, and public servants within the political and legal framework in particular, can be motivated by something more that preference satisfaction or maximization of their utility functions prevents us from understanding the real alternatives that face us in the conduct of public policy. It is our view that "general respect for legitimacy" is necessarily tied to moral commitment—one we believe is possible within an Aristotelian framework, but not a Hobbesian one.

The importance of moral philosophy can be clearly seen when we consider the elements in Buchanan's constitutional contract. These are: (1) people must agree to disarm and accept the rules governing their behavior in exchange for others doing likewise; (2) rules determining how ownership is established and what ownership entails must be developed; (3) limitation on the powers of the enforcing agent must be fixed; and (4) the specification of the rules by which the political authority must operate in the future when it comes to the provision and financing of those goods that only a political authority can provide must be established.[48] Securing agreement on these four elements really amounts to securing agreement on four separate constitutional contracts, "for no one of the four could evolve out of the agreement concerning another without thereby becoming noncontractual. Increased opportunities for defection are now present in all areas . . . and this in turn threatens the stability of the social contract."[49] If Buchanan's constitutional contract is to be sustained, it needs to be based on more than people consenting to the constitutional contract because of its *perceived* advantages—they need to agree on the overall *purpose* of the constitutional contract. Moral philosophy can, and for the Aristotelian legislator must, enter into the story here to provide a unifying purpose for the constitutional elements.

For example, there is a possible complication in the disarmament agreement that we need to consider. It may be necessary for one party A to unilaterally give the other party B some goods to induce him to disarm. A might have to give some goods to B to get him to disarm, since

B has discovered that he can have more goods by engaging in predation than by engaging in production alone. The difference between this state and the state in which B agrees to accept some disarmament is the amount of unilateral transfer that A would need to provide. The amount of transfer would have to leave A better off than the natural distribution in the anarchist setting in order for such a transfer of goods to occur. So B cannot be too recalcitrant in the negotiations, although a unilateral payment by A from his stock of goods may be necessary for this initial agreement to emerge. As Buchanan states:

> There is no *necessary* basis for any initial agreement that will simply acknowledge the rights of persons to retain those stocks of goods that they can wrest from the natural environment by their own labor. Something other than the utility function employed by standard economic theory must be introduced to provide an explanatory foundation that legitimizes individuals' (families') claims to stocks actually produced by their own efforts independently from interference of others.[50]

We concur, of course, with Buchanan's observation that something other than a utility function is necessary to legitimize the stocks of goods that A and B have transformed from the environment. This illustrates the need for some extra-contractual purpose or standard for the constitutional contract.

As should be clear from our discussion of the natural right to property in Chapter 3, there is a wide latitude in the rules determining when one has established ownership and what that ownership entails. The exact determination of what rules will be used is beyond the purview of abstract moral and social theory. Such rules, *practically* speaking, depend on simply what people are willing to agree to—namely, a social contract. As Charles Jackson Wheeler has noted, "There is no one immutable Objective Legal Code, as some kind of Platonic *eidos*. Rights may be implemented in a variety of ways. . . . Within the form of objectivity and individual rights, the content of an objective legal code may be chosen by the philosophy of law from a number of equally viable alternatives".[51] Yet these rules must nonetheless meet two conditions to be morally legitimate (a) they must be universal—they must be applicable to everyone; and (b) they must be negative—they must set boundary conditions and thereby exclude others from the results of one's acts of transformation. In other words, constitutional element 2 cannot be determined merely through negotiation.[52] Some form of moral foresight or commitment would have to be present among the contractors.

The requirement that the second element in the constitutional contract be consistent with the two moral conditions that result from the natural right to property creates an interesting and important possibility regarding the aforementioned complication in the disarmament agreement. After the constitutional contract, when a legal system has been created, it might be shown that the unilateral transfer of goods by A to B for the purpose of inducing him to disarm violated A's property rights. Hence justice would require that B be legally compelled to repay A for this unilateral transfer of goods. Of course, this assumes that one could have a decent idea of who owned what in the anarchical setting at the time of the disarmament agreement and this, as we have already indicated, is quite difficult to determine apart from a social contract. Yet the possibility of such repayment does nonetheless exist, especially if the contracting parties come to believe that B held out *simply* for strategic reasons.

This possibility of repayment illustrates an important difference between the Lockean approach to the four elements in the constitutional contract and the Hobbesian approach. The content of these elements is both determined and limited by natural rights for the Lockean; for the Hobbesian, they are not and are determined solely by negotiation or bargaining. This becomes an extremely important point when one starts dealing with constitutional elements 3 and 4 and such issues as taxation, conscription, and public goods. We cannot, however, take up these complicated issues here, for that would carry us beyond the main purpose of this section.[53]

In Buchanan's theory there is nothing to prevent some leader from emerging who either by command or by ability to persuade the masses simply stipulates the content of element 2 or any of the other elements of the constitutional contract. The content of these elements cannot be determined by Buchanan's theory in any principled way. This is, of course, precisely why we have made use of only procedural social contract theory, argued for natural rights, and emphasized throughout that human beings *can* not only conduct themselves in accordance with moral principles but even agree to use such principles in giving content to the elements of a constitutional contract. This is exactly what we presume Madison and his compatriots to have done when they set about forming the constitution for this nation's legal system. It should be clear, therefore, that for the Aristotelian legislator the character of these elements must be in accord with the moral purpose for which such political authority exists—namely, the protection of individual rights.

Yet it might be asked, just what type of society would our Aristotelian legislator create? More precisely, what kind of human being would dominate this society? What virtues, if any, would predominate? If the Aristotelian legislator not only allows but morally legitimates human interaction on the basis of *perceived advantage* or, as we have described the situation earlier, considers friendships of advantage the dominant form of human interaction, what hope can there be that there will be character-friendships or, for that matter, any other moral virtue? In other words, and to put it bluntly, have we not in this chapter really sold our Aristotelian souls in our desire to provide a moral defense of the commercial society?

COMMERCIALISM, VIRTUE, AND CHARACTER

A common criticism of commercial orders is that they fail to promote virtue, or at least not the highest and most significant forms of human virtue. Our discussion in the preceding two sections has shown that advantage-friendships are a means for linking commercialism to Aristotelianism. But even if all that came before were true, it has not yet been shown that commercial orders produce the kinds of persons of virtue an Aristotelian would most admire. Indeed, the opposite may seem to be the case. Commercial orders are said to produce persons skilled in strategy, calculation, utility, and the low virtues of thrift and honesty; but the upper reaches of human excellence would be lost in such a social order. Our question, then, is what type of person is the commercial order likely to produce? And does this person in any way reflect the ideals that form the core of a teleological eudaimonistic ethic?

Our question is not a new one, even if we ignore critics of commercial orders. Adam Smith and Montesquieu, for example, both offer defenses of commercialism as well as characterizations of the type of person likely to dominate such orders. Indeed, both regard the commercial order as defensible, but at a cost. For Smith that cost was mediocrity and a lowering of educational standards.[54] Montesquieu had similar worries, as did Tocqueville.[55] One might sum these worries up under the title 'the lowest-common-denominator objection'. This objection, in its various guises, is the most common one among *defenders* of commercial orders. Critics charge, in addition, that commercial orders produce greedy, self-ish, exploitative, manipulative, amoral individuals. Yet in this case, it seems to us more instructive to deal with the objections arising from those sympathetic to commercial orders rather than the critics. One reason is that when added together, these criticisms become self-contradictory—not all of them can be equally true of commercial orders. Secondly, the most interesting insights into an issue are often found among the criticisms of those most sympathetic to that same issue (such as Orwell's criticisms of socialism).

A good place to begin our discussion is with an essay by Ralph Lerner entitled 'Commerce and Character: The Anglo-American as New-Model Man'.[56] Lerner concentrates on some of the main defenders of commercial orders—or more broadly, liberal republican orders—such as Smith, Montesquieu, Hume, and Tocqueville. He describes in some detail how these thinkers pictured the "new-model man" that would arise in commercial society and how such a man differed from the type that characterized aristocratic-based societies of the past. Not only does Lerner describe these thinkers' views of the emerging new man, but also their concerns with the loss of what was valuable in the old. Indeed, the losses seem to be what is most instructive about the essay, since the gains have presumably become an ordinary part of our present culture.

Lerner, echoing a now-familiar theme, argues that political thinkers can be divided into 'ancients' and 'moderns', with the latter being will-ing to sacrifice the higher virtues touted by the regimes of the ancients for a workable and peaceable social order. Ancient regimes, such as Sparta, were criticized by commercial republicans for being excessive in their pursuit of virtue.[57] Commercial republicans would settle for 'less nobility'—attain a more felicitous and secure polity. Lerner can no doubt muster sufficient support among the 'moderns' for his interpretation. Our concern is, however, not historical but philosophical. Two main philo-sophical postures are maintained by Lerner throughout his essay: (1) a posture about the nature of virtue; and (2) a posture about the role of the civil order in producing virtue. The last is most significant for our purposes, but in many ways depends upon the first.

The posture on virtue taken by Lerner, Strauss,[58] and others falls into the category of what we labelled earlier as the 'dominant-end' theory. As the writings of particular thinkers such as Plato, Aristotle, Aquinas, and the like get merged and distilled into the category 'ancients', the concept of virtue also hardens into one or two dominant virtues being exemplified in ancient polities. These could be one of a number of intangible goods mentioned by Lerner versus the tangible values advocated by commercial republicans. Whatever the values, they become translated into a few unshakable virtues that stand above all others. It is no accident that the example Lerner uses of both excess from the modern perspective, and the 'reliance on virtue' of the ancients, was Sparta. Although one is led to wonder how the Spartan pursuit of "heroic virtue" qualifies as more intangible than the commercial pursuit of peace or benevolence, the point here is that the type of interpretation being offered by Lerner suggests a dominant-end understanding of virtue. Ancient regimes may differ about what the dominant end should be, but all seem to agree that the purpose of the polity is to promote that virtue which it regards as best.

If we assume, for the sake of argument, that Lerner and others have gotten it right about the debate between the ancients and moderns, it is clear from our own discussion that both parties to the dispute have misunderstood the nature of virtue itself. For as we saw in an earlier chapter, virtue is not correctly characterized in terms of a dominant end. The choice, in other words, is not between whether to pursue a given form of excellence or to forget about the question entirely and settle for a workable common denominator. Virtue is more correctly considered in the abstract as an inclusive end of many salutary qualities, each of which may be more or less emphasized by the particular individual who pursues them. On the dominant-end theory, both the ancients and moderns would have to be correct: the moderns because the pursuit of one dominant end is indeed excessive; and the ancients because the loss of a concern for excellence does indeed lend itself to mediocrity. Both must, in addition, be incorrect: the moderns for believing that since we cannot all be models of virtue X all the time, the virtue approach is mistaken and we must embrace subjectivism, relativism, historicism, and other modern philosophical 'isms'; the ancients for believing that anything less than an all-consuming focus on virtue X will generate not only an absence of X, but of other virtues as well.

On the dominant-end interpretation of virtue, the debate between the ancients and moderns is unresolvable. It must be so, because the nature of virtue is distorted by both sides, and that distortion lends itself to a choice between undesirable (or equally desirable) alternatives. If virtue were initially understood to be an inclusive end, or more properly, if human excellence were understood in terms of an inclusive set of virtues, the debate over virtue would be more accurately centered on the role, if any, politics plays in promoting it. This naturally leads us to the second assumption mentioned above—namely, civil order and the promotion of virtue.[59]

Antiquity (for example, Plato and Aristotle) seems to take the self as the basic object of ethics, with our behavior towards others being a function of the requirements for self-perfection. Ethics is *essentially* a theoretical investigation of the principles of self-improvement and only secondarily or derivatively an investigation of interpersonal relations. As an example, consider Plato's definition of *justice* as "having one's soul in proper order"[60] This definition is virtually unintelligible to the modern mind because we think of justice as being essentially concerned with rules about appropriate behavior *towards others.* But the definition illustrates that the first and primary object of ethics (justice) is self-perfection or the development of character. If our character is properly developed, our actions towards others will tend to be appropriate as well. The reverse, however, is not necessarily true. The same point could be made about Aristotle, who devotes an entire book (Book II) of the *Nicomachean Ethics* to character development. From the perspective of Plato and Aristotle, no amount of rules on how to behave towards others, however obligatory, can replace the central role of self-perfection. Even the excessive propagation of rules found in Plato's *Laws* seems to reflect his misguided belief that such rules will help in the quest for *self*-perfection or the development of character.

Modern philosophy, however, reversed the emphasis. Ethics became primarily concerned with others and only secondarily concerned with self. Morality became thoroughly infused with the social. The two leading ethical theorists of the modern era, Kant and Mill, labor mightily, and probably in vain, to keep some semblance of self-perfection within the scope of their ethical theories. There are, nevertheless, some good reasons for the modern rejection of ancient politics. Antiquity gave a more-or-less significant role to the state with respect to the development of self—Plato being one of the more extreme examples, but Aristotle is not to be excluded. Modernity discovered that societies organized to promote virtue were dismal failures. Virtue was lacking, especially among those in charge of promoting it; and the value of freedom was often forgotten. It became more plausible to argue that the state was not the appropriate instrument for promoting virtue. The state should instead focus upon interpersonal conflict and freedom—ends it could reasonably accomplish.

The modern position on the state's ability to secure virtue is, as we shall mention below, correct, but it carried with it a fatal flaw. Despite the criticism of the state as an inappropriate vehicle for promoting virtue, the modern era never really severed the connection between state and virtue. At best, modernity simply lessened the number or kinds of virtues the state could control. One tendency was to associate virtue with interpersonal relations and ignore self-perfection. States and communities could do little about self-perfection anyway, but since they could observe interpersonal relations, virtue came to be increasingly understood in interpersonal terms. Arguments then developed about the degree to which states or communities should control interpersonal relations. Liberalism answered such questions by saying 'only to a small degree', while various forms of statism answered 'to a large degree'. Neither answer challenged the proposition that morality is essentially concerned with interpersonal relations.

The other main tendency was moral scepticism and/or relativism. Since states and communities were so unsuccessful in securing virtue, and since vice was everywhere to be found, even in the face of efforts to wipe it out, perhaps there are no general principles of virtue (or vice) after all. Perhaps we can say no more about virtue than that, if it has any meaning at all, it must refer to keeping society going by not allowing people to harm one another. This sort of minimalism and/or scepticism is at the heart of much of both classical and modern liberalism.[61] But more importantly, the minimalist/scepticist approach left unchallenged the idea that virtue, if it were to exist, was an appropriate item for state action. Indeed, it is not uncommon for contemporary classical liberals (such as Buchanan) to believe that if we knew what virtue was, there would be nothing to stand in the way of the state forcing us to adhere to it.

The implications of all this with respect to the arguments we have advanced in this book are as follows. Two main propositions about virtue, accepted by *both* ancients and moderns, must be rejected: (1) that virtue is a communal phenomenon or achievement, and (2) that virtue is necessarily connected to the state. [62] If both these propositions are rejected, the debate over whether the state should promote virtue becomes a red herring. From our perspective, the result of rejecting both propositions would be that the moderns were correct about politics, the ancients about ethics, and each incorrect about the other.

The reason that the state is not an appropriate vehicle for the promotion of virtue is that coercion is necessarily destructive of moral agency, and that moral agency must be present for virtue to be present. [63] Moral agency refers to neither intention alone, nor simply to the behavior or action of the agent. As Aristotle understood, [64] moral agency involves both elements linked together by the purpose of the agent. Coercion obliterates one or both elements of moral agency (not to mention the link between them). It can force a behavior that is 'good,' but at the expense of the presence of a good intention. It can effectively destroy intention altogether (whether good or bad) by forcing actions (either good or bad), which are performed simply because they are forced, and for no other reason. Finally, by severing the connection between intention and action, coercion can encourage good intentions which result in evil (harmful) actions. This is so because the separation tends to create the illusion that the manner in which the action is undertaken (for example, coercively) is not a factor in determining the moral character of the action. Thus if the intention is 'sincere', 'heartfelt', or 'compassionate', that is thought to be enough to qualify it as 'good'. The *means* by which the intention is fulfilled becomes a practical, not a moral matter. Self-directedness, however, is not only a necessary condition for an action being moral, but is itself necessarily a constituent of the morally good. The means by which an action is promoted cannot, therefore, be ignored when determining its moral character.

Since coercion destroys moral agency, a necessary condition of virtue is freedom or liberty. The social side of the argument, therefore, is that for a society to be virtuous, it must also be free. This is not to say that freedom is a sufficient condition of virtue; it is not. But whatever further sufficient conditions there may be for attaining virtue, they cannot come at the expense of the necessary condition. This implies that although a free society cannot be totally immoral (because basic rights are respected), it may be a society whose citizens adhere to a minimalist (simply rights-respecting) morality. Higher levels of moral excellence could be ignored. This thesis raises questions that we shall deal with in a moment.

Yet even if the coercive methods of the state were not at issue, the collectivist understanding of virtue would be.[65] It makes little difference whether the virtues in question are liberal republican or aristocratic. The tenuous and contingent character of virtue is not a function of the difficulty in getting virtuous men and women to rule, but is rather correlated to a central component of our brand of eudaimonism: individualism. As we have argued in Chapter 2, values are pursued, gained, and lost by individuals; and it is only individuals that can have values, not collectivities. Virtue, being the pursuit or possession of good values, must also be achievable only by individuals. And if virtue must be understood along individualist lines, collective efforts to attain virtue would constitute a virtual contradiction in terms. Virtue is solely and exclusively an achievement of individuals. Collective action, if it can do anything at all, can only lay the foundation for the achievement of virtue.

For us that foundation is the protection of individual rights. Efforts to go beyond that foundation by collectively prescribing appropriate courses of action may achieve conformity of behavior with moral principles, but not virtue. Virtuous actions are willed for their own sake by the agent undertaking them. Appropriate behavior without the corresponding understanding and will of the individual agent is not sufficient for producing virtue. Thus even if the state, *per impossibile*, could noncoercively direct or encourage appropriate forms of behavior, there would still be no virtue because of the missing intentional component on the part of the individual agent. That intentional component must be supplied by the individual agent himself. Just as economic prosperity cannot be achieved on collectivist principles, so also must collectivism fail with respect to moral prosperity. Conservatives cannot create productive lifestyles or humane sexuality by wars on drugs and pornography any more than liberals can create compassion and charity by redistribution schemes. All that can be accomplished by such collective efforts is a restriction on the opportunity for vice, which simultaneously restricts the opportunity for virtue. In the end such efforts promote not moral excellence, but a drab form of moral mediocrity and conformity.

It is no response to try and argue, as have some conservatives, that coercively induced behavior can instill appropriate habits in the populace such that later on people can come to will the actions for their own sake. In the first place, this argument assumes that the use of coercion does not itself instill the wrong kind of habits. We see the result of this process in our own litigious society where every inconvenience seeks redress through state action. Secondly, there are serious questions about whether the kinds of habits instilled will transform themselves into the sorts of virtuous actions desired. For if one is simply made to do 'right', it is not at all clear where and how one learns about the free choice of the good. And how would one be able to tell anyway whether a person was pursuing the good for the right reasons or from fear of reprisal? Finally, the argument for coercive habituation assumes that in the absence of threats all inducements to virtue will disappear. But the market order, unhindered by state intervention, carries its own set of regulatory properties, at least with respect to the 'low' virtues. And as to the 'high' virtues, these seem most susceptible to the problems raised by our second objection.[66]

All that remains, then, is the question of the role of virtue with respect to community (as opposed to state). In light of the principles we have argued for in this book, there is significant mutuality among persons only when those persons freely associate under mutually agreeable terms. The 'human' nature of this significant mutuality is defined by the centrality of choice and judgment. Respect for persons is shown by grounding communities in a recognition of the central role of individual judgment and choice. And since virtue must be achieved by individual judgment and choice, virtue and community are connected by the same conception of personhood. This means that virtue is not a phenomenon achieved by or descriptive of communities, but rather is an achievement of individuals. The role of community is secondary; it serves to make possible the achievement of self-perfection. In this sense, communities serve individuals, not individuals communities.

If one accepts our line of argument, it is clear that efforts to promote virtue by political means are not only vain but morally suspect. Statecraft is not, cannot, and ought not to be soul-craft, to paraphrase the title of a popular book. But to say this does not quite address Lerner's question, which was: What kind of man would be produced by the (now) free society? There is also the question of whether the *conditions* for virtue just mentioned ought to be a part of the political and communal efforts. The answer to this latter question is simply yes. What should be done here was described in the last two chapters. Nothing further in terms of state action would be consistent with our principles. The first question is more complicated, but it should be noticed immediately that the question is now a purely sociological one, not a moral or philosophical one. If the type of man produced by the free order is not to our liking, it would certainly not follow that the mechanism of politics ought to be called in to correct the problem. We are left, therefore, with sociological speculation.

To consider the sociological question it may be instructive to back-track a little and consider an ostensibly philosophical work: Adam Smith's *Theory of Moral Sentiments* (*TMS*). Although this work appears to offer a moral theory, that theory is marred by an insoluble dilemma: the "impartial spectator" who makes the final judgment about moral propriety must either make that judgment on the basis of his sentiment or not. If so, what justifies that sentiment over the others being observed in the actions considered? If not, a standard other than sentiment is being used, which seems disallowed by the theory itself and would require its own justification. [67] Nevertheless, it is possible to ignore this problem and treat the work as expressing a theory of moral sociology. If we do this, the actions of the impartial spectator can be considered as descriptive of moral attitudes rather than justificatory, and the work as a whole could be regarded as an account of how moral attitudes and norms are generated in a free society.

The relevance of all this to our point is the following: the free society undoubtedly allows for the free-flowing of the passions, or sentiments. Assuming that people are guided more by their passions than anything else,[68] it is plausible to conclude that the most common personality of such a society would reflect the most common passions, and that such a person's judgments about propriety and impropriety would in some way be described by Smith's account of the development of moral sentiments. Smith claims that benevolence is the highest and most endearing of the passions.[69] Clearly the 'liberal' or 'soft' virtues are favored by Smith, and logically so. For if the program is one of sentiment, the most comfortable sentiments are likely to predominate. The hard virtues are difficult to bear and uncomfortable to experience. Thus, as Lerner suggests, the "new-model man" of the modern world is likely to favor the soft virtues over the hard ones of antiquity.

But our last conclusion may be too quick. What is actually more likely in a pluralistic society is that different sentiments will predominate in different sub-cultures. Although there may be an overall tilt towards the liberal sentiments, a person in the military or an entrepreneurial business may develop a different set of sentiments and values from a college professor or a person with inherited wealth. Smith recognizes and describes these possibilities.[70] What does seem generally evident, in any case, is that moral discussion and debate will proceed in terms of sentiment. In this respect Smith's *TMS* was *predictive* of moral discussion in a free society. We need only observe our own culture to find the validity of Smith's prediction, *even among those most critical of Smith and his system of "natural liberty"*. We can, for example, criticize wealth by pointing to the presence of the poor and imagining ourselves in their place. Indeed, the anticapitalist literature is filled with images appealing to sentiments: 'sweatshops', 'greed', 'selfishness', 'exploitation', 'price gouging', and numerous others could be cited. And political battles are generally won or lost today on the basis of how appealing or evocative the issue in question can be made to the general public. In essence, moral discourse has resulted in what Smith describes in his opening chapters: simply putting oneself in another's place and reflecting upon one feelings.[71] Feelings are decisive; rational analysis serves to clarify, not justify, the sentiments.

Unfortunately, a deeper problem with respect to the prospects for freedom is raised by this scenario. To appreciate this problem, a brief look at the production of moral sentiment as Smith understood it is in order. Essentially, moral sentiments are dependent upon what Smith calls the "correspondence of sentiment."[72] A and B, for example must adopt sentiments that each can experience. This requires that each moderate his sentiment so that the other can enter into it. Extremes of joy or sorrow, for example, cannot be appreciated by an observer, so the one who experiences these will have to modify the sentiment to receive the act of sympathy from another. Smith gives numerous convincing examples of this process,[73] but to mention just one, he observes that displays of public affection are offensive because the observer cannot experience the pleasure enjoyed by the participants.[74] Therefore, their behavior will have to be modified to gain the support of the impartial spectator. (This example was chosen because of what we say later.) The impartial spectator in Smith's theory serves, in effect, to generalize the process just described. For actions to receive approbation or disapprobation, anyone and no one in particular must be able to sympathize with the motives and actions in question. This requires an act of 'standing outside of oneself', or disinterestedness, to accomplish. The impartial spectator is what the name suggests: a disinterested observer.

It is clear that this system of observing the actions and motives of others and reflecting on our feelings does occur, can generate norms of behavior, and can go some distance in explaining current attitudes. But assuming we are still uninterested in the question of why any of this explains how we ought to live, there is the further question of whether this system provides the sort of guidance expected of a moral theory. For if A and B must compromise their sentiments to reach accommodation, where that accommodation will be reached depends on how far apart A and B are at the outset. If A and B are culturally homogeneous, then reaching accord will take little effort. But if they are far apart, not only will more effort be required, but *the point at which correspondence is reached is likely to differ from the case where A and B are homogeneous.* And if A and B reach accord but C is some distance away, then accommodating C will naturally pull A and B away from the point they would have reached without C. This is all because what is 'excessive', and thus in need of moderation, is relative to the sentiments of others in the society. To return to our previous example, public kissing may make eighteenth-century British gentlemen blush, but today public fornication (in the form of pornography) barely raises an eyebrow.

In the system just described, the stability of the norms is a function of the stability and homogeneity of the participants to the sympathetic enterprise. Yet in large pluralistic societies, there is serious doubt that normative stability can be maintained. Without it, however, the guidance sought from ethical principles will be lessened or lost. Now the same picture can be painted of political/moral principles. If sentiment is all that rules, is there any safe haven for private property, rule of law, free and open markets, and the like? Presumably a correspondence of sentiment must be reached with those who have negative feelings about such principles. Depending on the degree and depth of those feelings, these principles will be modified accordingly. Herein lies the problem mentioned above: if the free society unleashes the passions, creating an ethics of sentiment, does it not at the same time threaten those often severe procedural rules designed to maintain the free society itself, especially if the citizenry is heterogeneous?

The problem identified here is one that has been beneath the surface throughout this chapter; for whether one speaks of advantage-friendships, contractarianism, or modern man, the preceding expositions all rest upon a foundation of feeling, sentiment, or desire. In all these cases something else was needed to keep the associations involved from breaking down. What that 'something else' is is usually described in political terms. For some, advantage-friendships need to be replaced by friendships of virtue. For others, the social contract needs to be solidified in constitutional rules. And for still others, the state should dictate virtue if not populate itself with those who possess it. It has been our contention throughout the book that the problem ultimately lies not here, but in the abandonment of an objective theory of value and the effort to recover by political means from the problems that abandonment entails. In making this point, however, we have also implied something relevant to our sociological discussion, namely, the role of intellectuals and ideas in a culture.

There is nothing in a free society that prevents, or even discourages, the pursuit of virtue and human excellence. Indeed, we have argued here that the free society is a precondition for virtue and may in some cases encourage it. We are also not so starry eyed as to believe that the problems we have been discussing in this last section can be solved and a society of virtuous men and women created simply by respecting individual rights. Because virtue is an attribute of individuals and difficult to obtain, it is likely to always be rare. But it does seem plausible to conjecture that if there is a crisis in this area it has more to do with a general lack of respect for the concept of virtue than it does with appropriate political or social mechanisms. Clearly, modern intellectuals have abandoned the traditional conceptions of human excellence and virtue, and this is bound to affect the environment of character development.[75] For when intellectuals abandon a notion, the permeation of the abandoned idea into a culture is difficult or impossible. Intellectuals still stand as that class which validates a culture's beliefs; and that which is not validated is unlikely to remain an object of respect or aspiration.

We are not arguing here that the classical moral perspective should be adopted. We have done that elsewhere in this book. Our point here is sociological: the self-conceptions and values of a culture are largely dependent upon the beliefs of the intellectual class. The ideas that emerge from this class not only influence how the society is structured, but also how it perceives and maintains itself. The "new-model man" is at best only partially a product of the actual characteristics of the system in which he lives. Ignoring the individual's own judgment and choices for the moment, modern man is more a function of his intellectual heritage than his socio-economic background. The same would presumably hold true for antiquity—if virtue were more evident among the regimes of antiquity, that was more likely because of the intellectual commitment to virtue than because of aristocratic rule.

It is beyond our competency as philosophers to endeavor to prove our contention about the significant role of intellectuals upon a society's moral climate. But by indicating that there is no theoretical conflict between the free society and virtue, we have by implication shown that Lerner's alternative of ancient or modern model men is not thereby an alternative among logically connected political forms. In a free society, the degree of virtue exhibited by the citizenry will be up to them—as it should be. Only the Smithian problem of the free-flowing of the passions remains as an intrinsic feature of the free order, and therefore as a possible ultimate threat to liberty itself. But the Smithian problem is not unique to Smith or the free society. The lack of a rational commitment to appropriate principles is the essence of the *political* problem identified long ago by Plato in the Allegory of the Cave. The problem is endemic to all regimes, whether ancient or modern. Plato, and others of his era, were mistaken to associate the structure of one's soul with the structure of a political regime. But he was most certainly correct in his conviction that the identity of a regime is a function of the philosophy that underlies it and that it is, in the end, philosophy that contributes most to the character of the citizens' souls.

6

CONCLUSION

In Locke explicitly, and implicitly in all natural rights theorists, claims about natural rights presuppose claims about natural law. By natural law is meant here the theory that there are certain moral necessities, certain principles of conduct, which flow directly from an independently identifiable human good. The matrix of any theory of natural rights, then, is an account of natural law. In the absence of an account of natural law, indeed, natural rights theories are not wholly coherent or defensible: the rights they yield are stillborn, deprived of the environment in which they can be conceived and brought to birth.

—John Gray, *Liberalism*

Liberal political theory grew out of a tradition other than the Aristotelian one. For the most part, liberalism can be roughly categorized as an outgrowth of British empiricism, since liberalism's founding fathers include such figures are Hobbes, Locke, Hume, and Adam Smith. Nevertheless, certain continental thinkers—such as Voltaire, Kant, and Spinoza—have also factored into the development of the liberal political tradition. Virtually all of these thinkers share a rejection of Aristotelianism, although the degree and explicitness of that rejection varies. We, on the other hand, have tried to lay the foundations for a liberal political theory within the Aristotelian tradition. The liberalism for which we have chosen to seek a moral foundation is one which justifies itself by reference to natural rights. Whether we have succeeded is not for us to judge; but a moment spent on some of the thematic characteristics of our project should be an appropriate way to conclude this volume.

By the standards of modern times (the last 300 years), classical political philosophy, such as that produced by Plato and Aristotle, could not be classified as liberal. Liberty is not one of the core values of antiquity, and it can be doubted whether the thinkers of antiquity fully appreciated the value of the individual person. Moreover, the Strausseans claim that Plato was the seminal thinker of classical political theory, indicating an antiliberal tendency within that tradition. And MacIntyre has recently argued that the chief foe of Aristotelianism is the Enlightenment. Yet both classical and modern political philosophy saw the need for theories about human co-operation in a social setting and tended to base those theories on certain conceptions of human nature.

Since our discussion here is thematic, let us work with two basic categories—co-operation and personhood. Let us further adopt the terminology of speaking of either category in terms of being 'thick' or 'thin'. A theory of the person is thin if the general characteristics of personhood are few in number, especially as those characteristics affect action and motivation. Hobbes, Spinoza, and Hume, for example, would have a thin theory of the person, since these thinkers see human beings in terms of two general principles—reason and desire—with all the complexities of human nature being ultimately reducible to one or the other of these two basic features of human existence. Another example would be the economist's commitment to *homo economicus* which, of course, is simply a more rigorous extension of the theories advocated by the philosophers just mentioned. A thick theory, on the other hand, would see the person as characterized by a complex set of principles and would tend to avoid reductionistic conceptions. Plato's tripartite version of the soul as well as Aristotle's hierarchical and multifunctional 'types' of soul would be examples here.

If we consider the concept of co-operation, 'thickness' or 'thinness' is determined by the number of regulating principles that must be adhered to for co-operation to be said to have been completed. The fewer the number of regulating principles, the thinner the theory of co-operation. Hobbes, for example, would have a thin theory of co-operation because obedience to the sovereign is all that is required for co-operation to be completed. Plato, on the other hand, would have a thick theory of co-operation, because of the numerous categories of conduct whose rules one must obey for social co-operation to be realized.

With this convention in mind, we can characterize liberal political theory (both past and present) as having a thin theory of the person and a thin theory of the requirements for co-operation. Since liberal social theorists have tended to see persons as moved primarily or exclusively by their desires (or interests, wants, preferences, or passions), the areas of rules for co-operation are limited in number and tend to concern ways in which the problem of conflicting desires can be solved. Liberty is given primacy of place because all desires are essentially equal, thus removing any justification for giving one set of desires (values) priority over another. What remains, therefore, is the task of making room for as many different expressions of desire as possible. This, in turn, seems to require as few rules as possible. The rules that *are* formulated are generally universal and negative.

If liberalism is characterized as a thin theory of the person coupled with a thin theory of co-operation, antiliberal theories are generally of the sort that have a thick theory of the person and thus a thick theory of co-operation. For the most part, the Aristotelian tradition has not been sympathetic to the liberal political tradition, which is not to say that tradition has ignored the importance of liberty in human life. But our discussions of people like Finnis, Maritain, MacIntyre, and others should indicate a basic dissatisfaction these thinkers have with the foundations of liberalism and often with the conclusions of liberal political theory. This dissatisfaction arises because the Aristotelian tends to see the person as more than, say, a rational utility maximizer or a slave to passion. The atomistic implications of these conceptions seem to violate the Aristotelian thesis about man's sociability, not to mention the more restrictive range of ends such theories postulate. It would seem, therefore, that there must be more to co-operation than simply negative liberty, and this insight translates into a more extensive state than classical liberals would allow.

In this book we have attempted to break the mold by selecting one of the two remaining alternative approaches to these two categories. One of these alternatives is to have a thin theory of the person and a thick theory of co-operation. This alternative is the one that seems to be adopted by modern liberals. They tend to see the person in much the same way as the classical liberals, but since they distrust market mechanisms, emphasis is placed upon state imposed solutions to conflicts among diverse desires. We see classical liberalism as more consistent than this approach; but in any case, this is not the remaining alternative we have selected. What we have done here is to argue for a thick theory of the person and a thin theory of the requirements for social co-opera-tion. In other words, we have tried to avoid the reductionistic tendencies of classical liberalism (and certain contemporary versions of libertarian-ism) while at the same time remaining true to the minimalist tenets of liberalism and libertarianism.

Our own position is made possible by our agreement with one fun-damental principle of modern political philosophy in opposition to the classical political philosophy of Plato and Aristotle, and with one central principle of classical political philosophy in opposition to modernity. If we take both traditions as attempting to find solutions to the problem of human social co-operation, the central disagreement between them seems to center around the basic meaning of *co-operation*. Following Hobbes, modern political theory takes *co-operation* to mean peace (the absence of war). This is why social contract theories have been and are so prevalent in the liberal political tradition—they provide test cases for conceptualizing the principles of peace. Classical political philosophy, on the other hand, regards moral perfection as the true standard of co-opera-tion. A mere reconciliation of desires can never solve the problem of co-operation in the long run, because it is the very need to control and di-rect desire that makes sociality possible.

The arguments of the preceding chapters indicate our agreement with modern political philosophy that social co-operation does not depend upon the realization of moral perfection. But instead of denying the meaningfulness of a concept like moral perfection, and instead of seeing liberty and natural rights as merely a mechanism for solving the problem of conflict, we have sought to give liberty moral significance by showing that the natural right to liberty is a social and political condition neces-sary for the possibility of our moral perfection. In this latter way, we are agreeing with antiquity that social theory must always have an eye to-wards moral perfection. Moreover, we also agree with antiquity that unless the prime social values are regarded as moral commitments, con-flict resolution will remain simply a function of academic theorizing.

The paradigm of the two basic world views (modern and classical) we have presented is not so rigid as we have made it seem. Liberalism actually leaves the possibility of moral perfection open. All it says is that we must first solve the problem of social conflict before we can worry about perfection. And antiquity is not necessarily opposed to the idea that perfection must be achieved in stages and that such stages may involve certain preconditions that must be met and maintained if further advancement is to be achieved. Furthermore, antiquity is not necessarily committed to the notion that the state must be the vehicle by which people are directed to their proper ends. These logical openings in both traditions are what make our position possible. What we have done is to take advantage of them and to indicate a possible means of reconciling morality and liberty.

In the end, our project might be understood as an effort to resuscitate the founding philosophy of the American political tradition. For it is evident from the Declaration of Independence that our Founding Fathers were committed both to moral truth (through natural rights) and liberal political institutions. At present the connection between them has been severed. Different quarters on the contemporary scene are engaged either in attacking the idea of moral truth or engaged in attacking liberal politics. In other words, neo-Hobbesians reject the commitment to objective values while various communitarian forces find fault with the Enlightenments commitment to pluralism and the private pursuit of interest. Since we have endeavored to steer clear of both approaches, our project can be considered as a defense of the American political tradition. We do, however, concede that the balance of moral truth with liberal politics is an uneasy one. It requires a certain kind of philosophical backing—one not adequately found in traditional Enlightenment doctrines. We believe the Aristotelian tradition offers the appropriate backing. That tradition is perhaps the only remaining unexplored source for providing liberalism with the kind of secure moral footing it desperately needs.

NOTES

CHAPTER 1

1. In some cases, not all the thinkers discussed offer direct attacks on Aristotelian ethics, and so we will in these cases 'manufacture' criticism out of available positive theories. Our purpose in these instances will be to discover why Aristotelian ethics was ignored.
2. Our purpose here is not to critique competing theories but to open the door for our own. Thus we feel it to be beyond the scope of this chapter to show that our theory is 'superior' by directly critiquing an alternative theory. We do so, as noted, only when we believe our response is thereby clarified.
3. The one sense in which they are not diverse is that they might all fit under the general heading of *analytic philosophers.*
4. More general critiques of themes in twentieth century ethics can be found in Alasdair MacIntyre, *After Virtue* (Notre Dame, Indiana: University of Notre Dame Press, 1981) and Henry Veatch, *For An Ontology of Morals,* (Evanston, Illinois: Northwestern University Press, 1971).
5. Charles King, 'Moral Theory and the Foundations of Social Order' in *The Libertarian Reader,* ed. Tibor R. Machan (Totowa, New Jersey: Rowman and Littlefield, 1982), 17.
6. *Ibid.* Similarly, John Gray has declared that "Aristotle supports his moral theory with a metaphysical biology which depends in the last resort on a *mystical* conception of nature as a system tending to perfection. There seems little room for Aristotelian. . . ideas of final causes or natural ends in a modern scientific worldview which has expelled teleology from itself . . . . That is to say, in short, that the conception of natural law needed to support a theory of natural rights is incompatible with modern empiricism". (*Liberalism* [Minneapolis: University of Minnesota Press, 1986], 46, emphasis added.) Also, MacIntyre in *After Virtue* states: "Any adequate generally Aristotelian account must supply a teleological account which can replace Aristotle's metaphysical biology". (152) We explicitly deal with these sorts of objections in Chapter 2. But see also Tibor R. Machan, 'Natural Rights Liberalism', *Philosophy and Theology* (Spring 1990).
7. King, 'Moral Theory and Foundations of Social Order', 23

8. E3P51.

9. King, 'Moral Theory and the Foundations of Social Order', 21.

10. Charles King, 'Life and the Theory of Value: The Randian Argument Reconsidered' in *The Philosophic Thought of Ayn Rand*, ed. Douglas J. Den Uyl and Douglas B. Rasmussen (Urbana and Chicago: University of Illinois Press, 1984), 102–121.

11. See Douglas B. Rasmussen, 'Logical Possibility: An Aristotelian Essentialist Critique', *The Thomist* 47 (October 1983): 513–540.

12. King, 'Life and the Theory of Value: The Randian Argument Reconsidered', 74.

13. *Ibid.*, 75.

14. *Ibid.*, 77.

15. See *Nicomachean Ethics,* 1102a5–1103b2 and *De Anima*, 433a1–433b30.

16. Gilbert Harman, 'Human Flourishing, Ethics, and Liberty', *Philosophy and Public Affairs* 12 (Fall 1983): 307–322. There have been recent applications of Harman's version of relativism—most notably David Gauthier. See *Morals by Argreement* (Oxford: Oxford University Press, 1986), Chapter 2.

17. Gilbert Harman, 'Libertarianism and Morality', *The Libertarian Reader*, 231.

18. Harman calls these "inner judgments". See Gilbert Harman, 'Moral Relativism Defended' in *Relativism: Cognitive and Moral,* ed. Jack Meiland and Michael Krausz (Notre Dame, Indiana: University of Notre Dame Press, 1982), 190.

19. *Ibid.*

20. Gilbert Harman, 'Justice and Moral Bargaining', *Social Philosophy and Public Policy* 1 (Autumn 1983), 114.

21. Harman, 'Moral Relativism Defended', 191.

22. *Ibid.*, 196.

23. It is worth noting here that someone for whom Harman should have some sympathies—Thomas Hobbes—*did* see agreement as a kind of ritual. Hobbes argued that for a contract to be meaningful, "sufficient signs" must be given by all parties to the contract (*De Cive* II, 4).

24. Harman, 'Libertarianism and Morality', 232.

25. Harman, 'Justice and Moral Bargaining', 129.

26. Harman would then be denying the existence of, rather than explaining, moral principles contrary to one's interests.

27. 'Justice and Moral Bargaining', 130–31.

28. *Ibid.*, 130.

29. Benito Mussolini, *Diuturna*, 374–77. Quoted by Henry B. Veatch, *Rational Man* (Bloomington, Indiana: Indiana University Press, 1962), 41.

30. Robert Nozick, *Philosophical Explanations* (Cambridge, Massachusetts: Harvard University Press, 1981), 410.

31. *Ibid.*, 505ff.

32. See Robert Nozick, 'On the Randian Argument' in *Reading Nozick,* ed. Jeffrey Paul (Totowa, New Jersey: Rowman and Littlefield, 1981), 206–31.
33. Douglas J. Den Uyl and Douglas B. Rasmussen, 'Nozick On the Randian Argument', *Reading Nozick,* 232–269.
34. Nozick, *Philosophical Explanations,* 515. John Gray makes objections along similar lines: *Liberalism,* 47–50.
35. Jennifer Whiting, 'Aristotle's Function Argument: A Defense', *Ancient Philosophy* 8 (Spring1988): 33–48 argues persuasively that Aristotle did not hold the view Nozick attributes to him.
36. Whiting (*Ibid.,* 38–39) points out that the formal and final causes coincide in the *ergon* argument. We cannot understand what an organism essentially is without knowing something about what benefits it.
37. When trying to determine whether Q and P are necessarily related, Nozick assumes that if he can imagine (picture) Q without P or if the definition of Q does not involve P or vice versa, then he can 'suppose' or 'conceive' of Q without P and thus show that they are only contingently related. This entire way of arguing fails to consider how the definitions of Q and P were determined or what it is that allows us to decide what our pictures picture. It further treats the significance of concepts as if it were determined by some criterion-in-mind and ignores what the natures of Q and P involve. Overall, this way of arguing assumes that a procedure of *inspectio mentis* is a legitimate procedure for determining whether a state-of-affairs is possible. An Aristotelian approach to conceiving rejects this procedure in toto. See Rasmussen, 'Logical Possibility: An Aristotelian Essentialist Critique', 513–540.
38. Nozick, *Philosophical Explanations,* 516.
39. It is worth noting that Aquinas held angels don't reason. *Summa Theologiae* I, Q. 58. art. 4.
40. In this regard, Nozick is similar to Quine. See Douglas B. Rasmussen, 'Quine and Aristotelian Essentialism', *The New Scholasticism* 58 (Summer 1984): 316–335.
41. Alan Gewirth, *Reason and Morality* (Chicago: University of Chicago Press, 1978).
42. Rocco, Porreco, ed., *The Georgetown Symposium on Ethics* (Lanham, Maryland: University Press of America, 1984).
43. *Ibid.,* 70.
44. *Ibid.*
45. *Ibid.,* 71.
46. *Ibid.,* 72–73.
47. *Ibid.,* 73.
48. *Ibid.,* 74.
49. *Ibid.*
50. *Ibid.,* 76.

51. *Ibid.*, 77.
52. *Ibid.* See also note 36 above.
53. *Ibid.*, 80.
54. See Henry B. Veatch, *Rational Man*, 217–218.
55. Rocco, *Georgetown Symposium on Ethics*, 77–79.
56. *Ibid.*, 79–84.
57. *Ibid.*, 80.
58. We shall ignore the important question of whether general agreement necessarily indicates truth.
59. *The Georgetown Symposium on Ethics,* 80.
60. Veatch, *Rational Man*, 136.
61. For a further discussion of this point see Douglas J. Den Uyl, *The Virtue of Prudence* (New York: Peter Lang, 1991), Chapter 8.
62. Cf. *Discourse on Method*, Part III.
63. This theme is given more sustained treatment in the next chapter.
64. Cf. Murray Rothbard, *Egalitarianism As a Revolt Against Nature and Other Essays* (Washington, D.C.: Libertarian Review Press, 1974).

CHAPTER 2

1. See Douglas B. Rasmussen, 'Logical Possibility: An Aristotelian Essentialist Critique', *The Thomist* 47 (October 1983): 513–540.
2. See Douglas B. Rasmussen, 'Quine and Aristotelian Essentialism', *The New Scholasticism* 58 (Summer 1984): 316–335 for an account of the empirical character of real definitions as well as a critique of Quine's criticisms of Aristotelian essentialism.
3. See Douglas B. Rasmussen, 'The Open-Question Argument and the Issue of Conceivability', *Proceedings of the American Catholic Philosophical Association* 56 (1982): 162–172, especially pages 168–170.
4. See Douglas B. Rasmussen's review essay of Roger Trigg's *Reality at Risk* in *Reason Papers* 9 (Winter 1983): 85–90.
5. It should be further noted that the Kantian turn in epistemology (which conflates the mode of cognition with the content of cognition) need only be made if one accepts the assumption that percepts and concepts are what we know rather than that by which we know. See Douglas B. Rasmussen, 'Ideology, Objectivity, and Political Theory' in *Ideology and American Experience*, ed. J.K. Roth and R.C. Whittemore (Washington, D.C.: Washington Institute Press, 1986), 45–71.
6. See Tibor R. Machan, 'Epistemology and Moral Knowledge', *The Review of Metaphysics* 36 (September 1982): 23–49.
7. See Baruch Brody, *Identity and Essence* (Princeton: Princeton University Press, 1980), 84–134 for a discussion (and qualification) of these criteria.
8. Aristotle, *De Anima* II, 5 (Oxford Translation), 417b18–25, emphasis

added. '*Wishes*' refers to rational desire rather than mere whim. Fred Miller, Jr. called this passage to our attention.

9. Conceptualizing "is not a passive state of registering random impressions. It is an actively sustained process of identifying one's impressions in conceptual terms, of integrating every event and every observation into a conceptual context, of grasping relationships, differences, similarities in one's perceptual material and of abstracting them into new concepts, of drawing inferences, of making deductions, of reaching conclusions, of asking new questions and discovering new answers and expanding one's knowledge into an ever-growing sum." Ayn Rand, 'The Objectivist Ethics' in *The Virtue of Selfishness* (New York: New American Library, 1961), 20.

10. For convenience, *generic potentialities* is used here, and throughout the text, to refer not only to those potentialities that a being has in virtue of belonging to a certain genus but also to those potentialities a being has in virtue of belonging to a certain species.

11. Simply because something is a potentiality, something which can be but at present is not, does not, in and of itself, provide any reason why it is to be actualized.

12. We interpret living rationally or intelligently not to be merely the life of contemplation, *theoria,* but the practical life of man as possessing reason. We heartily concur with Henry Veatch's observation that man's true end is to *live* intelligently, since knowing is for the sake of living, not vice versa. See Henry B. Veatch, *Rational Man* (Bloomington, Indiana: Indiana University Press, 1962), 67.

13. Cf. Douglas J. Den Uyl and Tibor R. Machan, 'Recent Work on Happiness', *American Philosophical Quarterly* 20 (April 1983): 115–134.

14. Tibor R. Machan, *Human Rights and Human Liberties* (Chicago: Nelson-Hall, 1974), 74–75.

15. W.F.R. Hardie, 'The Final Good in Aristotle's Ethics' in *Aristotle: A Collection of Critical Essays*, ed. J.M.E. Moravcsik (Notre Dame, Indiana: University of Notre Dame Press, 1968), 297–322.

16. Immanuel Kant, *Foundations of the Metaphysics of Morals*, trans. Lewis W. Beck (New York: Bobbs-Merrill, 1959), section I, 11–14.

17. *Ibid.*, 15.

18. Roger J. Sullivan, 'The Kantian Critique of Aristotle's Moral Philosophy: An Appraisal', *The Review of Metaphysics* 28 (Summer 1974): 24–53.

19. Kant himself recommends that happiness be pursued as a duty (*Foundations of the Metaphysics of Morals,* 15). This is because those who are happy are more likely to do their other duties. But this whole recommendation is contradictory on Kant's part. In the first place, pursuing happiness for the sake of doing our other duties violates the very principle of duty, since any duty must be done for its own sake. Secondly, how can one pursue the satisfaction of inclinations without satisfying the inclination of hap-

piness itself? But if one satisfies the inclination of happiness, then the Kantian prescription that all duties must be fulfilled without recourse to inclination will be violated.

20. Aristotle, *Nicomachean Ethics* 2.4 1105b5–9.
21. Andrew G. Oldenquist, *Moral Philosophy: Texts and Readings* (Boston: Houghton Mifflin Co., 1978), Chapter 1.
22. Aristotle, *Nicomachean Ethics*, 2.4 1105a32–35.
23. See Fred Miller, Jr., 'The State and the Community in Aristotle's *Politics*', *Reason Papers* 1 (Fall 1974): 63–64.
24. See Tibor R. Machan, *The Pseudo-Science of B.F. Skinner* (New Rochelle, New York: Arlington House, 1974). Also see Machan, 'Essentialism Sans Inner Natures', *Philosophy of the Social Sciences* 10 (1980): 195–200. This article is a reply to Larry Briskman, 'Skinnerism and Pseudo-Science', *The Philosophy of the Social Sciences* 9 (1979): 81–103, which is a critique of Machan's book. Further, Briskman has a rejoinder, 'Essentialism Without Inner Natures?' *The Philosophy of the Social Sciences* 12 (September 1982): 303–09. However, see finally Machan, 'Epistemology and Moral Knowledge'.
25. See Marjorie Grene, 'Aristotle and Modern Biology' in *Topics in the Philosophy of Biology*, ed. Grene and Mendelsohn (Dordrecht, Holland: D. Reidel, 1976), 3–36; David Lowenthal, 'The Case for Teleology', *Independent Journal of Philosophy* 2 (1978): 95–105; Francisco J. Ayala, 'The Autonomy of Biology as a Natural Science' in *Biology, History, and Natural Philosophy*, ed. Breck and Yourgrau (New York: Plenum Press, 1972), 1–16; Allan Gotthelf, 'Aristotle's Conception of Final Causality', *The Review of Metaphysics* (December 1976): 226–254; Gotthelf, ed., *Aristotle On Nature and Living Things* (Pittsburgh, Pa.: Mathesis Publications and Bristol, England: Bristol Classical Press, 1985); Allan Gotthelf and James Lennox, eds., *Philosophical Issues in Aristotle's Biology* (Cambridge: Cambridge University Press, 1987); Michael Bradie and Fred Miller, Jr., 'Teleology and Natural Necessity in Aristotle', *History of Philosophy Quarterly* 1 (April 1984): 133–146; and Harry Binswanger, *The Biological Basis of Teleological Concepts* (Los Angeles: Ayn Rand Institute Press, 1990).
26. Gotthelf, 'Aristotle's Conception of Final Causality', 231.
27. Bradie and Miller, 'Teleology and Natural Necessity in Aristotle', 143.
28. Gotthelf, 'Aristotle's Conception of Final Causality', 253. Also, see Bradie and Miller's 'Teleology and Natural Necessity in Aristotle' for a discussion of how the "irreducible potential for form" interpretation of teleology does not require irreducibility at all levels of explanation.
29. Allan Gotthelf, 'The Place of the Good in Aristotle's Natural Teleology' in *Proceedings of the Boston Area Colloquium in Ancient Philosophy,* vol. IV, ed. John J. Cleary and Daniel C. Shartin (Lanham, Maryland: University Press of America, 1989), 133.

30. Eric Mack, 'How to Derive Libertarian Rights' in *Reading Nozick*, ed. Jeffrey Paul (Totowa, New Jersey: Rowman and Littlefield, 1981), 294.
31. *Ibid.*, 291-302.
32. Rand, 'The Objectivist Ethics', 17.
33. *Ibid.*
34. Patrick M. O'Neil, 'Ayn Rand and the Is-Ought Problem', *Journal of Libertarian Studies* 7 (Spring 1983): 85. Also, see Jeffrey Paul, 'Substantive Social Contracts and the Legitimate Basis of Political Authority', *The Monist* 66 (October 1983): 517–528 for a version of this difficulty as it applies to contractarianism, and Paul, 'On the Foundations of Natural Rights', *Reason Papers* 13 (Spring 1988): 48–66, as it applies to natural-end ethics.
35. See Douglas J. Den Uyl and Douglas B. Rasmussen, 'Nozick On the Randian Argument' in *Reading Nozick*, 232–269; Douglas B. Rasmussen, 'The Groundwork for Rights: Man's Natural End', *The Journal of Libertarian Studies* 4 (Winter 1980): 65–76; and Douglas J. Den Uyl and Douglas B. Rasmussen, 'In Defense of Natural End Ethics: A Rejoinder to O'Neil and Osterfeld', *Journal of Libertarian Studies* 7 (Spring 1983): 115–125.
36. William K. Frankena, 'The Naturalistic Fallacy', *Mind* 48 (October 1939): 471. This is also Jeffrey Paul's basic objection in 'On the Foundation of Natural Rights'.
37. See Henry B. Veatch, *For An Ontology of Morals* (Evanston, Illinois: Northwestern University Press, 1971), especially chapters 2, 3, and 6.
38. See Frankena, 'The Naturalistic Fallacy'.
39. For the purposes of this discussion, we will include natural-end ethics in the category of naturalistic theories. We do this for the sake of simplifying the discussion but do not assume that one can move directly from any 'is' to an 'ought'.
40. Frankena, 'The Naturalistic Fallacy', 473.
41. In *Nicomachean Ethics* 1.6 Aristotle denies that goodness is a single identical property. Further, the Aristotelian tradition does not consider goodness something capable of definition *per genus et differentiam*. Goodness is one of the 'transcendentals'. Panayot Butchvarov in 'That Simple, Indefinable, Nonnatural Property Good', *Review of Metaphysics* 36 (September 1982): 51–75 and in *Skepticism in Ethics* (Bloomington and Indianapolis: Indiana University Press, 1989) has argued that the claim that goodness is indefinable is simply that it cannot be defined *per genus et differentiam*. We have no objection to Butchvarov's interpreting this claim this way. Yet, we would only note (as Butchvarov recognizes) that the fact that a definition *per genus et differentiam* for goodness cannot be offered does not imply that nothing can be said about what goodness really is (and must be) or that goodness does not exist. Broadly speaking, *goodness* can be 'defined'. Aquinas does this sort of thing in, for example, *De Veritate*, Qu. 21 and 22. Further, it must be remembered that the fact that goodness is not univocal

does not imply that it is something totally equivocal. Goodness can be understood relationally. We will, however, discuss this point later in this section. Finally, see Jack Wheeler's discussion of the meaning of the good for Aristotle in his essay, 'Rand and Aristotle: A Comparison of Objectivist and Aristotelian Ethics' in *The Philosophic Thought of Ayn Rand,* ed. Douglas J. Den Uyl and Douglas B. Rasmussen (Urbana and Chicago: University of Illinois Press, 1984), 82–85.

42. See Panayot Butchvarov's *The Concept of Knowledge* (Evanston, Illinois: Northwestern University Press, 1970), 105-142 for a most devastating critique of the attempt to explain necessary truth in terms of analyticity. Butchvarov shows the various notions of analyticity used by modern and contemporary philosophers to be inadequate to the task of explaining the necessity of logical truths themselves. Thus, the search for synthetic a priori truths—necessary truths that do not have self-contradictory denials—is largely beside the point. Milton Fisk in *Nature and Necessity* (Bloomington and London: Indiana University Press, 1973), 24–48, 123–149 makes a related point. Also, see Butchvarov's discussion of real definitions in *Being Qua Being* (Bloomington and London: Indiana University Press, 1979), 134–37.

43. We are only assuming that having a self-contradictory denial is a necessary condition for a proposition being a necessary truth.

44. Strictly speaking, the issue to be determined by the open-question argument is not whether it is *meaningful* to deny a naturalistic definition of goodness, but rather, is it *self-contradictory.* Self-contradictions are necessarily false, but they are not meaningless. By the same token, tautologies are also not meaningless; they are necessarily true. They do not, however, provide any *new* information. See Butchvarov, *The Concept of Knowledge.*

45. See Saul Kripke, 'Naming and Necessity' in *Semantics and Natural Languages,* ed. Donald Davidson and Gilbert Harman (Dordrecht: D. Reidel, 1972), 253–355; R. Harré and E.H. Madden, *Causal Powers* (Totowa, New Jersey: Rowman and Littlefield, 1975); and Brody, *Identity and Essence.*

46. See 'The Open-Question Argument and the Issue Of Conceivability', 162–172.

47. See Veatch's *For An Ontology of Morals,* 108–110 for a discussion of goodness as a supervenient or consequential feature.

48. *Ibid.,* 106–124.

49. Gotthelf, 'The Place of the Good in Aristotle's Natural Teleology', 139.

50. Veatch in his *For An Ontology of Morals,* 113, follows Aquinas by explaining potentiality as a kind of *appetitus*—an appetite or desire for the relevant actuality—that pervades, albeit analogously, all of reality. See also Peter Simpson, *Goodness and Nature* (Dordrecht: Martinus Nijhoff, 1987), 135–36.

51. Machan, *Human Rights and Human Liberties,* 66.
52. Ayn Rand, 'What Is Capitalism?', *Capitalism: The Unknown Ideal* (New York: New American Library, 1967), 22.
53. John Rawls, *A Theory of Justice* (Cambridge, Massachusetts: Belknap Press of Harvard University Press, 1971), 24–26, and William K. Frankena, *Ethics* (Englewood Cliffs, New Jersey: Prentice-Hall, 1963), 13.
54. W.D. Ross, *Aristotle* (New York: Barnes and Noble, 1966), 188. Yet Ross does state in a footnote that at times teleology is immanent for Aristotle and thus "the good act is a means to the good in the sense that it forms an element in the ideal life". *Ibid.*
55. John M. Cooper, *Reason and Human Good in Aristotle* (Cambridge, Massachusetts and London, England: Harvard University, 1975), 88.
56. Robert Nozick, 'On the Randian Argument', *Reading Nozick,* 215.
57. *Foundations of the Metaphysics of Morals,* 30–31.
58. Aristotle, *NE* 1.7 1098a5–7, *NE* 10.6 1176b2–4. John Finnis notes the neo-Aristotelian maxim: "*omne ens perficitur in actu:* flourishing is to be found in *action.*" *Fundamentals of Ethics* (Washington, D.C.: Georgetown University Press, 1983), 39.
59. If we consider the animal kingdom, the same can be said of automatic guiding mechanisms provided by nature to the animal. Animals which are not prevented for environmental reasons from pursuing the types of actions nature has dictated for that species are successful in both the productive and expressive senses. We have recognized this fact in recent years in zoos, which have endeavored to establish more 'natural' habitats for their animals to avoid the psychological and health problems found under the old conditions.
60. It is interesting to note that Henry Veatch argues that consequentialism is ultimately just another form of deontologism since, for example, the happiness principle in utilitarianism functions precisely as a deontological rule. See Henry Veatch, ' Telos and Teleology in Aristotelian Ethics' in *Studies in Aristotle,* ed. Dominic J. O'Meara (Washington, D.C.: Catholic Univ. of America Press, 1981), 279–296.
61. The opposite, e.g. paternalism, is also false. Others are in no better position, and probably a worse one, to know what will benefit one either. An Aristotelian ethics simply challenges the assumption that one is necessarily possessed of self-knowledge or that one can attain it by simply, and effortlessly, examining one's 'interests'.
62. Veatch, 'Telos and Teleology in Aristotle's Ethics', 287.
63. Harman states: "A second feature of this approach to ethics is that it tends toward utilitarianism or consequentialism. 'Human Flourishing, Ethics, and Liberty', *Philosophy and Public Affairs* 12 (Fall 1983): 313.
64. Our interpretation and understanding of human flourishing or eudaimonia has benefited from Cooper's *Reason and Human Good in Aristotle,* particularly Chapter 2, 'Moral Virtue and Human Flourishing'.

65. *Ibid.*, 124.
66. Aristotle, *Nicomachean Ethics*, 1099b25–29.
67. Cooper, *Reason and Human Good in Aristotle*, 123.
68. Neither is human flourishing a single, dominant end which allows no other ends to have value except as a means to it, but this shall be discussed later.
69. It must be remembered that an Aristotelian ethics never claims greater certitude than its subject matter allows.
70. For an alternative view, see John Cooper, 'Aristotle On The Goods of Fortune', *The Philosophical Review* (April 1985): 173–196. Our position regarding the goods life requires is developed in the next chapter, in our discussion of property.
71. See Douglas J. Den Uyl, *The Virtue of Prudence*, (New York: Lang, 1991), Chapters 8–9.
72. See Rand, 'The Objectivist Ethics'.
73. See Nathaniel Branden, *Honoring the Self* (Los Angeles: Jeremy P. Tarcher, 1983), 24–25.
74. Henry B. Veatch, *Aristotle: A Contemporary Appreciation* (Bloomington, Indiana: Indiana University Press, 1974), 108–09.
75. Veatch, *Rational Man*, 93.
76. Aristotle, *Nicomachean Ethics*, 1166b19–22.
77. David Norton, *Personal Destinies* (Princeton: Princeton University Press, 1976), 222.
78. J.L. Ackrill, 'Aristotle on Eudaimonia' in *Essays on Aristotle's Ethics*, ed. Amelie O. Rorty (Berkeley and Los Angeles: University of California Press, 1980), 23.
79. However, what makes these virtues so essential is precisely the fact that they cannot be properly understood *without* reason or intelligence. This is perhaps why the moral virtues are given such importance by Aristotle. Their very exercise demands intelligence.
80. See John M. Cooper, 'Aristotle on the Forms of Friendship', *The Review of Metaphysics* 30 (June 1977): 619–648.
81. John M. Cooper, 'Friendship and Good in Aristotle', *The Philosophical Review* 86 (1977): 310.
82. *Ibid.*, 299.
83. *Ibid.*, 305.
84. *Ibid.*, 310.
85. Fred D. Miller Jr., 'Aristotle on Rationality in Action', *The Review of Metaphysics* 37 (March 1984): 499–520.
86. This passage was brought to our attention by Fred D. Miller, Jr.
87. See Norton, *Personal Destinies*, Chapters 1, 6, and 7.
88. See Douglas J. Den Uyl, 'Freedom and Virtue' in *The Libertarian Reader*, ed. Tibor R. Machan (Totowa, New Jersey: Rowman and Littlefield, 1981); and 'Freedom and Virtue Revisited' in *Man, Economy, Liberty: Essays in*

Honor of Murray Rothbard, ed. Walter Block and Llewellyn H. Rockwell Jr. (Auburn, Alabama: Ludwig von Mises Institute, 1988).

89. In this sense it is, strictly speaking, the potentiality for being an end-in-oneself that matters politically, not the actuality. Ends signify accomplishments. Simply existing is not an accomplishment, so *pace* the usual understanding, one is not an end-in-onself simply because one exists. One must, however, be treated as a being capable of achieving self-perfection, capable of being an actual end-in-oneself.

90. Immanuel Kant, *Fundamental Principles of the Metaphysics of Morals*, trans. Thomas K. Abbott (Chicago: Henry Regnery, 1949), section 2, 53.

91. See Alasdair MacIntyre, *After Virtue* (Notre Dame, Indiana: University of Notre Dame Press, 1981), 44–45.

92. For a discussion and defense of the scientific legitimacy of self-directedness, see Roger W. Sperry, *Science and Moral Priority: Merging Mind, Brain, and Human Values* (New York: Columbia University Press, 1983), 21–39; 'Mental Phenomena as Causal Determinants in Brain Function' in *Consciousness and the Brain: A Scientific and Philosophical Inquiry*, ed. G.C. Globus Maxwell and I. Savodnik (New York: Plenum Press, 1974), 163–177; 'Changing Concepts of Consciousness and Free Will', *Perspectives in Biology and Medicine* 9 (Autumn 1976): 9–19; and 'Mind, Brain, and Humanistic Values' in *New Views of the Nature of Man*, ed. J.R. Platt (Chicago: University of Chicago Press, 1965). Also, see Joseph M. Boyle, Jr., G. Grisez, and O. Tollefsen, *Free Choice: A Self-Referential Argument* (Notre Dame, Indiana: University of Notre Dame Press, 1976) for an argument against the very coherence of the claim that there is no self-directed human action.

93. Commonsensically, we would say of this person that he has no self-respect. Metaphysically, we would say that he denies that he has the potentiality to be an end-in-himself.

94. Mack, 'How to Derive Libertarian Rights', 291.

95. It can also be said that according to this account of Aristotelian natural-end ethics, the human good is 'agent-relative' and yet objective and universalizable. An elaboration of these concepts is found in the next chapter.

CHAPTER 3

1. Robert Nozick, *Anarchy, State and Utopia* (New York: Basic Books, 1974), 33.

2. Isaiah Berlin, *Four Essays on Liberty* (London: Oxford University Press, 1969), 137.

3. Nozick never claimed to be presenting a moral foundation for individual or Lockean rights. "This book does not present a precise theory of the moral

basis for individual rights". (*Anarchy, State and Utopia*, xiv.) Moreover,
Nozick did not claim to know whether his later work on the foundations of
ethics would be able to link up with a notion of Lockean rights or lead to a
completely different view. See *Philosophical Explanations* (Cambridge,
Mass.: Harvard University Press, 1981), 498–99. In his most recent work,
The Examined Life: Philosophical Manifestations (New York: Simon and
Schuster, 1989), Nozick claims that the position propounded in *Anarchy,
State and Utopia* seems inadequate because it "did not knit the humane
considerations and joint co-operative activities it left room for more
closely into its fabric. . . . There are some things we choose to do together
through government in solemn marking of our human solidarity, served by
the fact that we do them together in this official fashion." (286–87) Nozick,
however, has very little to say in defense of his new position. In Chapter 4
we seek to show how the view of rights presented in this chapter is
not only consistent with the natural sociality of man, but also the basis
for human solidarity. Also, the importance of understanding commercial
and civil society in terms of 'friendships of advantage' is discussed in
Chapter 5.

4. Eric Mack, 'How to Derive Libertarian Rights' in *Reading Nozick*, ed. Jeffrey Paul (Totowa, New Jersey: Rowman and Littlefield, 1981), 288.

5. Alasdair MacIntyre, *After Virtue* (Notre Dame, Indiana: University of Notre Dame Press, 1981), p. 67.

6. Leo Strauss, *The Political Philosophy of Hobbes* (Chicago: University of Chicago Press, 1966), 155.

7. John Finnis, *Natural Law and Natural Rights* (Oxford: Oxford University Press, 1980), 206–07.

8. Michael Villey, *Seize Essais de Philosophie de Droit* (Paris: Dalloz, 1969).

9. Richard Tuck, *Natural Rights Theories: Their Origin and Development* (Cambridge: Cambridge University Press, 1979), 7–13.

10. *Ibid.*, 49.

11. Alan Gewirth, *Reason and Morality* (Chicago: University of Chicago Press, 1978), 100ff.

12. M.P. Golding points out, for example, that "the Romans can be said to have 'had' the concept of a right even if it is true that, contrary to the practice of modern jurisprudence, they did not make the conception of a right the basis of their arrangement of legal doctrines". 'Justice and Rights: A Study in Relationship' in *Justice and Health Care,* ed. Earl E. Shelp (Dordrecht: D. Reidel, 1981), 28. See also M.P. Golding, 'The Concept of Rights: A Historical Sketch' in *Bioethics and Human Rights* (Boston: Brown & Co., Little, 1978), 44–50.

13. See Golding's 'Justice and Rights' and 'The Concept of Rights'; as well as A.P. d'Entrèves, *Natural Law*, rev. ed. (London: Hutchinson University Library, 1970), chapter 4, especially p. 62.

14. See Golding, 'Justice and Rights'; Golding, 'The Concept of Rights', and d'Entrèves, *Natural Law*.

15. Nevertheless, the individualism of subjective rights does not necessarily imply a rejection of the primacy of justice or a general theory of the objectively right. It may be that the rights individuals possess are ultimately grounded in principles of justice. In this case, modernity would not have broken so radically from antiquity. Consider the following by Martin Golding: "All the classical and early modern writers we discussed do agree on one point: To the extent that they acknowledge rights at all, they agree that rights derive from justice or, to put it in other words, that subjective rights must be subordinated to the objectively right. It could be said that the emergence of a liberty notion of rights throws this assumption into question." 'Justice and Rights', 33. Golding has not yet discussed Hobbes when he makes this statement.

16. W.N. Hohfeld, *Fundamental Legal Conceptions* (New Haven: Yale University Press, 1919).

17. As Fred D. Miller, Jr., has noted: "What are crudely referred to as particular 'rights' in the law, such as property rights, are really very complex bundles of rights-relationships. Corsicus's right to a jar of olive oil includes the claim-right against Callicles's taking it without permission, the liberty-right to use or dispose of it himself, the power-right to offer it for sale or enter into a contract promising its future sale, the immunity-right from Callicles selling it without Corsicus's permission. And, in general, Corsicus's right (*in rem*) to the jar of olive oil involves many other rights-relations with many other act-descriptions against an open-ended set of individuals (Callicles, Thrasymachus, etc.)." 'Are There Any Rights in Aristotle?' 7–8, an unpublished paper presented at a Conference in Honor of Father Joseph Owens on Aristotle and Islamic Philosophy, sponsored by the Society of Ancient Greek Philosophy, on October 29, 1984, at Baruch College, New York.

18. John Hospers, *Human Conduct*, 2nd ed. (New York: Harcourt Brace Jovanovich, 1982), 245.

19. See Eric Mack, 'Introduction' and Tibor R. Machan, 'Moral Myths and Basic Positive Rights' in *Positive and Negative Duties*, vol. 23 of *Tulane Studies in Philosophy*, ed. Eric Mack (New Orleans, Louisiana: Tulane University, 1985), 1–8 and 35–41, respectively. Also, see Hospers, *Human Conduct*, 245–46.

20. Meta-normative principles do not provide an individual guidance in how to conduct his life, be it alone or in the company of others. Rather, meta-normative principles provide guidance in the creation of a constitution whose legal system provides the social and political condition necessary for individuals to apply the principles of normative ethics to their lives among others. Meta-normative principles are *meta*-normative in the sense that they

underlie or provide the context in which people pursue the good or perform right actions in society. These principles are not meta-normative if this is taken to mean that they are, somehow, not moral principles. They are, however, a unique type of moral principle; for though their moral justification is based on the nature of human flourishing, they only have a point in the legal creation of a social and political context. If human beings were not social and political animals—if, in other words, human flourishing were not such that it required that human beings live among others—then there would be no need to emphasize the meta-normative character of rights; for living among others in a political community would be merely an option a human being could choose, like choosing which flavor of ice cream to eat. Yet since human beings can only flourish when their lives involve others, special attention needs to be given to the creation of the social and political condition necessary for any life among others to have a possibility that it might flourish. We attempt to highlight this situation by calling rights 'meta-normative' principles.

21. Herbert Morris, 'Persons and Punishment', *The Monist* 52 (October 1968): 494.

22. Early in Chapter 2, we noted that Aristotelian essentialism was to be differentiated from Porphyrian essentialism because Porphyrian essentialism treats the natural kind term *man* as referring to a metaphysical element—'manness'—which exists 'in' individual men, while Aristotelian essentialism treats *man* as signifying (though not specifying) the entire identity of individual men. It was further noted that the real definition of man—the *genus per differentiam*—was not something which an Aristotelian essentialism would determine in an a priori manner. The fundamental defining characteristics of an entity are determined by an empirical, scientific process which involves a consideration of vast amounts of information regarding the entity in question. Further, the process involves an awareness of the features of many other entities from which the entity to be defined is differentiated. Thus, the differentiating feature of human beings—the capacity to reason and choose—does not exhaust what *man* signifies, but rather represents to date the fundamental distinguishing feature of human beings. Therefore, it is quite possible for there to be many beings who share many of the characteristics of beings who are animals with the capacity to reason, but do not as yet have this capacity to reason, such as, the unborn and infants, or those who have had the capacity to reason but through accident or disease have now lost this capacity, and yet are classifiable as human beings. Since the term *man* signifies more than rational animal or even what can be deduced from it, and given what we know about infants and the mentally disabled, it seems appropriate to include them in the class of human beings and therefore as having certain rights due them. Yet since they do not yet have the ability to reason and choose or once had such an ability

and now no longer have it, the character of these rights, at least in terms of their implementation, will no doubt be different from that of healthy adults. Yet a more detailed discussion of this problem is beyond the concerns of this chapter. (The issue of the unborn and when they should be included in the class of human beings is a much more complicated issue with which we also, fortunately, do not need to deal at this time.) We only mention these difficulties so that the reader might realize that our understanding of the nature of man is in no way Platonic or based on a Cartesian process of *inspectio mentis*. Further, there is nothing in our understanding of Aristotelian essentialism that precludes, if warranted, revising our definition of human beings or the existence of 'borderline cases'. "Aristotelian essentialism is compatible with those cognitive developments that sometimes occur at the edges of science which require that the fundamental distinguishing characteristic(s) of an entity be changed or that an entity be identified descriptively and not grouped into a class—as for example, certain primitive organisms are treated in biology because they share characteristics with both plants and animals. It must be remembered that definitions are classificatory devices which serve a cognitive function by allowing man to order his knowledge of reality, and though they reflect (if carefully developed) the structure of the world, they are nonetheless tools or instruments for knowing, not reality as such. . . . Metaphysically speaking, the nature of X is not determined by human cognition. A thing is what it is. Epistemologically speaking, the real definition of X is dependent on human knowledge—on all that is known about X—for the essential defining feature of a being is not, and indeed cannot be, determined in a vacuum." Douglas B. Rasmussen, 'Quine and Aristotelian Essentialism', *The New Scholasticism* 58 (Summer 1984): 329.

23. Tibor R. Machan, *Human Rights and Human Liberties* (Chicago: Nelson-Hall, 1975), 114.

24. Though rights are based on one's capacity to reason and choose, there is a question of interpretation. Could someone *through their own choices* alienate their right not to be used by other people for purposes they have not chosen? Consider Mary, who knows with certitude that an excruciatingly painful death awaits her in the near future unless she grants to William, who is in no way responsible for her dire situation, the moral liberty to do with her what he pleases. Though William could also put Mary to painful death, Mary chooses to be William's slave to avoid—at least for the time being—a painful death. This is to say, Mary consents to a situation in which her consent is no longer necessary when it comes to how she is to be treated. She is, therefore, not in a postion where she can have any rights-based moral complaint regarding her treatment by William. Is this because (1) she has alienated her right to liberty, or (2) because of her exercise of the right to liberty, or (3) is this entire situation a self-contra-

diction? (1) Eric Mack in his unpublished paper, 'The Alienability of Lockean Natural Rights', argues that Mary has indeed alienated her rights by her choice. According to Mack, simply because rights are based on human nature—the fact that human beings have the capacity to reason and choose—does not require that human beings cannot choose to alienate their fundamental rights. Mary can alienate her rights, and William can have a legally enforceable agreement. (2) If, however, we distinguish (a) waiving the right to have others forbear from (b) placing ourselves in a position in which we have no legitimate right to complain, could Mary's choice be considered an exercise of her inalienabile right? If I say to you, 'You have my permission, slap me', I have not alientated my right that others not interfere without permission. Rather, I have put myself into a relationship in which this right no longer applies with respect to a specified person. Could Mary's choice be so interpreted? She puts herself into a most peculiar relationship and yet a relationship that would have moral and legal force because it is an exercise of her inalienable right to live according to her own choices—in this case, the choice not to be consulted regarding her future preferences. (3) Tibor R. Machan considers this type of situation a "self-contradiction", for the agent in this agreement, Mary *qua* rights possessing being, has 'logically' vanished. She has become the property or tool of William. Yet she must exist as an agent for this agreement to be legally enforceable. If Mary refused to comply with her agreement with William, there would be no agent for the law to demand compliance with the agreement of. (See note 26.) Finally, it seems to us that Mary has the right to choose to enter this relationship, but her choice will not change what she fundamentally is and thus the rights she has in virtue of her nature. William cannot claim a right to use Mary without her consent. She can, of course, continue to choose to follow William's wishes, but William could not claim that because of Mary's choice she no longer has the right to refuse to submit to his wishes.

25. Morris, 'Persons and Punishment', 486.
26. Machan, *Human Rights and Human Liberties*, 116. Machan also considers the issue of whether one can sell himself into slavery and argues that it is a contradiction in terms. Yet he does differentiate this from contracting oneself for permanent or long-term service and sets up the conditions that are necessary for this to be achieved. See Tibor R. Machan, 'Human Rights: Some Points of Clarification', *Journal of Critical Analysis* 5 (July/October 1973): 30–39.
27. It should be noted that the adjudication of rights can be very troublesome and that for a particular case at a particular time there may not be a single judge who agrees on how to decide the case. Yet we agree with Dworkin that in and of itself such lack of agreement does not show that there is no right answer to that case or that rights do not have an important role to

play. Dworkin's justification for rights, as well as his conception, is much different from ours. Yet for this point see Dworkin's *Taking Rights Seriously* (Cambridge, Massachusetts: Harvard University Press, 1978), Chapter 13, 'Can Rights be Controversial?'
28. Hospers, *Human Conduct*, 254.
29. Tibor R. Machan, 'Prima Facie Versus Natural (Human) Rights', *The Journal of Value Inquiry* 10 (1976): 127
30. Henry Veatch's recent work, *Human Rights: Fact or Fancy?* (Baton Rouge and London: Louisiana State University Press, 1985) is a notable and worthy exception. He seems to argue for natural rights, yet he explicitly denies that they are absolute. We will consider Veatch's account of rights later in this chapter.
31. See Machan, 'Moral Myths and Basic Positive Rights' in *Positive and Negative Duties,* for a defense of the claim that negative rights are in fact different from positive rights.
32. See Mack, 'Introduction' in *Positive and Negative Duties.*
33. J. Roland Pennock, 'Rights, Natural Rights, and Human Rights—A General View' in *Human Rights: Nomos XXIII*, ed. J. Roland Pennock and John W. Chapman (New York: NYU Press, 1981), 6–7.
34. *Ibid.*, 7.
35. Iredell Jenkins, *Social Order and the Limits of Law* (Princeton: Princeton University Press, 1980), 250ff.
36. *Ibid.*, 250. By appealing to 'their minds' Jenkins means something like having a more explicit metaphysical foundation.
37. Martin P. Golding, 'The Primacy of Welfare Rights', *Social Philosophy and Policy* 1 (Spring 1984): 119–136.
38. *Ibid.*, 130.
39. Golding himself says that rights are interpersonal because they presuppose claimants and claims. But this will not do, because it is precisely the justification that stands behind the claims that will determine whether rights are inherently interpersonal. It is true that one can only make claims to others, but it doesn't follow from that that what one claims is interpersonal. We put people in mental institutions for making claims about phenomenon that are, in the last analysis, purely private. Furthermore, speaking in terms of 'claims' and 'claimants' begs the whole question about option versus welfare rights; for option rights are not so much claims about others as they are assertions about 'moral space' or 'boundaries', to use Nozickian metaphors. The claims are made *after* the boundaries are crossed or to a potential violator of those boundaries.
40. 'The Primacy of Welfare Rights', 134–35.
41. This is the first precept of the natural law according to Thomas Aquinas. It is based on the belief that the natural end of a thing is the good at which it aims. Regarding human beings, this means that "if a man is to become a

mature and responsible adult, there are certain things he must do, certain ways he must go about it; if he neglects these, it will mean that his natural end will not be achieved and his life will be, if not a downright failure, then at least not what it might or ought to have been." Henry B. Veatch, *For An Ontology of Morals* (Evanston: Northwestern University Press, 1971), 123. See 'The Is-Ought Problem' in Chapter 2 for our discussion and defense of the claim that human beings have a natural end.

42. Henry B. Veatch, *Rational Man* (Bloomington, Indiana: Indiana University Press, 1962), 93.

43. See Rasmussen, 'Quine and Aristotelian Essentialism', 316–335.

44. Henry B. Veatch, 'Ethical Egoism, New Style: Is Its Proper Trade Mark Libertarian or Aristotelian?' 27–28 of a manuscript included in a collection of essays by Veatch on ethics, entitled *Swimming Against the Current in Contemporary Philosophy* (Washington, D.C.: Catholic University of America Press, 1990) 194.

45. See Douglas B. Rasmussen, 'Liberalism and Natural End Ethics', *American Philosophical Quarterly* 27 (April 1990): 153–161.

46. Leo Strauss, *Natural Right and History* (Chicago: University of Chicago Press, 1953), 248.

47. As we observed in an essay on the ethics of Ayn Rand, "Rand's view of the self is neither Kantian (some *Ding an sich* totally unrelated to life) nor Hobbesian (some bundle of passions and urges), but Aristotelian". Douglas J. Den Uyl and Douglas B. Rasmussen, 'Life, Teleology, and Eudaimonia in the Ethics of Ayn Rand', *The Philosophic Thought of Ayn Rand*, ed. Den Uyl and Rasmussen (Urbana and Chicago: University of Illinois Press, 1984), 77.

48. See Norman O. Dahl, *Practical Reason, Aristotle and Weakness of the Will* (Minneapolis: University of Minnesota Press, 1984) for an account of practical reason in Aristotle that shows why reason need not be a slave to the passions—be they egoistic or altruistic.

49. Strauss's comment might be viewed as strictly a historical report of the philosophical result of the rejection of natural ends by the moderns and not a statement about what a natural rights theory must reject. If so, we do not need to take exception to it here.

50. See also our discussion of Jacques Maritain's distinction between the good of the person and good of the individual in Chapter 4.

51. Mack, 'How to Derive Libertarian Rights', 290. (Some emphasis added.)

52. See Douglas B. Rasmussen, 'Essentialism, Values and Rights' in *The Libertarian Reader,* ed. Tibor R. Machan (Totowa, New Jersey: Rowman and Littlefield, 1982), 47. Most importantly, see Ayn Rand, 'The Objectivist Ethics', *The Virtue of Selfishness* (New York: New American Library, 1964), 19–20.

53. The human good is a supervenient property.

54. See in this connection, Douglas J. Den Uyl, 'Freedom and Virtue' in *The Libertarian Reader* and idem, 'Freedom and Virtue Revisited' in *Man, Economy, and Liberty: Essays in Honor of Murray N. Rothbard*, ed. Walter Block and Llewellyn H. Rockwell, Jr. (Auburn, Alabama: The Ludwig von Mises Institute, 1988).

55. There are situations in which someone is too young, old, sick, or injured to make such decisions, but these cases do not refute the claim that it is always better for a human being to be self-directed than not be self-directed. Rather, they merely show that there are situations in which this claim would have no point because of the ought-implies-can principle. Yet even in these situations the importance of autonomy is stressed; for in cases in which it is possible to determine by other means what the choices of the incapacitated party are (or reasonably project what the incapacitated party would choose), we try to honor those choices.

56. The relationship between self-directedness and human flourishing or self-perfection can be summarized as follows: the absence of self-directedness implies the absence of self-perfection, and the presence of self-perfection implies the presence of self-directedness; yet the absence of self-perfection does not imply the absence of self-directedness, nor does the presence of self-directedness imply the presence of self-perfection.

57. Mack 'How to Derive Libertarian Rights', 291.

58. Alasdair MacIntyre, *After Virtue*, 67.

59. *Ibid.*, 64–68.

60. *Ibid.*, 65.

61. We find it interesting that MacIntyre's rather Humean approach to this problem is so inherently modern and so inconsistent with the type of argument Aristotle would find acceptable or, for that matter, the type of argument most pre-modern thinkers would have found acceptable.

62. Thomas Aquinas, *Summa Theologiae* I-II, Q94, A4 and Q96, A2.

63. *Ibid.* Also, see Josef Pieper's discussion of Aquinas's distinction between demands of justice that are legally binding and demands that are only morally binding in *The Four Cardinal Virtues* (Notre Dame, Indiana: University of Notre Dame Press, 1966), 56–57.

64. MacIntyre, *After Virtue*, 153, emphasis added.

65. The sanctity and primacy of the individual which is emphasized by the Enlightenment may owe its origins to Christianity, which theologically sanctified the individual soul. See Shirely Robin Letwin, 'Romantic Love and Christianity', *Philosophy* 52 (April 1977): 131–145.

66. MacIntyre, *After Virtue*, 152.

67. A.P. d'Entrèves, *Natural Law*, Chapter 4.

68. See E.A. Moody, *The Logic of William of Ockham* (New York: Russell and Russell, 1965) for an account of Ockham which claims that Ockham was primarily arguing *against* the tendency among certain Scholastics to treat

genera and species as corresponding to *parts* of individual substances and *for* Aristotelianism free of any admixture of Platonic or Augustinian thought.

69. Loren E. Lomasky, 'Personal Projects as the Foundation for Basic Rights', *Social Philosophy & Policy* 1 (Spring 1984): 40–41. We have learned much from Lomasky's concept of 'personal projects'. He develops this concept more fully in his excellent book, *Persons, Rights, and the Moral Community* (Oxford: Oxford University Press, 1987). For a review of this book, see Douglas B. Rasmussen, 'Objective Value, Rights, and Individualism', *Liberty* 2 (September 1988): 64–67. See also, Douglas B. Rasmussen, 'The Right to Project Pursuit and the Human *Telos*', *Reason Papers* 14 (Spring 1989): 98–109 and Lomasky's response to this essay and others in the same volume, 110–129. Lomasky's understanding of an Aristotelian natural-end ethics differs greatly from ours: he seems to construe the human *telos* as a dominant end and to hold that it cannot be both objective and agent-relative.

70. Lomasky continues: "Ends are perfectly socialized. No matter who produced them, they belong to all equally, and all have an equal stake in advancing them. The fact that E is crucial to some deeply held project of mine creates no reason for its promotion by me. But then, in what sense can E still significantly be said to be my end? True, I brought it into being, but that gives me no proprietary rights. I am called upon to maximize utility in whatever way I am most able. If that involves pursuing E, it is no more than an accident. . . . [A utilitarian] can represent a person only as a convenient locus at which utility can be produced and as the instrument for producing utility at yet another loci. It is not persons as such that really matter, but rather the utility they can realize." 'A Refutation Of Utilitarianism', *The Journal of Value Inquiry* 17 (1983): 272–73.

71. We, of course, believe that Aristotelianism not only allows but demands a high degree of value pluralism.

72. This view is similar to Hillel Steiner's. See 'The Structure of a Set of Compossible Rights', *Journal of Philosophy* 74 (December 1977): 767–775. We recognize fully the difficulties in fine tuning such a set of compossible territories and thus why politics and revisions of the legal code are necessary in all political systems. But morally and philosophically it is still the basic framework that needs defense, which is the level we are operating at here.

73. To say that something is fundamentally other oriented is different from saying that something is only applicable in the presence of others. It is the latter idea that applies to our conception. This distinction is lost on David Braybrooke who, in a response to Samuel Wheeler, tries to argue that all rights are 'social'. See *Nous* 14 (May 1980): 195–202.

74. Veatch, *Human Rights: Fact or Fancy?*, 160–196.

75. *Ibid.*, 160–66.
76. We do not wish to imply that violating rights is consistent with self-perfection. We believe that generally it is not.
77. In fact, Veatch is quite explicit about this: "But on a natural law theory of ethics. . . a person's rights are strictly conditioned upon that individual's life, liberty, and property being the necessary means of his living wisely and responsibly and of his becoming and being the person that a human being ought to be." *Human Rights: Fact or Fancy?*, 205.
78. Regarding the individual who engages in nonperfecting conduct, Veatch states: "The actions that he takes and the conduct that he pursues are then no longer right at all; nor can his natural right to life, liberty, and property be said to entitle him so to live in the way he has foolishly and unwisely chosen to do. In other words, that one should abuse one's right [viz., engage in nonperfecting conduct] must not itself be taken to be right, or even one's right in any strict sense." *Ibid.*
79. Rand, 'Man's Rights' in *The Virtue of Selfishness,* 92.
80. Machan, *Human and Human Liberties,* 107, (emphasis added). In a more recent book, *Individuals and Their Rights* (La Salle: Open Court, 1989), Machan still describes rights as "the principles we need to inform us about the requirements of proper conduct vis-a-vis our fellow humans" (60). Yet it should be noted that he also states that "members of a community ought to establish and preserve a constitution of natural rights" (96). Even here, however, Machan does not directly note that the function of rights is to provide guidance in the creation of a constitution.
81. Eric Mack brought this example to our attention.
82. Further examples of the importance of treating rights as meta-normative concepts will be seen in Chapters 4 and 5.
83. Rand, 'Man's Rights' in *The Virtue of Selfishness*, 94.
84. Allan Gibbard, 'Natural Property Rights', *Nous* 10 (1976): 77.
85. Laurence C. Becker, *Property Rights: Philosophic Foundations* (London: Routledge and Kegan Paul, 1977), 18–22, especially note 11, 120.
86. *Ibid.*, 1.
87. George Mavrodes, 'Property' in *Property in a Humane Economy*, ed. Samuel L. Blumenfeld (La Salle: Open Court, 1974), 183.
88. David Kelley has noted that the argument for private property must show why human beings are entitled to not merely the possession of property, but exclusive control, use, and disposal of it. 'Life, Liberty, and Property', *Social Philosophy and Policy* 1 (Spring 1984): 112. He also notes that any argument which purports to justify the natural right to private property must employ a substantive moral theory. Kelley says that appeal should be made to an ultimate end. "Some fundamental end—life, happiness, self-realization—is an ultimate end, the source and standard of *all values*." *Ibid.*, 109. This section of this chapter makes just such an appeal.

89. *Ibid.*, 117.
90. These ideas follow the essence of the concept of entrepreneurship offered by Israel M. Kirzner's *Competition and Entrepreneurship* (Chicago: University of Chicago Press, 1973). See also his essay, 'Some Ethical Implications for Capitalism of the Socialist Calculation Debate', *Social Philosophy and Policy* 6 (Autumn 1988): 163–183. These same ideas are found in Ayn Rand, *For the New Intellectual* (New York: New American Library, 1961), 183.
91. See David Kelley and Roger Donway, *Laissez Parler: Freedom and the Electronic Media* (Bowling Green, Ohio: Social Philosophy and Policy Center, Bowling Green State University, 1983) and Arthur S. DeVany et al., *A Property System Approach to the Electromagnetic Spectrum* (San Francisco, California: Cato Institute, 1980) on the ownership of commercial airwaves.
92. Becker, *Property Rights*, 109–111.
93. Becker is, of course, correct to suggest that inequity might have political repercussions.
94. Mavrodes, 'Property', 187, and see 198, where he makes a claim opposite from our own.
95. See 'Defining the Good—Part II' of Chapter 2.
96. See, for example, Julian L. Simon, *The Ultimate Resource* (Princeton, New Jersey: Princeton University Press, 1981).
97. This is, of course, different from saying that there will not be other types of interests in the results.
98. We regard the right to free speech as a derivative right. It results from an exercise of the basic natural right to liberty.
99. Robert Nozick, *Anarchy, State, and Utopia*, 175.
100. Mavrodes, 'Property', 189, 195, and passim.
101. Gibbard, 'Natural Property Rights', 78.
102. Mavrodes implicitly endorses an idea of a positive right to an opportunity to acquire property. It should in general be noted that we understand the concept 'equal opportunity' to signify that the basic natural, negative right to liberty is legally protected and implemented for all members of the political community. This does not involve 'an equal distribution of opportunities' in the sense of requiring the distribution of goods and services in accordance with some principle of equality.
103. The only way out, at this general level, is to take the collectivist premise seriously and argue that *all* one's actions have attached to them obligations to serve the interests of others such that *no* actions are ever really one's own. We need not comment here about how contrary such a position is to all that we have written.
104. It should by now be evident that without a moral principle which determines ownership, there would be no way of determining which of two

incompatible uses of objects or regions of space was consistent with the basic right of every person to live according to their own choices and which was not. There simply could be no way for there to be a com-possible set of moral territories—namely, no system of natural rights—consistent with the individualized and self-directed character of human flourishing. There need to be property rights if people are to have the right to live their lives according to their own judgments. There needs to be a moral principle which provides a basis for assigning ownership to objects and regions of space.

105. F.A. Hayek, *The Mirage of Social Justice*, vol. 2 of *Law, Legislation, and Liberty* (Chicago: University of Chicago Press, 1976).

106. Mavrodes, 'Property', 194–96.

107. Yet despite the absence of a ready metaphysical principle, he goes on to argue why some of these rules should be prefered over others. We stick more directly to his basic claim that there is no way to decide in the abstract apart from what we say below. Of course, in concrete situations there may be reasons to prefer one abstract rule over another within the legitimate latitude of rules available. But this carries us beyond what moral and political theorists can legitimately do in the abstract.

108. See, for example, the discussion of rights in James Buchanan, *The Limits of Liberty* (Chicago: University of Chicago Press, 1975), Chapters 1–4.

109. Gibbard and Mavrodes both seem to place extraordinary emphasis upon agreement in their analyses. What we are arguing is that agreement is only politically decisive, not morally so. Thus, to use Mavrodes's example, if society decides upon rule 1 and another upon rule 5, perhaps the only way to avoid conflict would be adopt rules 6 or 7. This would not give such rules moral sanction, but only political feasibility; and for that reason alone we might be willing to concur in the adoption of that rule.

110. Samuel C. Wheeler, 'Natural Property Rights as Body Rights', *Nous* 14 (May 1980): 171–193.

111. On the whole we find David Braybrooke's response to Wheeler to be unconvincing; but on this point we agree with him. See 'Our Natural Bodies, Our Social Rights: Comment on Wheeler', *Nous* 14 (May 1980): 195–202.

112. Wheeler, 'Natural Property Rights as Body Rights', 188ff.

113. *Ibid.*, 181.

114. We do believe that institutional arrangements that respect the basic rights we have outlined in this chapter will also most likely produce the most favorable consequences relative to any alternative arrangement; but that is not our point here.

115. See Richard A. Epstein, *Takings* (Cambridge, Massachusetts: Harvard University Press, 1985) for a discussion of the complications and benefits of the legal aspects of a private property system.

CHAPTER 4

1. The natural right to liberty involves both the right to life and the right to property. Like the right to liberty, these rights are rights to actions—that is, the right to take all the actions necessary for the support and further-ance of one's life, that is, in order to flourish, and the right to the action of producing or earning something and keeping, using, and disposing of it in accordance with one's goals. These are negative rights and are sometimes referred to as 'individual rights'. See Ayn Rand, 'Values and Rights' in *Readings in Introductory Philosophical Analysis,* ed. John Hospers (Englewood Cliffs, New Jersey: Prentice.Hall, 1968), 381–82. Also, see Eric Mack, 'Individualism, Rights, and the Open Society' in *The Libertar-ian Reader,* ed. Tibor R. Machan (Totowa, New Jersey: Rowman and Littlefield, 1982), 3–15.

2. See D.J. Allan's discussion of this claim and related issues in his essay, 'Individual and State in the *Ethics* and *Politics*' in *La 'Politique' D'Aristote,* vol. 11 of *Entriens Sur l'Antiquité Classique* (Geneva: Found-ation Hardt, 1965) 55–95.

3. Though the terms *society* and *community* do not always mean the same thing, the differences in their usage do themselves differ; so there is little advantage in attempting to work out all their various meanings here. We will follow the same procedure as John Finnis regarding this difficulty: "what is here said of 'community' might equally well be said of 'society'". *Natural Law and Natural Rights* (Oxford: Clarendon Press, 1980), 135. We would only add "and vice versa" to this statement, for we see nothing cru-cial in the use of one term over the other.

4. D. J. Allan, 'Individual and State in the *Ethics* And *Politics*', 84

5. John Wild, *Introduction to Realistic Philosophy* (New York: Harper and Brothers, 1948), 186.

6. Henry B. Veatch, *Human Rights: Fact or Fancy?* (Baton Rouge: Louisiana State University Press, 1985), 85.

7. See the last chapter of Jacques Maritain's *The Person and the Common Good* (see note 8) for a discussion of the deviant political theories and their defects.

8. Jacques Maritain, *The Person and the Common Good* (South Bend: Uni-versity of Notre Dame Press, 1966). Although our judgment of Maritain will be harsh, justice demands that we note Michael Novak's claim that Maritain came to be much more favorably disposed towards a liberal social order later in his life. See Michael Novak, *The Spirit of Democratic Capi-talism* (New York: Simon and Schuster, 1982), 20. Also, Novak in his re-cent book, *Free Persons and the Common Good* (Lanham, New York, and London: Madison Books, 1989) has argued that a marriage of Aristotelian and classical liberal political traditions is possible and desirable and that

Maritain's conception of the the common good of the political community is the proper starting point. Regrettably, Novak seems to accept Maritain's bifurcation of human beings into persons and individuals. Further, he never really gets around to showing how a *principled* marriage of the two traditions is possible. This is, of course, our concern. Yet there is much that is interesting and worthwhile in this excellent work. Had this book appeared sooner, we would have had more to say about it.

9. Maritain, *The Person and the Common Good*, 33.
10. *Ibid.*, 37
11. *Ibid.*, 38ff
12. *Ibid.*, 43
13. *Ibid.*, 43
14. Thomas Aquinas, *Summa Theologiae* I, Q. 76, A. 1.
15. *Ibid.*, A. 5.
16. David Norton, *Personal Destinies* (Princeton: Princeton University Press, 1976) 9.
17. Tibor R. Machan, *Human Rights and Human Liberties* (Chicago: Nelson-Hall, 1975), 119. In *Nicomachean Ethics* 2.4 1105a26–33 and *Eudemian Ethics* 1248b40–1249a8, Aristotle claims that virtuous actions must be chosen for their own sakes. Also, Fred Miller, Jr. in a recent series of articles has argued that practical rationality—the means by which the end of human conduct is fully articulated—involves insight which must be exercised at the time of action and only by the individual agent himself. See 'Rationality and Freedom in Aristotle and Hayek', *Reason Papers* 9 (Winter 1983): 29–36; 'Aristotle on Practical Knowledge and Moral Weakness' in *The Georgetown Symposium on Ethics,* ed. Rocco Porreco (Lanham, Maryland: University Press of America, 1984), 131–144; and 'Aristotle on Rationality In Action', *The Review of Metaphysics* 37 (March 1984): 499–520.
18. Ayn Rand, 'From My "Future File"', *The Ayn Rand Letter* 3, September 23, 1974: 4–5. Similarly, D.J. Allan has observed that Aristotle does not "credit the politician, in his capacity as lawgiver, with the power of manufacturing happiness or virtue, but represents him as *establishing a framework* within which happiness can be attained". 'Individual and State in the *Ethics* and the *Politics*', 66.
19. *The Person and the Common Good,* 49. (Emphasis added.)
20. *Ibid.*, 49
21. *Ibid.*, 52
22. It may be that for Maritain the common good is a supernatural phenomenon. This form of 'theologism' (what Gilson referred to as reducing philosophy to theology) would, of course, place Maritain outside the boundaries of philosophical theorizing that we have put him in for purposes of this exposition.
23. *The Person and the Common Good*, 57. One is reminded here of

Wittgenstein's 7th thesis in the *Tractatus*: "What you can't say, you must pass over in silence".

24. *Ibid.*, 60–70

25. *Ibid.*, 60

26. John Finnis, *Natural Law and Natural Rights*, 156.

27. Mortimer Adler claims that " because each man as a person is an end not a means, and in relation to human beings the state is a means not an end, the good that is common to and shared by all men *as men* (the *bonum commune hominis*) is the one and only ultimate end or final goal in this life. The good that is common to and shared by all men as members of the political community (the *bonum commune communitatis*) is an end served by the organized community as a whole, and a means to the individual happiness of each man and of all". 'Little Errors in the Beginning', *The Thomist* 38 (January 1974): 39. There is much in this quotation that we find correct; but there are ambiguities, especially with respect to the concept of the community as a whole having an end. See below for a discussion of this matter.

28. David Wiggins has argued that in Aristotle's *Politics*, "that form of government is held to be best in which everyman, whoever he is, can act well and live happily. But the theory does not subserve a program for social action to maximize anything. . . . Insofar as it suggests a social program, the program is only for the removal of the public impediments to eudaimonia". 'Weakness of Will, Commensurability, and the Objects of Deliberation and Desire', *Essays on Aristotle's Ethics,* ed. A.O. Rorty (Berkeley, Calif: University of California Press, 1980), 261.

29. Ayn Rand, 'The Ethics of Emergencies' in *The Virtue of Selfishness* (New York: the New American Library, 1964), 47.

30. The example also assumes that neither man has any prior moral claim to the plank nor that it is in any way possible for each man to take turns in using the plank or in any other way 'share' it.

31. See James Sterba, 'Response to Rasmussen' in Douglas Rasmussen and James Sterba, *The Catholic Bishops and the Economy: A Debate* (Bowling Green, Ohio: Social Philosophy and Policy Center, and New Brunswick and London: Transaction Books, 1987), 88–92. This objection assumes that having what it takes to live well is the same thing as living well (human flourishing). Sterba also conflates autonomy or self-directedness with human flourishing when he claims that protecting the autonomy of the rich reduces the autonomy of the poor. Sterba makes this same argument in *How to Make People Just* (Totowa, New Jersey, Rowman and Littlefield, 1989).

32. The starving man situation assumes that the man has only sufficient strength and time to take the bread and thus cannot ask for help and live.

33. See our discussion of rights as 'meta-normative' principles in Chapter 3.

34. It would, however, be a non sequitur to claim in situations in which indi-

vidual rights are not appropriate that therefore some sort of collectivism or dictatorship is the preferred alternative.

35. It should be emphasized, however, that other moral principles (virtues) do still apply.

36. It is, however, vital to note the following: "[As the simplest] evidence of that fact that the material universe is not inimical to man and that catastrophes are the exception, not the rule of his existence—observe the fortunes made by insurance companies." Rand, 'The Ethics of Emergencies' in *The Virtue of Selfishness*, 49.

37. James Sterba, 'Response to Rasmussen', *The Catholic Bishop and the Economy*, 87.

38. Admittedly, this commits us to holding that the range of a concept's applicability is in important ways fixed by the identity of things to which they apply, and not solely by human convention, but we see no reason to take up this issue here. Also, see Douglas B. Rasmussen, 'Quine and Aristotelian Essentialism', *The New Scholasticism* 58 (Summer 1984): 316–335.

39. Yves Simon, *Philosophy of Democratic Government* (Chicago: University of Chicago Press, 1951), 19–20.

40. Simon's claim about the impossibility of unanimity is not so compelling as appearances may suggest. Utilizing a distinction between acting within a set of rules and designing the rules themselves, James Buchanan imposes a unanimity rule on participants to a hypothetical social contract. Under what Buchanan calls a "veil of uncertainty", there are in fact strong incentives for the contractors to reach unanimous agreement, since they know that whatever rules they arrive at they will have to live under, but they do not know their future social positions. The tendency will thus be to generate rules all think are 'fair' and which all can agree to. Simon's scepticism about unanimity is an observation about actors within a set of rules where the tendency is to protect one's own interests.

41. See F.A. Hayek's discussion of this fallacy, *The Mirage of Social Justice,* volume 2 of *Law, Legislation and Liberty* (Chicago: University of Chicago Press, 1977), passim.

42. Traditionally, such things as money, postal service, dams, and bridges were regarded as common enterprises that required government direction or supervision. Yet it is not at all clear that these could not be provided by the market. See Walter Block, 'A Free Market in Roads', and Tibor R. Machan, 'Dissolving the Problem of Public Goods: Financing Government Without Coercive Measures' in *The Libertarian Reader.*

43. See Mortimer J. Adler, *The Times of Our Lives* (New York: Holt, Rinehart, and Winston, 1970), Chapter 16 and notes 6, 7, and 8 for that chapter.

44. Fred D. Miller, Jr.,'The State and the Community in Aristotle's *Politics*', *Reason Papers* 1 (Fall 1974): 63.

45. *Ibid.*, 64.

46. Finnis, *Natural Law and Natural Rights,* 136–38.
47. See Hayek's *Rules and Order* in *Law, Legislation and Liberty,* vol. 1, for a discussion of these concepts.
48. Finnis, *Natural Law and Natural Rights,* 170–71.
49. *Ibid.,* 153. (Emphasis added.)
50. *Ibid.,*
51. *Ibid.,* 155.
52. *Ibid.*
53. *Ibid.,* 166.
54. *Ibid.,* 167
55. For example, see Robert Poole, Jr., *Cutting Back City Hall* (New York: Universe Books, 1978).
56. Finnis, *Natural Law and Natural Rights, 170.*
57. *Ibid.,* 113.
58. *Ibid.,* 187.
59. *Ibid.,* 110n11.
60. *Ibid.,* 231.
61. *Ibid.,* 232.
62. *Ibid.,* 233.
63. See Douglas J. Den Uyl, 'Freedom and Virtue' in *The Libertarian Reader,* 211–225.
64. There is some similarity between traditional means/end reasoning and our procedural/determinate end distinction. However, in the former case the value of the means is established solely by the value of the end. Procedural ends, on the other hand, can be expressive of something with value in its own right (e.g., liberty) and some determinate ends can be a means to more final ends. Also, we would regard W.F. Hardie's distinction between inclusive and dominant ends to be a distinction within the category of determinate ends.
65. Norton, *Personal Destinies.*
66. *Ibid.,* 310.
67. *Ibid.,* 311.
68. *Ibid.,* 333.
69. *Ibid.,* 321–22.
70. *Ibid.,* 314.
71. *Ibid.,* 342.
72. *Ibid.,* 341–42.
73. *Ibid.,* 352.
74. *Ibid.,* 353.

CHAPTER 5

1. Bernard Yack, 'Community and Conflict in Aristotle's Political Philosophy', *Review of Politics* (1985): 92–112.
2. John M. Cooper, 'Aristotle on the Forms of Friendship', *The Review of Metaphysics* 30 (June 1977): 619.
3. These ideas and the description to follow of Cooper's views can be found in *Ibid.* Unless we quote directly from Cooper, we shall allow the foregoing note to serve as the reference for the discussion that follows.
4. *Ibid.*, 631.
5. *Ibid.*, 638–39.
6. These may not yet be friendships of character, but that is only because Cooper has arrested the development of the friendship before it reached that stage and not because Cooper has explained advantage-friendships.
7. St. Thomas Aquinas, *Commentary on the Nicomachean Ethics* (Chicago: Henry Regnery, 1964), vol. II, 714. See also *NE* 1156a10–20 for a clear statement on Aristotle's part of what Aquinas is saying.
8. 'Aristotle on the Forms of Friendship', 639.
9. *Ibid.*
10. *Ibid.*
11. Martin Ostwald, 'Glossary of Technical Terms' in *Nicomachean Ethics*, trans. Martin Ostwald (Indianapolis, Indiana: Bobbs-Merrill, 1962), 311–12. We wish to thank Henry Veatch for pointing this out to us.
12. *Wealth of Nations* (henceforth *WN*) (Oxford: Oxford University Press, 1916); Liberty Press/Liberty Classics edition, 26.
13. It may be objected that this claim only relates to apparent or subjective good. But as Aristotle points out: "Do men love, then, *the* good, or what is good for *them*? These sometimes clash. . . . Now it is thought that each loves what is good for himself, and that the good is without qualification lovable, and what is good for each man is lovable for him; but each man loves not what is good for him but what seems good. This however will make no difference; we shall just have to say that this is 'that which seems lovable'". (*NE* 1155b20–27)
14. Do legally governed credit transactions fall under the legal or the moral category? It is likely Aristotle would put them under the former, but his discussion creates ambiguity on this point.
15. The term *clearly* must, of course, be understood relative to less formal relationships. No matter how specific, e.g., a law might be, there always seems room for dispute. *Clearly* should not be understood to mean beyond interpretation or dispute.
16. James Buchanan, *The Limits of Liberty* (Chicago: University of Chicago Press, 1915), Chapter 2.
17. Our litigious society seems to refute this argument, but we attribute this

largely to a weakening commitment to live up to one's contracts, continual changes and complication of law, generous awards by the courts, and a utilitarian push towards expediency rather than principle. Yet even under saner circumstances, disputation will always be present because of the nature of advantage-friendships. Nevertheless, unless coercive authority is used to resolve the problem, more stability will be present than not if the conditions just mentioned are absent.

18. We hold to the 'legal-recognition' theory of corporations as expounded, for example, by Robert Hessen, *In Defense of the Corporation* (Palo Alto: Stanford University Press, 1982).

19. Yack, 'Community and Conflict in Aristotle's Political Philosophy', 97–98.

20. *Ibid.*, 105–06.

21. Buchanan, *The Limits of Liberty*, Chapter 2.

22. Patriotism, e.g., in athletic events at the Olympics, is a product of the good will engendered by a mutual sharing of those formal principles that govern all members of the same society.

23. Aristotle had a strongly agrarian and anti-growth prejudice. See Barry Gordon, *Economic Analysis Before Adam Smith* (New York: Harper and Row, 1975), Chapter 2.

24. T.J. Lewis, 'Acquisition and Anxiety: Aristotle's Case Against the Market', *Canadian Journal of Economics* 11 (February 1978): 69–90.

25. Scott Meikle, 'Aristotle and the Political Economy of the Polis', *Journal of Hellenic Studies* 99 (1979): 57–73.

26. *Ibid.*, 87–90.

27. *Ibid.*, especially sections II and III.

28. *Ibid.*, 60.

29. Meikle has a footnote (p. 60, note 8) claiming that Aristotle's low estimation of *chreia* is damaging to the marginal utility interpretation. This is not suprising if Aristotle is looking for an intrinsic standard. But Meikle does not explain how it is damaging. Furthermore, such a claim seems to contradict Meikle's own argument that *chreia* cannot be translated as 'demand'.

30. The actual proportions would vary from exchange to exchange, but the equality remains. The rich person and the poor person are equals with respect to a potential exchange with each other although the relevant costs to each might differ. To search for a defined 'proportion' for all exchanges is to search for an intrinsic value to the goods which, we claim, is not present.

31. See Henry Veatch, *Human Rights: Fact or Fancy?* (Baton Rouge and London: Louisiana University Press, 1985).

32. Jeffrey Paul, 'Substantive Social Contracts and the Legitimate Basis of Political Authority', *The Monist* 66 (October 1983): 518–19.

33. See Douglas B. Rasmussen, 'A Critique of Rawls's *Theory of Justice*', *The Personalist* 55 (Summer 1914): 303–18; and 'Liberalism, Contractarianism, and the Choice of Liberties: A Response to Gray', *The Restraint*

of Liberty, vol. 7 of *Bowling Green Studies in Applied Philosophy,* ed. Attig, Callen, and Gray (Bowling Green, Ohio: Bowling Green State University, 1985), 26–36. Also see Douglas J. Den Uyl, 'Sociality and Social Contract: A Spinozistic Perspective', *Studia Spinozana* 1 (1985): 19–51.

34. Besides criticizing 'substantive' social contract theory, Jeffrey Paul's essay, 'Substantive Social Contracts and the Legitimate Basis of Political Authority', also criticizes most effectively the claim that consent, by itself, can be a sufficient defense for political authority.

35. See Buchanan, *The Limits of Liberty,* Chapters 1 and 4.

36. James Buchanan, *Freedom in Constitutional Contract* (College Station and London: Texas A & M University Press, 1977), 25.

37. *Ibid.,* 127, (Emphasis added.)

38. *Ibid.,* 130. Agreement on rules of the 'game', we might add, is for Buchanan by *all* players, not, as in Rawls's case, all *rational* players.

39. F.A. Hayek attempts, we believe quite unsuccessfully, to do this in *Rules and Order*, volume 1 of *Law, Legislation, and Liberty* (Chicago: University of Chicago Press, 1973).

40. Buchanan, *Freedom in Constitutional Contract,* 38.

41. Den Uyl, 'Sociality and Social Contract: A Spinozistic Perspective,' 40.

42. As should be obvious, we do not mean by this that Buchanan needs to become a 'substantive' social contract theorist like Rawls and Gauthier. Rather, we only mean that normative knowledge and a wider view of human motivation is necessary for his constitutional contract to be sustained. We have throughout this book tried to provide a foundation for these.

43. Starting with real as opposed to some allegedly 'just' set of endowments also underscores the Aristotelian legislator's advocacy of Lockean rights and rejection of three assumptions present in the Rawlsian social contract. These assumptions are (1) inequality of natural endowments is something a conception of justice must rectify; (2) the inapplicability of the concept of justice to natural endowments somehow implies that the products which result from their use are neither deserved nor something one has a right to; and (3), even more incredibly, others somehow deserve or have a right to some of these products. See Rasmussen, 'A Critique of Rawls's *Theory of Justice*' Fred D. Miller, Jr., 'The Natural Right to Private Property' in *The Libertarian Reader*, ed. Tibor R. Machan (Totowa, New Jersey: Rowman and Littlefield, 1982), 215–281 for detailed criticisms of these assumptions.

44. *The Limits of Liberty,* 68–69. (Emphasis added.)

45. D.J. Allan, 'Individual and State in the *Ethics* and *Politics*' in *La 'Politique' D'Aristote,* vol. II of *Entriens Sur l'Antiquité Classique* (Geneva: Foundation Hardt, 1965), 66.

46. This is what we also understand to be the central problem with liberalism. See Rasmussen, 'Liberalism, Contractarianism, and the Choice of Liberties:

A Response to Gray'; and Den Uyl and Warner, 'Liberalism and Hobbes and Spinoza', *Studia Spinozana* 3, (Fall 1987).

47. James Buchanan, 'Boundaries of Social Contract', *Reason Papers* 2 (Fall 1915): 26–27. (Emphasis added.)
48. Buchanan, *The Limits of Liberty*, 71-72.
49. Den Uyl, 'Sociality and Social Contract: A Spinozistic Perspective', 39.
50. *The Limits of Liberty*, 63.
51. Charles Jackson Wheeler, 'Justice and Anarchy', *The Personalist* 52 (Spring 1971): 399.
52. There is reason to believe, however, that the contracting parties might come close to this realization on their own—that is, that the rules should be universal and negative. It seems to us that this is one of the reasons Buchanan believes that the social contract approach can actually defend liberalism and is not purely descriptive.
53. The reader is directed to the following articles, which deal with these issues in great detail from the perspective of Lockean natural rights: Tibor R. Machan, 'Individualism and the Problem of Political Authority', *The Monist* 66 (October 1983): 501–515 and 'Dissolving the Problem of Public Goods' in *The Libertarian Reader* 201–08; Eric Mack, 'The Ethics of Taxation: Rights Versus Public Goods', *Taxation and the Deficit Economy*, ed. Dwight R. Lee (San Francisco, California: Pacific Research Institute for Public Policy, 1986); and Roger Lee, 'The Morality of Capitalism and Market Institutions', *The Main Debate: Communism versus Capitalism*, ed. Tibor R. Machan (New York: Random House, 1987), 92–93.
54. *Wealth of Nations* (Oxford: Oxford University Press, 1976), Vi, pp. 784–88; Liberty Press/Liberty Classics edition.
55. See Ralph Lerner 'Commerce and Character: The Anglo-American as New-Model Man', *William and Mary Quarterly* 36 (January 1979): 3–26.
56. *Ibid.*
57. E.g., *Ibid.*, 12–13.
58. E.g., see Leo Strauss, *Natural Right and History* (Chicago: 1974), 300.
59. Much of what follows is taken from Douglas J. Den Uyl, 'Freedom and Virtue Revisited', in *Man, Economy, and Liberty: Essays in Honor of Murray N. Rothbard*, ed. Walter Block and Llewellyn H. Rockwell, Jr. (Auburn, Alabama: Ludwig von Mises Institute, 1988).
60. Plato, *Republic*, Book IV, 443d–e
61. The latter sees itself as offering a different interpretation on what it means to be harmed, and not as expanding the state's role in the direct promotion of morality or virtue.
62. Interestingly enough, one facet of modern political theory—Marxism—combines 1 and 2 through its historicism. Unlike liberal moral scepticism or relativism, Marxism does not necessarily reject virtue, but 'historicizes'

it. Thus, antiquity can have its virtues, capitalism a different set, and the coming new age its own and different set.

63. This sketch is based upon the conclusions of the following: Douglas J. Den Uyl, 'Freedom and Virtue', *Reason Papers* 5 (Winter 1979); reprinted in revised form in *The Libertarian Reader*, also reprinted in *The Main Debate*.

64. Aristotle, *Nicomachean Ethics*, Book II, Chapter 4, 1105a30–35.

65. It is here that a great debt is owed to Ayn Rand's novels; for she, more than anyone else, has severed the connection between moral perfection and the collectivist premise that had always been tied to it.

66. The model here seems to be one used by many colleges and universities. If we force students to listen to classical music or read Shakespeare, they may come to appreciate it. Those who have taught such courses know that this works in a few cases, but generally fails on most students. It would be fallacious to infer from this, however, that because we recommend abandoning state-induced virtue for society at large that we also recommend a laissez-faire approach to university curricula. Our argument is not that no efforts should be made to habituate virtue, but rather that no *coercive* efforts should be made. Students and parents still have the right of exit and tend to *choose* universities on the basis of their educational programs and philosophies.

67. For further details, see Den Uyl, 'Self-Interest and American Ideology' in *Ideology and American Experience*, ed. John K. Roth and Robert C. Whittemore (Washington D.C.: Washington Institute, 1986) 101–119.

68. If this is true, however, the point would apply to ancient as well as modern regimes. Whatever virtue was touted by a regime on the ancient model would have to be translatable into a sentiment to be politically workable. But in doing so, there is some question as to whether the 'virtue' remains a virtue, or at least a question about the translation leading to excess. If, for example, regime R focuses upon courage, that can easily translate into a people prone to belligerence, power lust, brutality, and the like.

69. Adam Smith, *Theory of Moral Sentiments* (*TMS*) (Oxford: Oxford University Press, 1976) VII.ii.3.4.

70. *TMS*, V.2ff.

71. Smith does elaborate and refine this process as his work proceeds.

72. *TMS*, I.i.3.3ff.

73. *TMS*, I.i.5-I.ii.5.4.

74. *TMS*, I.ii.2.1.

75. A somewhat related theme appears in Allan Bloom, *The Closing of the American Mind* (New York: Simon and Schuster, 1987).

INDEX